GETHSEMANE TO GOLGOTHA

40 DEVOTIONS ON CHRIST'S REDEMPTIVE SUFFERINGS

JOSHUA HERSHEY

Gethsemane to Golgotha
Copyright © 2023 Joshua Hershey
Published by Jubilee
All rights reserved.
ISBN: 978-1-7344241-2-6

CONTENTS

Forward

Gethsemane to Golgotha. A sacred period in history Christians call *Christ's Passion.* 'Passion' comes from a Latin word that means "to suffer." Christ's *sufferings* began in the garden of Gethsemane and culminated when He gave up His spirit on the cross at Golgotha. Though there are several chapters in all four Gospels that cover this episode of Christ's life in great detail, everything that transpired from Gethsemane to Golgotha took place in less than a day. Why so much space given to these final hours? Why not devote more space to the many miracles the Evangelists didn't have room to record? (John 21:25) The reason is simple. This was Christ's *greatest* miracle. He was not merely helping the situation of one person, or even an enormous crowd, rather, what Jesus accomplished in His Passion was nothing less than *eternal salvation for anyone and everyone who would believe* (John 3:16).

The number of books that have been written on the Passion are extensive. So, why this book? Is it really needed? Well, I'm sure the church can get along just fine without it. And if you choose to put it down right now with the intention of never picking it up again, all I ask is that you pass it along to someone else, or at least take it to the nearest thrift shop. Ultimately, whether ten people need to be touched by this book, or ten thousand, I know *I needed to write it.* I'm in just as desperate need of hearing the Passion story, rehearing it, and being able to communicate it, as anyone else. Though many great books have been written before, there will always be a need for people in every generation to *tell* and *retell* the Good News. New books, new sermons, new videos and drama skits of the Passion will always be important to the church. We all need to *own the Story* ourselves.

So, why *this* book? Is there anything *unique* about it? Whether there are unique insights in this book or not, I cannot say, for I have not read everything that has been written or said as it would take me many lifetimes to do so. What I can say is that the format of the book is one I have yet to come across. I do not know of another book that breaks the Passion Narrative into forty four-page devotions. The idea for this format came about soon after I published my thirty-one day December devotional on the Christmas Story. I figured if I did do another devotional it would have to be about the Passion. But, how long? That is when the season of Lent came to mind. A traditional period in the church that is observed for *forty days prior to Easter morning* (plus Sundays). While these forty devotions can be read at any time of the year, or in one sitting for that matter, the season of Lent is an especially useful occasion to think deeply upon the Passion. For if you are denying yourself, or participating in some form of fast, you especially need the encouragement of the story of Christ's own self-denial and His superabounding grace!

Over the past ten years, I have taught the 14 Biblical Stations of the Cross to my church on Good Friday at least six times. Each year I have been forced to reflect upon the Passion Narrative in a fresh way. I begin each station by reading one of the fourteen sections of the Passion, then I generally put up some artwork that depicts that scene as I read a prayer/meditation that I have written. All in all, my congregation has always given me feedback that they are greatly blessed by this tradition that we observe at our church. Well, in 2023 I decided to take these Passion reflections to a whole new level. During the season of Lent I preached seven long sermons on the Passion. In preparing for each sermon I not only digested many commentaries and books, but also wrote (most of) the forty devotions you now hold in your hands.

As far as how one should approach this book as a *daily devotional*, it is important to read the scripture verses under the title of each chapter first. Read the Bible humbly. Don't rush past it. Ask the Lord to speak to you. Then, after your own meditation on the text, read the devotion. The goal of these devotions is ultimately for the truth of the Gospel to penetrate you to the core of your being. *For you to know who Christ is, what Christ has done, and how the 18-hours from Gethsemane to Golgotha literally changes everything.*

Robert Bellarmine was spot on when he said, "The only reason that can be assigned for our sloth and folly is, that we neither meditate on the Passion of Christ, nor consider His immense love for us with that earnestness and attention we ought to. We content ourselves with reading the Passion hastily, or hearing it read, instead of securing fitting opportunities to penetrate ourselves with the thought of it."[1] So, take all the time you need. Whether ten minutes a day, or an hour, allow the truths within the Passion Narrative to wash over and transform you from the inside-out. What is happening in the suffering of Christ is God's great display of love for *you* (Rom. 5:8). It is not a tragic story of a man who dies, but rather a triumphant story of a God-Man who defeats death by His own death!

It is remarkable how much of the Gospel as expounded by the apostles in their letters can be found *within* the Passion narrative. Over and over again we see Christ portrayed as the Lamb of God who takes away the sin of the world. Over and over again we see the significance of Christ's blood being poured out for the forgiveness of sin. Over and over again we see the longsuffering love of Christ on display. Pastors and evangelists would benefit from drawing more heavily from the Passion narratives for their Gospel presentations. For the narratives speak just as loudly as Paul or Peter's letters. Though the Passion Narrative is sufficient in itself to tell the Good News, Appendix B aims to help further elucidate the meaning of Christ's Death in light of the Sacrificial Victim in both the Old and New Testament. Appendix A also gives exciting insights concerning an important historical artifact that gives witness to the Passion and is a great apologetic tool for defending the faith. These appendices are designed to further deepen your passion for His Passion. Don't miss out on them!

One last detail to consider. My Christmas Devotional, *A New Day Dawns*, has beautiful colored pictures that go along with each devotion. Though that is nice, this devotional just had too much information to cover, and *I could keep the production cost down* keeping everything black and white. But, there are four pictures on the cover to keep you *pondering the movement from Gethsemane to Golgotha*. The four pictures represent the four primary settings of the Passion Narrative. The picture in the Upper Left, by William Black, depicts *Heaven's strength and encouragement throughout* Christ's suffering in Gethsemane. The picture in the Upper Right, by Julius Schnorr von Carolsfeld, depicts Christ's bold testimony in the high priestly household before Caiaphas and the Sanhedrin. The picture on the Bottom Left, by Antonio Ciseri, depicts Pilate calling on the crowd to *'Behold the Man'* who had just been scourged and who they had chosen to be handed over to death *in place of Barabbas*. The picture on the Lower Right, by Matthias Grünewald, depicts Jesus hanging on the cross with John the Baptist pointing to Him as *the Lamb of God* while the beloved disciple and Mary receive His words of life. Behind these four pictures Grünewald's painting is *juxtaposed* with *Agnus Dei* ('Lamb of God') by Francisco de Zurbarán. For Christ as the Sacrificial Lamb is the theme that undergirds the entire devotional and both appendices. Ponder these images as you read through the Passion and these short devotions. Let the Almighty Love of Christ saturate *you* and conform *you* to Himself!

DAY 1
The King Crosses The Kidron
(John 18:1-3)

It was a cold spring night in Jerusalem (John 18:18). The population had swelled to its yearly high. Nearly 200,000 Jewish pilgrims were jostling in the streets and surrounding hillside, excitedly making preparations for the celebration of Passover—a festival that commemorated God's deliverance of His people from slavery in Egypt. Passover received its name because death 'passed over' the homes of all who trusted God's word to take a lamb as a substitute, slaughter it, eat it, and splatter its blood on their doorposts. They were spared judgment on their firstborn son (a picture of the extension of their own life) because a first-born male lamb bore the deserved judgment in their place.

The multitudes in Jerusalem in AD 33 were not simply looking forward to this sacred festival, they were also bubbling with excitement about the ministry of a rabbi from Galilee. A rabbi many believed to be the long awaited Messiah. A common belief about the Messiah at this time was that he would deliver Israel from Roman oppression in a similar way to how Moses delivered them from Egyptian oppression. Just four days earlier crowds had welcomed this Nazarene with shouts of, "Hosanna to the Son of David!" (Matt. 21:9). Hosanna means, "Save now!"

This rabbi's name was Jesus. In Hebrew, Yeshua. A name meaning "Yahweh's salvation/deliverance." For three years Jesus had astonished many within Israel—drawing multitudes to witness His teaching and miracles. He opened blind eyes and mute ears, walked on a stormy sea, fed thousands of famished people on two occasions with just a few loaves of bread, turned water into wine, cast out multitudes of demons, cleansed lepers, and even raised a man who had been in a tomb for four days! Though He was admired by a great many Jews, and even some Gentiles, Jesus also drew the ire of many Jewish leaders.

The Pharisees, Sadducees, Herodians, scribes, and chief priests had been interrogating Jesus—seeking to *trap* Him from Monday through Thursday leading up to Passover (Mark 11:27-12:34). During this same exact time, beginning on Monday, the lambs for Passover were being inspected—making sure they were spotless, without fault, and permissible as sacrifices (Ex. 12:3). Though Jesus, as the Lamb of God, passed each test with flying colors, the chief priests were still intent on finding a way to put Him to death. They believed He was a *rabble rouser*, a *blasphemer*, and that a swift execution would benefit the nation (John 11:50).

After four days of confrontation, parables of judgment, and prophetic foretelling from Jesus, Passover finally arrived. As the sun sank over the hills of Jerusalem on the 14th of Nisan, their Holy Passover began. Jesus, fully aware of the prophetic significance of this most holy day, decided to eat the sacred meal with His disciples at the beginning of Passover rather than the following evening with the rest of the Jews.[2] He had something *far more important* to accomplish when the rest of the Jews were slaughtering their lambs and preparing their own celebrations. He would *be* the Passover Lamb (1 Cor. 5:7).

The meal Jesus shared with His most loyal followers is often referred to as His 'Last Supper'—*a time when He took the elements of the meal that signified the events of the Exodus, and showed how they would signify a new and greater Exodus (His Passion).* Throughout the

Gospels, especially Matthew, Jesus is portrayed as a New Moses.[3] In fact, He is far greater than Moses. He spoke to Moses from the burning bush (John 8:58), is far superior to the manna Moses provided (John 6:32, 51), and is the very Presence upon the rock that Moses struck (1 Cor. 10:4). He is a *divine* deliverer.

At the end of the meal, right before His journey to the garden, Jesus and His disciples "sang a hymn" (Mark 14:26). The only time we are ever told Jesus sang was *at this moment*. He sang as He marched into the *darkness*—physical and spiritual—and prepared for His greatest battle. If Jesus was following the later Jewish liturgy of Passover Night He very likely was singing the Hillel Psalms. One could faithfully imagine Him singing, "The stone which the builders rejected has become the chief cornerstone", and "Bind the sacrifice with cords to the horns of the altar" (Psalm 118:22, 27). As the *Author* and *Inspiration* behind these songs, He sang knowing those Scriptures spoke of Him. He was that Stone and Sacrifice. In the strength of His own prophetic song, Jesus marched to the garden ready to fulfill *all* that had been written about Him. Ready to be *rejected*, *bound*, *tortured*, and *killed*. He "rejoiced in the Lord at all times" (Phil. 4:4).

As Jesus exited the city, and walked to the Mount of Olives, "He went out with His disciples over the Brook Kidron" (John 18:1). The Kidron was a murky, shallow water source in the valley just outside the city and temple. *Great pools of excess blood from the temple sacrifices would drain there.* It also had been the site where pagan images and altars were pulverized and washed away (2 Kings 23:12). As Jesus saw that murky river that symbolized the washing away of sin and idolatry, He likely thought of the work that lay before Him. He had told His disciples at the Last Supper that His blood would be poured forth "for the remission of sins" (Matt. 26:28). In that dark valley, where heinous crimes had been committed (like child sacrifice), picture Jesus preparing to bear the penalty for the most egregious sins. There is no sin too great that it cannot be cleansed by the holy blood of Jesus. It truly reaches *the highest mountains* and flows to *the lowest valleys*, a river of life that washes and purges recipients of "all sin" (1 John 1:7).

Though Jesus went willingly, even joyfully, to the garden, He was soon besieged by *great anguish*. The image of Jesus crossing the Kidron in great anguish echoes the story of another great king, David. Toward the end of David's life his eldest son, Absalom, had secretly won the hearts and allegiance of many Israelites. Upon learning of his son's treachery we are told that David "crossed over the Brook Kidron…[and] went up by the Ascent of the Mount of Olives, and wept as he went up" (2 Sam. 15:23, 30). While *weeping*, David learned that not only his eldest son had conspired against him, but also *one of his best friends*—Ahithophel (2 Sam. 15:31). Many believe David penned Psalm 55 as a result of this dual betrayal. He wrote, "Fearfulness and trembling have come upon me, and horror has overwhelmed me" (Ps. 55:5) for betrayal came from "my equal, my companion and my acquaintance" (Ps. 55:13). A fitting description not just of David, but also Jesus! We will enter more deeply into the *trembling, horror,* and *betrayal* Jesus experienced in the garden in the coming days.

Lord Jesus, because of Your abundant love You came to Earth, took on flesh, and became my elder brother. For four days after entering Jerusalem You were inspected like all the lambs at the temple, proving You are my perfect sacrifice. You were inspected, so I could be accepted. Thank you for approaching Your suffering with a prophetic song and a resolute march. May I be filled with that same song, conviction, and resolve. For without You, I easily waver. But with You, I can do all things (Phil 4:13). You crossed the Kidron knowing You would be betrayed, rejected, bound, and tortured. All this was done so MY sin could be washed away and I could be redeemed. Thank you!

DAY 2
A Garden Called Gethsemane
(Matt 26:36; Mk 14:32; Lk 22:39-40; Jn 18:2)

After Jesus, the Son of David, crossed the Kidron we are told He entered a garden. Matthew and Mark both tell us the garden's name was Gethsemane. Luke adds that it was Jesus' "custom" to go there, and John plainly says "Jesus had often met there with His disciples." Because John also states the garden needed to be "entered", many believe it was a walled, privately owned space, near the base of the Mount of Olives. The word 'Gethsemane' means 'wine/oil press', and we can assume the garden likely housed an oil press where olives from the surrounding area, or from the garden itself, were brought to be crushed and pressed into that precious ancient commodity.

For Jesus to have frequented this site gives the impression that one of His wealthy followers had given Him access to the garden whenever He was in Jerusalem so He could either spend alone time in prayer there, or have discussions with disciples and friends. In fact, there is an old tradition that says the owner of this garden was the father of John Mark. Whatever the case, this was a space that had been important to Jesus throughout His ministry. By bringing His disciples "often" to a "garden", He was wanting to impress important imagery on their hearts and minds. Imagery that would make a lasting impact.

A *garden* is very important to the Biblical story. Before man was called to venture out into the world, God wanted them to be grounded in *the atmosphere of a garden*. In fact, immediately after God formed Adam from the dust of the ground we are told He "planted a garden eastward in Eden, and there He put the man whom He had formed" (Gen. 2:8). God didn't place man in Havilah, Cush, Assyria, or any of the other named zones in His newly created world. Rather, He wanted man in the eastern part of Eden—a place that means 'delight' or 'pleasure'—where there was a specially crafted garden, uniquely designed for him.

This garden would have been the most beautiful place the world has ever known—specifically planted and designed by God Himself in the pre-fallen world. In fact, we are told it was filled with *beautiful* plants, *nourishing* and *delicious* fruit bearing trees, and most importantly, the *manifested and special presence of God* (Gen. 2:9). It was meant to be humanity's hub in the world. The place where they were based, and gained rest and strength before and after fulfilling their commission to "take dominion" and Edenize the rest of the world as God's image-bearers (Gen. 1:26-28).

This primal garden of delight was situated near the top of a mountain (Ezek. 28:14). A river flowed through the garden, and then split off into four rivers that brought that water of life and blessing to the surrounding world (Gen. 2:10). Sadly, man rebelled against God and was banished from the garden—with cherubim guards watching over the gates with flaming swords (Gen. 3:24). But, God's intention was always for *restoration* and *return*. The altars that the patriarchs built were 'mini-mountains' that pictured a return to fellowship with God on that mountain. When God met Moses at the top of Sinai, in a sense, it was also a return to the garden, but, of course, Moses came in contact with the closed gates of Eden and the cherubim with fiery swords guarding God's glorious presence (Ex. 19:16-20).

So, what was God's solution to reopen the garden? Well, out of His great love, God made a way for humanity to have a *partial* return, that also pictured a *full* return in the future. This was done when God gave the tabernacle blueprints to Moses at the top of Sinai, and the temple blueprints hundreds of years later to David. The entire tabernacle/temple system pictured how seriously God's holiness took sin, as well as how great God's love was that desired to bring redemption from that sin. He would be righteous to judge sin, and loving to be the One who ultimately would pay the price for that sin Himself! (Rom. 3:20-26)

The tabernacle, and two later temples, are filled with Edenic imagery. Flowers, pomegranates, palm trees, and cherubim were etched on walls, woven into curtains, and stitched into priestly garments. Large portions of *Exodus, 1 Kings, Ezra*, and *Ezekiel* are devoted to the construction of these 'new Edens'—God's special dwelling place among His people. The prophets also pictured return from Babylonian exile as a return to Eden—partially because the temple, God's House, would be rebuilt. Ezekiel declared, "They will say, 'This land that was desolate has become like the garden of Eden'" (Ezek. 36:35). Isaiah declared, "He will make her wilderness like Eden, and her desert like the garden of the LORD" (Isa. 51:3). Jeremiah spoke of how not just the land, but the people, would be Eden-esque. He said, "Their souls shall be like a well-watered garden, and they shall sorrow no more at all" (Jer. 31:12). God was intent that the special garden in the land of Delight, where He strolled with humanity in the cool of the day, would return. No matter the cost, God would find a way to fully bring us back to Himself!

When Jesus stepped into *the garden* on the 14th of Nisan, AD 33, He began to reverse the tragedy that happened in the beginning. Adam disobeyed, Jesus obeyed. Adam didn't 'guard and keep' his bride, Jesus did 'guard and keep' His bride. Adam took the forbidden fruit in defiance to God's will from Eve's hand, Jesus took the cup of righteous indignation for that sin from His Father's hand in accordance with God's will. Jesus would suffer *in a garden*, pay for sin *in a garden*, and rise again *in a garden* while being mistaken for a *gardener* (John 20:15). The garden is central to the Passion Narrative from beginning to end. Comparing Adam and Jesus, Paul writes, "Therefore, as through one man's offense judgment came to all men, resulting in condemnation, even so through one Man's righteous act the free gift came to all men, resulting in justification of life. For as by one man's disobedience many were made sinners, so also by one Man's obedience many will be made righteous" (Rom. 5:18-19). The Last Adam has fully reversed the sinful consequences of the First Adam—and all of this was accomplished *in a garden*.

Jesus, You declared that You desire to manifest Your presence and make Your Home inside all who love You (John 14:21-23). You have called those You love Your "garden" (Song 6:2). Just as You "often met" with Your disciples in the Garden of Gethsemane, so You desire to "often meet" with me (John 18:2). Just as You wanted Adam's life rooted and grounded in the garden of delight in the beginning, so You desire my life to be "rooted and grounded" in Your delightful life and love (Eph. 3:17). You desire that I be "filled with all the fulness of God" (Eph. 3:19). Help me desire what You desire. Help me be more intentional to spend time with You and practice Your Presence.

I know spending time with You will change me from the inside-out. Moses came out of Your glory cloud at the top of the mountain with a shining face (Ex. 34:19). In some sense he was 'transfigured' by Your presence. I also desire to be 'transfigured' by Your Presence (2 Cor. 3:18; Rom 12:2). Thank you for reopening the gates of the garden. Thank you for gifting me an unfading glory in Your Light. Thank you that I can "shine like a star amidst a wicked and perverse generation" (Phil. 2:15). You sorrowed in the garden with an "exceeding sorrow" so that I might "sorrow no more" (Jer. 31:12; Rev. 21:4), at least, not with "worldly sorrow" (1 Thes. 4:13). May You grant me a greater sense of Your peace, a deeper awareness of Your presence, and may I blossom and grow as "a lily among the thorns" of this world (Song. 2:1), exuding the fragrance of Your new creation life!

DAY 3
Drinking The Bitter Cup
(Matt 26:37-46; Mark 14:33-42; Luke 22:41-42)

Upon entering the garden Jesus instructed eight of His disciples to sit near the entrance—likely where the oil press was in a cave or enclosed structure. He then proceeded to take Peter, James, and John with Him deeper into the garden, and with each step into that familiar space, the *weight of darkness pressed down upon Him*. A heavy burden began to descend over Jesus—body and soul. This was the "opportune time" Satan had been preparing for since His baptism (Luke 4:13). I imagine legions of demons gathered around Satan in order to make one final assault on Jesus, seeking to get Him to rebel against His Father's will and word. Would the Last Adam fall in the garden like the first?

As Jesus made His way deeper into the garden Mark tells us He began "to be troubled and deeply distressed." The word *troubled* can also be translated as "terrified" or "thoroughly alarmed." Though this trauma was outwardly apparent, in order to make His disciples fully aware of His great trial, He says, "My soul is exceedingly sorrowful, even to death. Stay here and watch with Me" (Matt. 26:38). Jesus then paced "a stone's throw" deeper into the garden, and in that alone space Matthew tells us He "fell on His face, and prayed" (Matt 26:39).

Being the Passover, there was a full moon in the sky. In that pre-modern world, with no light pollution, we can imagine shards of moon light being refracted through the olive trees falling as a mild spotlight on our Blessed Savior highlighting His agony as He lay prostrate on the ground. Maybe clouds overhead, or shadows from the trees, partially blocked Peter, James, and John from a full vision of their Master, but they were awake long enough to witness glimpses of His suffering and hear snippets of His "vehement cries" (Heb. 5:7). These three previously declared their willingness to share in Jesus' sufferings with Him (Mark 10:39, 14:31), and even declared their willingness to die with Him (Matt. 26:35). Would they live up to their commitments?

This is not the first time Peter and the sons of Zebedee were alone with Jesus. They had been private witnesses to some of His most glorious acts. They were in Jairus' house when his daughter was *raised from the dead* (Mark 5:41-42), and, even more important, they were with Jesus at the top of a mountain when Jesus was *transfigured in all His glory as His face shined like the sun* (Mark 9:7). While He was shining brightly we are told that Elijah and Moses spoke to Him about His "exodus" (Luke 9:31), and that the voice of the Father *thundered validation* over His "beloved Son" (Matt. 17:5). Even there, among His manifested glory, the three top apostles were "very sleepy" (Luke 9:32). The ones closest to Jesus were sleepy inwardly and outwardly. They didn't comprehend His mission, and they demonstrated that again in the garden.

In the garden, as the 'greater exodus' Elijah and Moses spoke to Christ about began, there was no longer a bright light or a booming heavenly voice. Yet, paradoxically, God's glory was on display in an even deeper way. For the eternal glory of God is nothing other than the *self-giving* and *self-emptying* love of the Triune God. The Father giving to the Son by the Spirit, and the Son giving back to the Father by the same Spirit. Power made perfect in apparent weakness. In fact, the cross is a sign of God's glory (John 12:27-33, 17:1-5). *The glory of the Great Shepherd is on full display when He lays down His life for His sheep, stands against the ravenous dark wolves, and is stuck for our salvation (Zech. 13:7).*

In the garden Jesus undergoes real suffering. His torture was no illusion. The real Jesus, the Jesus of Scripture, is not some kind of Gnostic, ethereal, impassible Spirit Being. Jesus is not of an angelic constitution, untouched by human trial and passion. Rather, Jesus is completely human—spirit, soul, and body. He has both a human and a divine will with a passible flesh that suffers and bleeds like the rest of humankind. In the garden we get a glimpse of Jesus' humanity that we have not seen elsewhere in the Gospels. While we have seen Jesus 'hunger', 'tire', 'weep', and express a whole host of other human behaviors, we have never seen the level of *suffering* and *deep distress* that is on display in Gethsemane. It is only here where His soul is described as "thoroughly alarmed" and "exceedingly sorrowful."

What could possibly cause the Almighty Lord, the One who had fed 5,000, walked on water, commanded legions of demons to leave, to experience such extreme pain, anguish, and inner turmoil? Certainly, knowing He would face Roman flogging and crucifixion—the most painful and humiliating form of capital punishment ever devised—would have caused any man to completely buckle. But, though Jesus knew those pains would be grievous to His flesh, I don't believe that was the primary cause of His torturous suffering and horror in the garden. Rather, the moment Jesus stepped into that olive press at Gethsemane, *He began to experience the crushing weight of our sin.* What was so soul-wrenching, to the point of breaking out in bloody sweat, was that the perfect, sinless, Son of God was being "made sin for us" as our substitute (2 Cor. 5:21). *A suffering far beyond all imagination.*

This is not to downplay the role of His physical sufferings. No man I am aware of would face the physical hell Jesus was about to face, and not run away. In fact, Jesus had seen many flogged and crucified victims throughout His life. He knew that trial would be grave, but the full suffering and pain Jesus was about to face was far worse than crucifixion. As the Lamb of God, as the Suffering Servant, He was being "crushed for our wrongdoings" (Is. 53:5, NASB), and He would experience the horror of God-forsakenness on our behalf. *He would be 'crushed' for every heinous sin in human history. The word 'Gethsemane' is twice in the Passion Narrative —two witnesses to Christ being completely crushed. He took the crushing penalty of our sin in order to ultimately gift us the oil of the Spirit of Life.*

Speaking of the sins our Savior bore, Sheen writes, "all sins were there…sins committed in the light that made even the wicked shudder; sins too awful to be mentioned, sins too terrible to name: Sin! Sin! Sin!…From the North, South, East, and West, the foul miasma of the world's sins rushed upon Him like a flood; Samson-like, He reached up and pulled the whole guilt of the world upon Himself as if He were guilty, paying for the debt in our name, so that we might once more have access to the Father…To most men, the burden of sin is as natural as the clothes they wear, but to Him the touch of that which men take so easily was the veriest agony."[4]

Almighty Savior, out of Your great love You chose to be "made a little lower than the angels, for the suffering of death" so that You "by the grace of God, might taste death for everyone" (Heb. 2:9). Angelic bodies cannot suffer or die. An angelic body could never pay the wages of MY sin. But the body You took on as You were woven together in Your mother's womb, could. Thank you for becoming fully man in order to drink the cup of wrath that I deserved. I am eternally indebted to Your mercy and grace! As I look to the suffering and trial You bore, I realize that my own sufferings and trials pale in comparison. Help me to be an imitator of You, and fall on my face before the Father in my own trials. Unlike Your disciples, help me "watch" and "be alert." Help me "tarry for an hour", or however long is needed, for the divine strength and help to fulfill Your will and perfect purpose for my life.

DAY 4
Touched By An Angel
(Luke 22:43-46)

The birth pangs of Jesus' suffering began when He entered Jerusalem on Palm Sunday. It was then that He declared, "Now My soul is troubled, and what shall I say? 'Father, save Me from this hour'? But for this purpose I came to this hour" (John 12:27). As He rode into Jerusalem, He "wept over" those who would reject Him (Luke 19:41). And this pain did not dissipate, rather, it *intensified*. A few days later we see Jesus agonizing over those who had been "unwilling" to "gather under His wings" (Matt. 23:37-39). A heart-breaking experience! But it was only once He entered the garden that Jesus went into full labor. It was there the birth pangs began to be *excruciatingly painful* and *bloody*. Right before entering the garden He compared His suffering to giving birth, "A woman, when she is in labor, has sorrow because her hour has come; but as soon as she has given birth to the child, she no longer remembers the anguish, for the joy that a human being has been born into the world" (John 16:21).

"For the joy that was set before Him", Jesus "endured the cross" (Heb. 12:2). He knew He was the *Suffering Servant*. He knew the Scriptures spoke of Him when they said, "Having suffered, he will reflect on his work, he will be satisfied when he understands what he has done. 'My servant will acquit many, for he carried their sins'" (Is. 53:11, NET). Though Jesus "offered up prayers and supplications, with vehement cries and tears" (Heb. 5:7), He knew that at the end of that bloody labor there would be an *eternal joy* and *satisfaction* over all the slaves of sin and death who had been remade into sons of God. Jesus endured *temporal* suffering and shame so we could experience *eternal* glory.

I mentioned that things got "bloody" in the garden. Luke, the doctor among the Evangelists, gives a detail Matthew, Mark, and John don't. He writes, "and having been in agony, He was more earnestly praying, and His sweat became, as it were, great drops of blood falling on the ground" (Luke 22:44, LSV). Interpreters disagree if Luke is communicating that the sweat was pouring so fast and profusely it was like blood leaking from open wounds, or whether Jesus was actually sweating blood. One of the earliest interpreters, Ireneaus, understood it as actual blood, and many others have agreed this was the case.[5] Today we call this medical condition *hematidrosis*—a state that usually is the result of the sudden onslaught of extreme fear and intense sorrow.

Dr. Barbet speaks of the condition of hematidrosis like this, "The blood mingles with the sweat, and it is this mixture which pearls over the whole surface of the body."[6] Interestingly, computer analysis of the three-dimensional images of the Shroud of Turin appear to reveal that the entirety of the Man of the Shroud's skin surface was soaked in blood—indicating that if the Shroud is indeed the burial cloth of Jesus, that Jesus did suffer *hematidrosis*.[7] Remember, Gethsemane means 'oil press.' Jesus was "crushed" like an olive (Is. 53:5). When olives are crushed under the weight of the press, the oil in the first press oozes out mixed with the crushed rinds. Before becoming *gloriously golden*, it pores forth *redemptively red*—mixed in the torn flesh of its outer sufferings. The Passionist, Fr. Ignatius, writes, "Behold, O my soul, behold your Redeemer sinking to the earth, overpowered with inward anguish, and bathed in His own Blood!...This Blood is not forced from His veins by the fury of His enemies, but wrung from His Heart at His own express desire, so we may understand the excess of His love for us."[8] *The first blood that poured was solely due to the crushing weight of our sin.*

In this intense state of *agony* Jesus cried, "Abba, Father, all things are possible for You. Take this cup away from Me; nevertheless, not what I will, but what You will" (Mark 14:36). Jesus certainly had no death wish. He was not suicidal. If salvation could've been accomplished some other way, He would gladly have gone that route. *But there was no other way, and Jesus obediently consented to the plan of Heaven. Salvation would rest in one source alone—the blood of the Lamb.* Earlier Jesus told His disciples that "He must go to Jerusalem, and suffer many things from the elders and chief priests and scribes, and be killed, and be raised the third day" (Matt. 16:21). *The cross was a "must", a divine necessity (Heb. 9:22).*

Christ prayed *three separate times* in the garden, and His human desire to embrace His suffering and cross grew stronger with each prayer. Though His closest companions had fallen asleep (three times), Heaven provided some encouragement. Luke writes, "Then an angel appeared to Him from heaven, strengthening Him. And being in agony, He prayed more earnestly" (Luke 22:43). *A creature came and strengthened the Creator!*

An angel once "strengthened" Elijah by providing him *angel cake* and a *jug of water* (1 Kings 19:5-8). An angel once "strengthened" Daniel by *touching him* and saying, "O man greatly beloved, fear not! Peace be to you; be strong, yes, be strong!" Daniel writes, "when he spoke to me I was strengthened, and said, 'Let my lord speak, for you have strengthened me'" (Dan. 9:19). In the wilderness, after Jesus was tempted three times by the devil, "angels came and ministered to Him" (Matt. 4:11).

Maybe the angel in Gethsemane said the same encouraging words that were spoken over Daniel. Maybe he spoke of the glories of His exodus in a similar fashion to Moses and Elijah during the transfiguration. Whatever the case, strength came to endure greater agony. For it was after the strengthening that the bloody sweat began to flow. Spurgeon theorized, "The angel may have whispered the promises; pictured before His mind's eye the glory of His success; sketched His resurrection; portrayed the scene when His angels would bring His chariots from on high to bear Him to His throne."[9]

Regardless of exactly what form the strengthening took, we do know it caused Jesus to pray "more earnestly." Jesus' prayer was *humble* (on His face), *relational* ('Abba, Father'), *persevering* (three times and likely three hours), *fervent* (earnest and heartfelt), *yielding* ('Thy will be done'), and *prevailing* (He rises in strength). His prayer in the garden is a model for our prayer in hours of trial. In fact, a model for prayer for every season of the soul.

The way the disciples were situated in the garden pictured the tabernacle. Eight disciples near the entrance were in the 'Outer Court' near the bronze altar (press). Three disciples were called to watch and pray like priests in the 'Holy Place.' A stone throw away, as our High Priest, Jesus was alone in the 'Holy of Holies.' Though we often fail in our prayer life and faithfulness like Peter, James, and John, the good news is Jesus has shed His blood for our forgiveness and "always lives to make intercession" when we are at our worst and have fallen woefully short (Heb. 7:25).

Lord Jesus, thank you for being pressed and crushed by the weight of my sin in Gethsemane. Thank you for being in full alignment with the will of the Father and shedding Your blood for my eternal salvation. Help me to pray as You have prayed, to trust as You have trusted, and to come boldly to Your throne in my need (Heb. 4:16). Though I falter at the exhortation to "pray without ceasing" (1 Thes. 5:17), as my Representative, You never fail!

DAY 5
'I AM' Betrayed With a Kiss
(Mt 26:47-50; Mk 14:43-46; Lk 22:47-48; Jn 18:2-9)

After praying for a third time alone, deeply distressed and prostrate before the Father, Jesus stood up. His garments were soaked and stained in the blood and sweat of those traumatic hours when He wrestled with what was about to transpire. As He walked back toward the garden gate He saw Peter, James, and John sleeping again. Though He could have justifiably berated them for their negligence and disobedience, as a tender, protecting, and forgiving Shepherd, He simply says, "Are you still sleeping and resting? Behold, the hour is at hand, and the Son of Man is being betrayed into the hands of sinners. Rise, let us be going. See, My betrayer is at hand" (Matt. 26:45-46).

The Man who emerged from this time of prayer was a Man of great strength. He rose from His bitter cries of agony to confront His captors, torturers, and death itself with *unwavering fortitude.* The devil truly found "no place" in Him, though he searched and prodded with all his might (John 14:30). He marched toward that garden gate, not as a reluctant victim, but as a triumphant and willing Victor. There He came face to face with a multitude of officers sent by the chief priests, elders, scribes, and Pharisees. The 'multitude' described by Mark was likely the 'police or court servants' who were at the disposal of the Sanhedrin, and the 'troops' described by John likely indicated the presence of "the Temple guard, commanded by the Temple colonel."[10] The top religious leaders in Jerusalem sent the largest forces under their command to go and arrest the peace loving and preaching Jesus!

Though Judas kisses Jesus to identify Him in the darkness to the captors (more on that in a moment), in John's Gospel we are told that Jesus is the One who confronts the mob. Jesus "went forward and said to them, 'Whom are you seeking?'" (John 18:4). Their response? "Jesus of Nazareth" (John 18:5). His response? "I AM" (John 19:5). Jesus of Nazareth *is* I AM! The one they were coming to arrest was none other than the enfleshed presence of God! The one they were coming out to arrest with "lanterns" and "torches", stumbling in their own darkness, was none other than the Light of the world! (John 8:12)

Upon saying "I AM", John tells us that the arresting multitude fell to the ground. The only time each year God's Name was pronounced by the high priest in Jerusalem was on Yom Kippur. After he would pronounce the name Jews would fall prostrate. That is what the Jerusalem guard does here. The big difference being that Jesus does not simply utter the Name, rather, He identifies as the Name! And this was not the first time He had done so. Earlier in the Gospel of John, when Jesus was in Jerusalem for the Feast of Tabernacles, He told the Jewish leaders, "Most assuredly, I say to you, before Abraham was, I AM" (John 8:58). This enraged them so much that they "took up stones to throw at Him" (John 8:59). But Jesus' hour had not yet come. Stoning, during the season of Tabernacles, was not how God providentially purposed to pay for our sin. So, Jesus slipped through their hands to live another day.

As the arresting multitude lay on the ground, Jesus could have walked away free. What transpires does not happen against His will. He *submits* to the arrest. He is the Commander in charge who essentially says, "Bind me!" The *innocent* willingly taking the place of the *guilty*. Sheen writes about this moment, "Love fettered Himself to unfetter man."[11] Though "the wicked" came upon Jesus, "they stumbled and fell", though "an army surrounded" Him, "His heart did not fear" (Ps. 27:2-3). For He knew, after His Passion was completed, He would see "the goodness of the LORD in the land of the living" (Ps. 27:13).

All three synoptic Gospels mention that the person who was betraying Jesus, Judas, was "one of the twelve." There is an emphasis upon the fact that our Lord was betrayed by a *close friend*. One He had specifically *chosen* (Mark 3:19). One who had been *entrusted* with His message and even *given a share* in His miraculous power (Luke 9:1). But though Judas had witnessed, and even experienced the wondrous power of God, his heart had not been fully changed. He was a *lover of money*. John tells us, "he was a thief, and had the money box; and he used to take what was put in it" (John 12:6).

Jesus taught that man cannot serve "God and mammon" (Matt. 6:24). In Colossians we are told that "covetousness is idolatry" (Col. 3:5). Judas had agreed with the Jewish leaders to betray Jesus for thirty pieces of silver (Matt. 26:15). That was equivalent to about four months wages. The average household income in America is about $70,000, so we could think of Judas receiving about $23,000 from the Jewish hierarchy. A sum that might appeal to the heart of one whose god is mammon.

The name Judas in Hebrew is Judah. *Judah betrayed Jesus.* The "Jews" get their name from the tribe Judah. In a sense, Judah betraying Jesus is a picture of all the Jews who rejected Him (John 1:12). In the Old Testament, Judah was the brother who hatched the plan to sell Joseph for twenty pieces of silver (Gen. 37:26-29). Joseph was the beloved son of Jacob (Gen. 37:3), just as Jesus is the beloved Son of the Father (Matt. 3:17). Both were betrayed by Judah and sold for silver. Yet, though betrayed, both would eventually rise to glory and rule all things (Gen. 41:41; Rev. 1:5). Both would provide 'salvation' even for the ones who had sold them into slavery (Gen. 45:20). In Hebrew, the name Judah is also the number thirty. "Thirty" sold Jesus for "thirty" pieces of silver. Thirty pieces of silver is also the compensation God commanded to be given for the death of a servant/slave (Ex. 21:32). The Suffering Servant was betrayed for the price of a servant. In fact, betrayed for the price of a servant's death!

The 'kiss' Judas gave Jesus was lavish. The Greek word used is the same word to describe the kisses the father of the prodigal gave to his son, or the kisses the sinful woman gave Jesus as she anointed Him and washed His feet with her hair (Luke 15:20; Luke 7:38). It was a kiss to draw attention. One 'savior figure' in the Old Testament who was betrayed partly by the lavish kisses of a lover was Samson. He was betrayed by Delilah, had his eyes gouged out, and was taken captive where he was chained to what appears to be an 'olive press' to grind oil for his enemies (Judges 16:21). In that moment of extreme suffering, Samson desired God's will to be accomplished through him one last time. So he began to *pray earnestly.* After being led into the temple of the pagan god 'Dagon', his arms were stretched between two pillars. He looked like Jesus stretched out on the cross! Pushing with all his might the demonic temple came crashing down! The betrayed one's *greatest deliverance in life* occurred *in his death* (Judges 16:30). Just like our Lord Jesus.

Father, open my eyes to perceive like never before that Jesus of Nazareth is none other than I AM. Open my eyes to perceive that Jesus of Nazareth is fully one with You (John 10:30). Lord Jesus, bind my heart to You in such a way that I would never consider choosing four months wages over the eternal inheritance that You have laid up for me in Heaven. May my desires and affections be free from covetousness. May I see You as the Pearl of Great Price, and be willing to forsake all, to simply have You (Matt. 13:46).

DAY 6
The Sword or The Cross?
(Mt 26:51-56; Mk 14:47-52; Lk 22:49-53; Jn 18:10-12)

The twelve Jesus had chosen to be His apostles were a *passionate* bunch. They longed for His kingdom to fully come. Jesus had promised they would "sit on twelve thrones, judging the twelve tribes of Israel" (Matt. 19:28). They took that literally and believed that day would happen *very soon*. In fact, Salome lobbied to get her two boys, James and John, the seats right next to Jesus. And it wasn't like the other ten were any humbler. When they heard about Salome's request, they were upset! They too desired those positions. Gently, Jesus corrected their wrongheadedness. He said, "whoever desires to be first among you, let him be your slave—just as the Son of Man did not come to be served, but to serve, and to give His life a ransom for many" (Matt. 20:27-28).

The zeal of Jesus' apostles is on display throughout the Gospels. John and James desire to call down fire upon the Samaritans and burn them to smithereens (Luke 9:54). One apostle is referred to as "Simon the zealot" (Mark 3:18), meaning he had been trained to use violence if necessary to usher in the Messianic reign. Peter was constantly putting his foot in his mouth, even zealously "rebuking" Jesus when He said the Son of Man must suffer and die (Mark 8:31-33). Certainly Christ's disciples are called to be "zealous" (Rom. 12:11; Tit. 2:14), *but it must be rightly directed zeal.*

Peter's zeal reached a high point in Gethsemane. As Jesus was being arrested by the great multitude of the temple guard, the reaction of Peter is an extraordinary display of both courage and incompetence—he began to swing one of the two swords that they brought to the garden that night! (Luke 22:38) And he struck first at the probable leader of the pack—the servant of the High Priest—cutting off his ear. Most certainly, Peter wasn't looking to cut off *ears*, rather, he was wanting *heads* to roll!

After Peter swung his sword Jesus immediately brought correction. He commanded Peter, "Put your sword into the sheath. Shall I not drink the cup which My Father has given Me?" (John 18:11) He then gave a proverb, "All who take the sword will perish by the sword" (Matt. 26:52). Peter was no civil magistrate (Rom. 13:4). He had no authority, or right, to kill Malchus. The sort of guerrilla warfare Peter's emotions had goaded him to engage in was unholy. If he had succeeded in taking a life in that manner, his life would have needed to be taken (Gen. 9:6). Jesus, as a Good Shepherd, wanted Peter alive. Maybe He even charged an angel to nudge Peter's sword ever so slightly in mid-flight so that only an ear was lopped off instead of a head. The Almighty and compassionate Prince of Peace understood Peter's heart that desired to protect Him, but He also gave a strong rebuke to Peter's misguided way of conducting himself.

The only thing Jesus had commanded His disciples to "take up" was a cross, not a sword (Matt. 16:24). A cross is an instrument of death. Paradoxically, it is also the means of victory. Had not Jesus taught them to love their enemies? (Matt. 5:44) Had not Jesus told them on several occasions that He must suffer, die, and rise again? (Matt. 16:21) Did Peter not see that Jesus was in complete control of the situation as the arresting party fell to the ground at the simple mention of His name? The disciples of Jesus had very thick skulls. They were slow learners. Yet, Jesus still patiently loved them. He reminded Peter, "Do you not think that I cannot now pray to My Father, and He will provide Me with more than twelve legions of angels?" (Matt. 26:53)

The largest military unit in a Roman army was a legion. It was enormous—six thousand men which included infantry, calvary, and even auxiliary. Jesus said instead of twelve puny disciples He could have twelve angel armies fight for Him in an instant! 72,000 spiritual warriors, some probably calvary riding flaming heavenly horses (2 Kings 6:17). We know one angel slaughtered 185,000 Assyrians in one night (2 Kings 19:35). What could 72,000 angels do? On top of this, Peter had seen Jesus have power to do anything He wanted. He saw Him *walk on water* and *raise Lazarus* after four days. Did he really think his puny sword was needed? *How quickly disciples of Jesus can become fleshly minded.*

After correcting Peter Jesus turned His attention to the *bludgeoned* Malchus. Luke says, "He touched his ear and healed him" (Luke 22:51). Imagine Jesus reaching out with His hand that had just been drenched in the bloody sweat of His suffering to touch and heal His enemy. In that moment He was bearing Malchus' sickness and disease, indeed, the sickness and disease of the whole world (Is. 53:4-5). The bearing of disease by the Suffering Servant was not solely spiritual and emotional, it was also *physical* (Matt. 8:17). The world gets a foretaste of that physical healing now, and one day will experience it forever in *resurrected bodies* (1 Cor. 15:42-43). Jesus experienced traumatic suffering inwardly and outwardly at the deepest levels in order to fully restore us. Be encouraged that Jesus heals even where His disciples have maimed. Though people might not be able 'to hear' the Good News *because of what disciples of Jesus have foolishly done,* Jesus, in His almighty mercy and grace, can cause them to hear again!

Jesus then turned to His captors and asked why He was being treated as a "robber." The Greek word is "lestai." It is probably best translated as "zealot" or "revolutionary"—for that is how Josephus uses the word. Jesus had regularly distanced Himself from revolutionary ideology, yet the Jewish leaders knew treating Jesus as a revolutionary was the only way they could get the Romans to put Him to death. In fact, Jesus ultimately ends up crucified between two revolutionaries (Mark 15:27). Though He asked this question, He knew exactly why He was being treated unjustly, at midnight, as a rebel. He says, "this is your hour, and the power of darkness" (Luke 22:53).

The power of darkness. The dark lord was present—prowling and seeking to devour. Doing his best to get Jesus to bow down and worship him. I imagine the darkness of that night was a "felt" darkness just like the darkness in Egypt (Ex. 10:21) Edersheim writes, "in that night the fierce wind of hell was allowed to sweep unbroken over the Saviour."[12] Yet, Jesus was unwaveringly resolute! The darkness did not move Him for He already gained the victory in prayer. But what about His disciples? They were prayerless men who were shaken like reeds. They all fled. One in particularly humiliating detail is recorded by Mark. He describes a young man who "fled from them naked" (Mark 14:52). *Naked in a garden. Running to hide. When have we seen that before?* Who will call out to this naked man, "Where are you?" (Gen. 3:9). Who will provide a sacrifice to re-robe this ashamed disciple? (Gen. 3:21) None other than the One being led away to be stripped naked, scourged, and offered as a sacrifice on his behalf! Only Jesus, and Jesus alone, can ever clothe man's nakedness (Rev. 3:17-20).

Lord Jesus, the misguided reaction of Peter in the garden has too often been my reaction. Though my spirit may be willing, my flesh also is weak. I have not prayed the way I ought. And as a result, I have too often sought to defend You by fleshly means. I also have found myself naked and ashamed when the power of darkness has descended and the accuser has shot his fiery arrows. Thank you for gently correcting me, healing those I have harmed, and dying in order that my nakedness and shame may forever be clothed in Your glory!

DAY 7
A Private Meeting With Annas
(John 18:13-14, 19-23; Luke 22:54)

The multitude that came with swords and clubs to arrest Jesus led Him away in fetters from the garden, through the winding streets of Jerusalem, to the house of the high priest. This was no ordinary house. Rather, it could properly be termed *a palace*. There was a large courtyard where many servants of the high priest and arresting party mingled (John 18:26). Mark indicates that it was two storied (Mark 14:66). We know that the Sanhedrin, a group of up to seventy-one men, met within one of the rooms in the house (Mark 14:53). From the narrative it appears most likely that Annas and Caiaphas both lived there— each residing in separate wings with their families on the lower floor. The upper floor appears to have had at least one large reception room where guests were entertained—likely where the 'trial' took place with the Sanhedrin (Luke 22:66).

This home was located in the upper city—the wealthiest part of Jerusalem. After Herod's palace, it was likely the nicest estate in Jerusalem, as it was owned and maintained by one of the wealthiest Jews of that day—Annas. We meet Annas three times in Scripture. He is mentioned as being "high priest" alongside Caiaphas at the beginning of John's ministry (Luke 3:2). He is mentioned in the Passion narrative as the first religious leader to *question Jesus* (John 18:13). Lastly, he is mentioned in the book of Acts as "the high priest" and is first in the list of named leaders before whom Peter and John are brought to be judged (Acts 4:6). He clearly is presented as a man holding a highly prominent position among the Jews. But how could he be "high priest"? Wasn't Caiaphas the high priest? What exactly is going on?

Well, our knowledge of Annas is not restricted to Scripture. Some of the outside sources help shed light on the sad condition the Jews were in. For one, we know the priesthood since the time right before the Maccabees—*nearly two hundred years earlier*—had been corrupted. Since this period there was no longer a high priest *descended from Zadok*, nor was his appointment for a *lifetime*, nor was it *hereditary*, nor was he *christened* upon holding the office. All in defiance of God's Word! And once Roman occupation arrived in 63 BC things grew even worse. The high priest position began to be auctioned off by Roman governors, and many of the most powerful aristocratic families bid against each other. From 37 BC until the fall of the temple in AD 70 there were twenty-eight high priests, from four Jewish families. These families would all intermarry to consolidate their power, and the most prominent family during this period was *the family of Annas*.

Annas 'officially' held the position of the high priesthood for nine years from AD 6-15. Josephus says he was "a bold man in his temper and very insolent; he was also of the sect of the Sadducees, who are very rigid in judging offenders, above all the rest of the Jews." He says Annas "had servants who were very wicked…[who] took away the tithes that belonged to the priests by violence: and did not refrain from beating such as would not give these tithes to them."[13] The Jewish Talmud agrees with this portrait of Annas. It refers to the temple market at the time of Jesus as the "bazaars of the sons of Annas." This detail is interesting because it sheds light on the 'temple cleansing' narratives at the beginning and end of Jesus' ministry. It was most likely *Annas' family*, foremost being his five sons, who were profiting off of the money changing booths and sacrificial sales!

Jesus drove them out and overturned *their* tables. (John 2:15; Matt. 19:12) I'm sure Annas received an earful about these incidents, and was more incensed than anyone, as his family profited greatly from their unjust exchange rates.

Though Annas was only high priest for nine years, his power and influence lasted much longer. For five of his sons, and a stepson, would also hold the high priesthood. Caiaphas being the stepson. Though Annas wasn't considered the official high priest by Rome, he is clearly presented in Scripture as being a "high priest" and calling shots. *The fact that Jesus was brought to the sixty-year-old Annas, before being led to the younger Caiaphas, shows Annas was still very powerful and was likely pulling many of the strings that night.*

When Jesus steps into this glitzy palace, surrounded by luxurious carpets and couches, He is met by this politically shrewd, wealthy, ticked-off whited sepulchre. While in private conference Annas "asked Jesus about His disciples and His doctrine" (John 18:19). Jesus, Good Shepherd He is, said nothing about His disciples so as not to put them in harm's way. Concerning His doctrine, He responded, "I spoke openly to the world", and, "Ask those who have heard Me what I said to them" (John 18:21). Jesus knew this private interrogation was a sham. Annas was simply seeking to expedite the process for Caiaphas, but Jesus would not oblige him. If they truly had a reason to arrest Him, they needed to *present the evidence*. They needed to *produce witnesses*.

Jesus had no problem letting Annas know He was not leading a movement that was cloaked in secrecy. There was nothing Gnostic about His ministry, nor was it like the mystery religions among the pagans, or the secret societies of today. Christianity and its teaching has always been very public. In fact, Jesus explicitly told His apostles, "Whatever I tell you in the dark, speak in the light; and what you hear in the ear, preach on the housetops" (Matt. 10:27). While there were times when Jesus told people to keep quiet about certain miracles for a short season so crowds wouldn't prohibit their access to villages, or to keep His identity as 'Messiah' under wraps because people had a wrong understanding of what the Messiah was, everything else He did and said was open for the world to see and hear.

Annas was silenced by Christ's response. He knew his scheme had been defeated. So, what happened? His servant "struck Jesus with the palm of his hand" (John 18:22). *People who don't get their way, and are exposed for who they are, tend to resort to irrational violence.* This strike in the face is the first mention of violence against Christ. It was with malice. It was unjust. Does Jesus respond in kind? No. He simply says, "If I have spoken evil, bear witness of the evil; but if well, why do you strike Me?" (John 18:23). Can they 'bear witness'? No. So their blood boils as they continue to seek a way to hand Him over to the Romans to be crucified.

Jesus, You are my Great High Priest. You descended from the unfading glories of Heaven and at the end of Your earthly life entered the fading glitzy palace of the corrupted high priests of that day. You knew the 'glory' Annas surrounded himself with paled in comparison to true Glory. You were neither in awe, nor taken aback. Though he sought to trap You, You saw right through his darkened soul. Indeed, You see right through all souls. Help me to seek Heavenly Glory rather than this-worldly glory that Annas sought. Help me set my "mind on things above, not on things on the earth" (Col. 3:2).

When 'reviled' and 'slapped' by Annas' servant, You did not revile in return. Rather, You turned the other cheek (1 Pet. 2:21; Matt. 5:39). Your Word says this is "an example" that I "should follow" (1 Pet. 2:20). Help me respond like You in times of injustice. Unlike Annas, You are the true and rightful high priest. An eternal "priest forever" (Ps. 110:4; Heb. 7:20-28).

DAY 8
Caiaphas and The Sanhedrin
(Matt 26:57-63; Mark 14:53-61; John 18:24)

Three examinations occur in the palace of Annas and Caiaphas after Jesus' arrest—an initial interrogation by Annas, a meeting in the dead of night before Caiaphas and some powerful council members, and an early morning confirmation 'trial' before at least a quorum of the Sanhedrin. After Jesus' first examination, "Annas sent Him bound to Caiaphas" (John 18:24). The servant who had just struck our Lord across the face, now led Him to another area in the palace precincts—likely a larger room where Caiaphas had been *making preparations* to conduct his own 'trial.'

This palace has already been spoken of as the site where some of the chief priests, scribes, and elders met to plot how they might "take Jesus by trickery and kill Him" (Matt. 26:3-4). They had reached a *predetermined verdict* before any sort of 'trial' would take place! Jesus truly entered a *kangaroo court.* The big dilemma for Caiaphas was how he could conduct a 'trial' with at least the outward semblance of justice—possibly for others on the council who were not yet fully on board with putting Jesus to death, or for the recorders who would make the proceedings of the trial more widely known. He wanted to at least appear righteous in putting this popular preacher and wonder worker to death.

Many scholars suggest the actual trial was overflowing with illegality according to the Sanhedrin's own rules. They say this based on the Jewish Mishnah which lays out many protocols. Based on the Mishnah trials could only be held in the day, they could not occur on Friday or the eve of a festival, and the accused could not be convicted on his own evidence. Also, the binding of a prisoner before a trial was not permitted unless they were resistant, and the judges in a trial were not permitted to be part of the arrest. All of these things were clearly violated in this 'trial' of Jesus during the Passover festival at night.

Because the Mishnah was not written until the third century, and because the Sanhedrin was filled solely with Pharisees at the time it was composed, it is impossible to know how closely it preserves what rules would have dictated the age of Annas and a heavily Sadducean court. Yet, it does seem that at least parts of the Mishnah were in play during the time of Jesus. For instance, in Acts we are told that Peter and John, though arrested in the evening like Jesus, were held in custody until a morning trial (Acts 4:3-5). Something similar happened with Paul (Acts 22:30). At the very least, what is happening in the trial of Jesus is 'shady' in terms of when they met, where they met, and how Jesus was arrested and the proceedings took place.

One thing that was definitely unjust is that "false testimony" was sought. The chief priests were acting like Jezebel who sought out "two scoundrels" to "bear false witness" against Naboth in order to kill Naboth and steal his vineyard for Ahab (1 Kings 21:10). Ahab, as the ruling authority, was supposed to *oversee* and *protect* that garden, not covet it. Earlier in the week Jesus taught a parable before the chief priests and elders about vinedressers who had been unfaithful at overseeing a vineyard—i.e. Israel (Matt. 21:33-46). Though the owner would send his servants to collect his fruit, the overseers would beat them up and kill them —seeking to have the fruit all to themselves. Ultimately, the owner sent his son. The overseers said, "Come, let us kill him and seize his inheritance." Then Jesus said, "So they took him and cast him out of the vineyard and killed him" (Matt. 21:39).

The chief priests and Pharisees "perceived He was speaking of them" (Matt. 21:45). A few days later, *they fulfilled Jesus' prophetic parable.* Caiaphas was a Jezebel attempting to secure God's garden for himself with his own "scoundrels" uttering "false testimony." *He, along with some other unjust overseers on the Sanhedrin, sought to kill the Son of the Owner of Israel to maintain their power.*

Though they had false witnesses lined up, they still went through the correct process of hearing them so the trial would have at least a pretense of justice. They cross-examined witnesses in accordance with the law's demand that two or three agree (Num. 35:30; Dt. 17:6; 19:16). Though they had very likely been coached and prepared as 'false witnesses' behind the scenes, they could not find two witnesses in agreement. Even though "many" came forward. I imagine as false witness after false witness disagreed before the Sanhedrin that Caiaphas' blood began to boil. How could these scoundrels not remember their lines!?

Finally, two false witnesses came forward that agreed enough to pass the test in the eyes of the council. They accused Jesus of saying "I will destroy this temple made with hands, and within three days I will build another made without hands" (Mark 14:58). Matthew and Mark seem to be in slight tension on how much these witnesses even agreed, but the tension can be relaxed when we realize that this was as close to two agreeing witnesses that the council could find (Mark 14:59; Matt. 26:61). Not perfect, but close enough for these men hell bent on getting a charge to 'stick' to Jesus before morning arrived.

While Jesus did have a lot to say about the destruction of the temple in His Olivet discourse, there is never a statement like the one the false witnesses report. Even in His metaphorical statement about the temple, when Jesus was speaking about His own body, He said, "Destroy this temple, and in three days I will raise it up" (John 2:19). He did not say He would destroy it, like the false witnesses maintained. Neither did He say "I will build another." Regardless, Caiaphas, who was desperate at this late point in the 'trial', seized on this accusation. He said to Jesus, "Do You answer nothing? What is it these men testify against You?" Jesus' response? *Silence.*

There was no reason to defend Himself to people unwilling to listen or hear the truth—something He reiterates a little later that morning (Luke 22:67). By His act of silence He was also fulfilling the prophecy of the *Suffering Servant,* "as a sheep before its shearers is silent, so He opened not His mouth" (Is. 53:7). His silence had the effect of magnifying the injustice. What was taking place was a sham 'trial' full of scoundrels bearing false witness. The injustice of it all spoke on His behalf.

At this point Caiaphas was in total desperation. He needed a verdict, and He needed it fast! So He placed Jesus under an oath, commanding Him to state whether He was the 'Messiah.' This was an accusation he likely felt naturally flowed from the temple accusation as some Jews of that day believed only the Messiah would rebuild the temple (2 Sam 7:13; Zech. 6:12). If he could get Jesus to claim to be the Messiah, he could deliver Him to Pilate, for a Messianic claim could be construed as *sedition* and *treason*—a capital offense in the eyes of Rome. (More on Jesus' response to Caiaphas' desperation tomorrow.)

O Lamb of God, You stood silent before Your shearers as a multitude of false accusations were leveled against You. What Your trial made clear was that You were 'the Just for the unjust' (1 Pet. 3:18). 'In You is no sin' (1 Jn. 1:8). You are 'the Spotless Lamb of God' (1 Pet. 1:19). Though I am guilty of sin, and deserve death, You have taken my place (Rom. 6:23). I join the choirs of Heaven in singing, 'Worthy is the Lamb!' (Rev. 5:12)

DAY 9
'Perceiving' the Son of Man
(Matt 26:64-66; Mark 14:62-64; Luke 22:66-71)

The sun was about to rise. The high priest, Caiaphas, moved from a seated posture in cross-examining witnesses to a place of deep emotion where he "stood up" ready to confront Jesus like never before (Mark 14:60). He knew he had no more time to waste for Roman trials only took place in the morning—so he needed to bring a charge to Pilate *quickly*, and it needed to be a charge that Rome would deem *dangerous*. Seeing Jesus remained silent about the temple charges, Caiaphas made sure He would remain silent no more. Raising his voice before our bound Lord, he cried, "I charge you under oath by the living God: Tell us if you are the Messiah, the Son of God" (Matt. 26:63, CSB).

This was the final card Caiaphas could play. It is the climactic moment of the entire trial. *Jesus was forced to speak*. He was bound by law, and so He would give one final declaration. Up until this point in the Gospels Jesus had made it very clear to His disciples and demons that they were not to talk about His messianic identity (Mark 3:12, 5:43, 8:30, 9:9). Scholars refer to this theme in the Gospels as *the Messianic secret*. The reason Jesus kept this under wraps is because He wanted to teach His disciples *the true role of the Messiah*. In the mind of His disciples, and the masses, it was an *earthly* and *political* role. He needed to correct that. After Peter declared Jesus was the Messiah, Mark writes, "He began to teach them that the Son of Man must suffer many things, and be rejected by the elders and chief priests and scribes, and be killed, and after three days rise again" (Mark 8:31).

Knowing the court would twist His words to mean something other than His own definition of 'Messiah', how does Jesus respond? He says, "You have said so" (Matt. 26:64, ESV). It is a qualified "yes." In fact, He follows that statement up with one that will get to the heart of His identity as the Messiah. He says, "But I tell you, from now on you will see the Son of Man seated at the right hand of Power and coming on the clouds of heaven" (Matt. 26:64, ESV).

This was a much bigger 'mic drop' moment than a simple messianic affirmation. We know that because Caiaphas tears his robes and screams "blasphemy!" while the other council members cry out that Jesus is "worthy of death." Jesus essentially said, "I am the 'Messiah', but not in the way *you* think. My messianic rule will be from a throne at the right hand of the Power in Heaven. Instead of having a political reign in Jerusalem, and overthrowing the Romans, I will rule the entire world as the Divine Son of Man that Daniel 7 and Psalm 110 prophesied about. I am the Supreme Judge, the Almighty Ruler, and you will begin to *perceive* that from this time forward!"

Five centuries before Jesus' time, the prophet Daniel had a vision of what would happen from his time until the coming of the Messiah. Describing a night vision, Daniel wrote, "behold, with the clouds of heaven there came one like a son of man, and he came to the Ancient of Days and was presented before him. And to him was given dominion and glory and a kingdom, that all peoples, nations, and languages should serve him; his dominion is an everlasting dominion" (Dan. 7:13-14, ESV). All the other kingdoms Daniel had described in his visions (Babylon, Media-Persia, Greece, Rome) would be given power for *limited periods of time*. But this "Son of Man" coming "with the clouds" was different. He would receive "an everlasting kingdom." In Daniel

2 His kingdom is described as "a great mountain" that "filled the whole earth" (Dan. 2:35). This is a kingdom that knows no bounds! A kingdom for all people! The glory of the King of this kingdom would cover the earth as the waters clothe the sea!

Many Christians think Jesus is talking about His coming at the end of history in this declaration before the Sanhedrin. That He will be coming on the clouds *to earth*. But that is not what Daniel is talking about. In fact, Daniel is very clear that He comes on the clouds *to the Ancient of Days*. This text is an *enthronement text*. Jesus was using the apocalyptic language of the Old Testament to make very clear to the Jewish leaders of His day that though they were going to put Him to death, ultimately He would be vindicated, and they would 'see' or 'perceive' that vindication. They would 'perceive' He was reigning next to *the Ancient of Days*!

This was not the first time in His ministry Jesus had used the language from Daniel 7 to refer to Himself. In fact, His favorite self-designation throughout the Gospels is that He is this 'Son of Man' figure. He quotes from Daniel 7:13 at least three times in His ministry. The first time is in Matthew 10 when Jesus sent the twelve out to preach "to the lost sheep of the house of Israel." Toward the end of His instruction He says, "I say to you, you will not have gone through all the towns of Israel before the Son of Man comes" (Matt. 10:23). Comes where? *Comes to the Ancient of Days*. They had gone through *most* of Israel by the time of Jesus' trial, but not all of it. Once Jesus had risen from the grave and was about to sit at the right hand of Power at the ascension, He told His disciples, "All authority in heaven and on earth has been given to me. Go therefore and make disciples of all nations" (Matt 28:18-19). Before they had been *forbidden* to go to all nations. Now they were *commanded* to go. What changed? *The Son of Man had come on the clouds to the Ancient of Days*. He is now the King of the World and the mission *must* go everywhere!

On the Mount of Olives Jesus told Peter, James, John, and Andrew their generation would "see the Son of Man coming on the clouds of heaven with power and great glory" (Matt. 24:30). Another reference to Daniel 7. Again, not about Jesus coming *to earth*, but rather Jesus coming *to the Ancient of Days in heaven*. Part of that generation being able to *see*, or *perceive*, that Jesus was in that position of power was that His prophetic word about the temple destruction would *come to pass in their generation—and it did!*

The other verse Jesus referred to in His trial was Psalm 110. A psalm He utilized earlier in the week to prove that He wasn't simply the son of David, but something far more than that, David's Lord (Matt. 22:42-46). David wrote, "The LORD said to my Lord, 'sit at My right hand, till I make Your enemies Your footstool" (Ps. 110:1). In other words, Yahweh said to Jesus, "Sit at My Right Hand." *A Glorified Man now sits as the Ruler of the Cosmos in Heaven—Jesus of Nazareth!* He is the Son of Man that rode on the clouds to the Ancient of Days! And the rulers began to perceive that truth as the church began to rapidly multiply, miracles were performed in Jesus' Name, and Judaism dwindled with its ultimate power structure ceasing to exist in AD 70 just as Jesus said it would. They could *see* and *perceive* it, but would they *believe* it? A question for people of every generation.

Jesus, You are the LORD of glory. You sit at the right hand of the Power and share in the glory of the Father (Jn. 17:5). You are the Messiah, the Son of Man, and the Son of God. May I have eyes to perceive Your present reign in Heaven. As the Supreme Judge, the Holy God, Purity Incarnate, You were unrighteously judged as deserving of death. Yet, even in that unrighteous sentence, Your death would give me access to everlasting life with You. In fact, You have made me sit with You in heavenly places even now (Eph. 2:6). Thank you for Your abundant grace and gift of righteousness so I can reign in life, and be an effective witness for You! (Rom. 5:17)

DAY 10
Blindfolded and Beaten
(Matt 26:67-68; Mark 14:65; Luke 22:63-65)

Jesus had just claimed to be the 'Son of Man'—the one who would 'come on the clouds to the Ancient of Days' and receive an everlasting kingdom. He also claimed that He would 'sit at the right hand of the Power' sharing in the enthronement and full authority of Yahweh. Earlier in the week Jesus had also appealed to Psalm 110 in making the claim that He was not simply the seed of David, but more importantly, "David's Lord" (Mark 12:35-37). Jesus was utilizing the two texts of Scripture (Daniel 7 and Psalm 110) that very clearly portrayed His divine nature. In the eyes of the Sanhedrin this claim was far worse than a claim to be the Messiah, it was *blasphemy*.

Both Matthew and Mark tell us "the high priest tore his clothes" as he screamed "blasphemy!" (Matt. 26:65; Mark 14:63). One reason this is significant is because God prohibited Israel's high priest from ever tearing their robe. Moses told Aaron and his sons, "Do not uncover your heads nor tear your clothes, lest you die, and wrath come upon all the people" (Lev. 10:6). The high priest was the representative of the people—for him to commit such a sin would entail "wrath coming upon all the people." Jesus had declared that the corrupt Jewish leaders were filling up "the measure" of their "fathers' guilt" (Matt. 23:32). He said the "days of vengeance" would descend on Jerusalem in that generation (Luke 21:22). While Jesus was at that very moment drinking the cup of wrath, the question ultimately to them would be—"Will you come to Me for forgiveness, as One who has taken the consequences of your sin, or will you die in your sins and experience destruction with your people?" Jesus *wept* for those who chose not to come to Him (Matt. 23:37-38).

The 'tearing of the robe' also signified that the old covenant was ending. Whatever authentic, God-ordained, spiritual authority Caiaphas may or may not have had, came to an end that night. All authority given to the high priest was transferred to Jesus—a high priest "according to the order of Melchizedek" (Ps. 110:4; Heb. 7:11). In fact, the very psalm that Jesus quoted to Caiaphas, Psalm 110, has to do not just with His divine Messianic status, but also His eternal high priesthood. Caiaphas tore his robes in the morning and God tore the temple veil in the evening—signifying the end of the Levitical priesthood and age of the temple. Jesus is the *new temple* and sole *eternal high priest*.

After the quasi-official night hearings in the high priestly palace, did the over-seeing officials allow witnesses to come forward to validate Jesus' claims? Did they allow those who were healed and raised from the dead to come and testify? Did they allow Peter, James, and John to testify about the transfiguration of Jesus and His walking on water? No. They are not interested in a proper trial. Instead, "they all condemned Him to be deserving of death" (Mark 14:64). If they had the legal authority from Rome, they might have stoned Him right then and there! But, they didn't have that authority, and it seems that instead of engaging in an illegal secretive stoning like they did for Stephen (Acts 7:58), they desired to make an example of Jesus. They wanted it to be absolutely clear in the minds of the people that Jesus was an *imposter* and *cursed* by God. They didn't just want Him stoned, they wanted Him *crucified*. They wanted this 'blasphemer' cursed by God for all to see! They will later shout "Crucify Him!, Crucify Him!" before Pilate, not "Stone Him!" (Luke 23:21).

Though they decided not to stone Him, all the members of the Sanhedrin that condemned Him that night engaged in a *symbolic stoning*. After each one voted that He deserved death they went up to Him and "spat in His face and beat Him" (Matt. 26:66). They threw *fists* instead of *stones*. Mark and Luke tell us that they blindfolded Jesus, and then took turns striking Him and beating Him, both in the face and the body, as His hands were bound behind His back. As Jesus was struggling for breath they mocked Him saying, "Prophesy! Who is the one who struck You?" (Luke 22:64). This is great irony. For Jesus had prophesied about this specific event multiple times. He even prophesied that they would "spit" on Him. In His words, "and they will mock Him, and scourge Him, and spit on Him, and kill Him. And the third day He will rise again" (Mark 10:34).

They were not just fulfilling Jesus' own prophecy, they were also fulfilling the prophecy of Isaiah, "I gave My back to those who struck Me, and My cheeks to those who plucked out the beard; I did not hide My face from shame and spitting" (Is. 50:6). He wasn't just beaten, mocked, and spit upon, but Isaiah testifies that portions of His beard were plucked out. Inflicting all sorts of pain, in all sorts of cruel manners! Numerous experts of the Shroud of Turin have pointed out that portions of the beard near the center of the chin and below the right side of the mouth have been plucked out. *An extraordinarily cruel beating, seeking to torture and humiliate Jesus before the ultimate humiliation of the cross.*

Luke adds a detail that Mark and Matthew don't have. He uses the Greek word 'derontes' for the beating the Sanhedrin inflicted on our Savior. It is a word that refers to a beating of the body. Jesus' entire body was *pummeled to a pulp*. Dr. McGovern writes, "By the time he reached Pilate early on Good Friday morning, he was exhausted and thirsty and had developed many tender areas of bruising and swelling on his face and body. His subsequent punishments would be magnified because the skin and soft tissues were inflamed and full of chemicals that mediate pain to the nervous system."[14]

It appears that this *symbolic stoning*, this beating of the face and body, mostly took place right after the 'second trial' in the dark of night. For the next few hours Jesus was held in 'custody' in the palace before a more 'official' final sentencing before a fuller Sanhedrin at dawn where the basic claims that were made that night were repeated (Luke 22:66-71). Jesus was probably in a dungeon or cellar that served as a make-shift prison, as His body was being primed to experience far greater suffering. He would be delivered to Pilate in the "early morning" (John 18:28).

Jesus, You are the Rose of Sharon and the Chief among ten thousand (Song. 2:1, 5:10). With King David I long to "behold Your beauty" and with the angels of heaven to sing "holy, holy, holy" (Ps. 27:4; Rev. 4:8). You have given us Your precious blessing when You told the high priests to speak over Your people, "The LORD bless you and keep you; The LORD make His face shine upon you, and be gracious to you; The LORD lift up His countenance upon you, and give you peace" (Num. 6:24-26).

Though You are beautiful beyond description, You came to us and we blindfolded and beat You. We put a veil over You to hide Your countenance. We mocked You, struck You, and pulverized You with the intent that You would die. We spat in Your face as a sign of ultimate disrespect (Deut. 25:9). Job in his abject humiliation said, "I have become one in whose face men spit" and "They do not hesitate to spit in my face" (Job 17:6; 30:10). Such were You as the Greater Job. The One who experienced humiliation, loss, and yet patiently endured until all was restored (James 5:11). While we spat at You in contempt, You gave life-giving spit to many (Mk. 7:23, 8:23; John 9:6). Thank you for enduring the symbolic stoning for MY sin!

DAY 11
Peter Denies & Curses Jesus
(Matt 26:69-75; Mark 14:66-72; Luke 22:54-62; John 18:15-18, 25-26)

While Jesus undergoes a trial by the Sanhedrin in the upper floor of the high priest's palace, his head disciple, Peter, undergoes a trial of his own in the courtyard below. Each Gospel juxtaposes these two trials. In Matthew and Mark Peter's denials are recorded *after* Jesus' night trial, though, it is clear that the denials occur simultaneously. In Luke the denials precede the morning trial—fitting seamlessly with Matthew and Mark. In John the first denial takes place around the time Jesus faces Annas, with the others occurring later. The four accounts harmonize well.

Peter was one of two disciples to follow Jesus "from a distance" to the high priest's palace. Earlier that night Peter had boasted, "Lord, I am ready to go with You, both to prison and to death" (Luke 22:33). As if that was not enough, he declared, "Even if all are made to stumble, yet I will not be" (Mark 14:29). Peter was puffed-up in self-confidence. He felt he was a cut above the rest and that nothing could make him stumble. He seems to be forgetting the proverb he was brought up on, "Pride goes before destruction, and a haughty spirit before a fall" (Prov. 16:18). Not only was he proud, but that pride allowed him to remain prayerless in the garden, and now careless in the courtyard—warming himself with the arresting party.

While around the fire the young servant girl who had let Peter through the palace gate questioned him if he was a disciple of Jesus. The brawny fisherman began to grow nervous. He tried brushing it off and said, "I neither know nor understand what you are saying" (Mark 14:68). As fear began to eat at Peter, he distanced himself from the crowd, hoping for a safer spot near the gate. Mark mentions that it was at this moment the cock crowed for the first time. A little later the same girl came back to him with some other servants or men from the arresting party. Together they claimed he was indeed a disciple of Jesus. His response? "He denied with an oath, 'I do not know the Man!'" (Matt. 26:72) The disciple who once declared Jesus was "the Son of the living God" now pretends that Jesus is simply a 'man' that he knows nothing about! *In fact, by taking an 'oath' he would have invoked God to witness his reiterated denial,* saying something like, "God is my witness that I do not know this man!"

About an hour later, one of the relatives of Malchus asked him, "Did I not see you in the garden with him?" (Luke 22:59; John 18:26) Fear seized Peter. Remember, he had just tried to lop Malchus' head off. At this moment he was likely planning his escape from the palace, and caught up in deep emotion, his Galilean accent became even more pronounced. He resorted to protecting himself by cursing and swearing. The New Testament scholar, R. T. France, writes, "first comes an evasive denial, then a direct denial on oath, and finally a much stronger response which is probably to be understood as actually uttering a curse against Jesus...If the verb here meant, as some versions have suggested, that Peter is putting *himself* under a curse if he is lying, it would require 'himself' as object, as it has in Acts 21:12, 14, 21. Here, where the object is not expressed, it means that Peter is cursing someone other than himself, and the most natural sense in this context would be that he now began to curse *Jesus*, as a way of dissociating himself from him; this was precisely what Pliny later required those accused of being Christians to do, in order to prove their innocence (Justin, 1 Apol. 31.6)"[15]

As Peter denies Christ for the third time and even begins to curse Him, Mark tells us that the cock crows for a second time (Mark 14:72). This was a fulfillment of Jesus' own prophecy earlier that night—"before the cock crows twice, you will deny Me three times" (Mark 14:30, KJV). The 'cock' likely was not a 'rooster' (which the Mishnah tells us was not allowed in Jerusalem for purity issues) but rather a 'man' who blew a trumpet in the temple precincts as priestly activity for the day began. Did Peter hear that trumpet blast from the temple as he sat in the courtyard of the high priest? Most certainly, as their residence was only a couple stone throws from the temple.

Both Matthew and Luke say that upon hearing the cock Peter "wept bitterly." The weeping was "with poignant grief", even "violently", as some lexicons put it. *We can imagine Peter's eyes gushing like a fountain as a result of hearing the cock and remembering the words of his Lord.* But it wasn't just Jesus' prophetic words that made his eyes water, Luke records that after the cock crowed, "the Lord turned and looked at Peter" (Luke 22:61). Much has been written about this "look" from Jesus. Tauler says, "How quickly did He look upon him with the eyes of His grace, and permitted the rays of divine light to shine into the dark depths of his soul!"[16] Philaret adds, "Jesus' gaze of love called Peter out of the bewitching darkness of sin" and his repentance was solely the result of "the life-giving gaze of Heavenly Goodness."[17] J. Groenings believes this "look of grace" caused "a *quick*, an instantaneous contrition...*sincere* and serious."[18] Martin Luther adds, "This consolation, like a mighty deluge, suffocated, yea, quenched the fire that had threatened to consume his heart."[19]

Peter's heart would have been flooded with emotion as he recalled what Jesus said to Him earlier that night—"I have prayed for you, that your faith should not fail; and when you have returned to Me, strengthen your brethren" (Luke 22:32). Peter's denials, oath, and cursing did not take Jesus by surprise. Our sins, even our most heinous and wicked sins, never surprise Jesus. If anyone was disqualified for ministry, it was Peter. He denied the Lord with an oath and cursed Him! But the Lord still saw him restored and a strengthening pillar in the church. We must have eyes of hope to see this for those who have fallen. God is not done with them yet. God is not done with *you* yet. The bitter weeping would last for a night, but the joy of restoration and new creation was just around the corner!

Upon His resurrection an angel commissioned by Jesus said, "Go, tell His disciples—and Peter—that He is going before you into Galilee" (Mark 16:7). Peter was singled out. All was forgiven and washed away by the blood! Jesus is sure to have him called 'Peter' instead of 'Simon'—that Rock which proudly professed faith in Christ (Matt. 16:18). And when He appeared to Peter in Galilee He gave Him a threefold commission to "feed My sheep" to restore him from his threefold denial (John 21:15-17). Peter would end up preaching the first Christian sermon and write two books of the Bible (Acts 2; 1-2 Peter). Jesus also said Peter would one day die like He did (John 21:18), and tradition tells us Peter was crucified upside-down in Rome to not take away from the glory of his Master. Truly a man fully restored.

Jesus, in observing Peter, I notice he not only escalated his denials from an evasive denial, to a direct denial with an oath, to uttering an actual curse against You, but that Peter also progressively moved farther away from Your Presence. He went from the fire, to the gate, and eventually fled outside the palace. Yet, even from a distance, You saw him! And, he saw You! Help me to see Your loving gaze fixed upon me at all times. As I see You, I know I will humble myself, confess You as my Lord, and have a strong sense of hope for my future. For You have forgiven me, You are with me, You are for me, and You have promised to never leave or forsake me. Thank you.

DAY 12
Judah's Sadness & Suicide
(Matthew 27:3-10)

Judas/Judah had just witnessed the Sanhedrin condemn Jesus as worthy of death. He knew they were intent on Rome crucifying Him. Suddenly, he was struck with pangs of regret! He knew Jesus did not deserve that sentence. The thirty pieces of silver jingling in his pocket, mixed with the other gifts of people who supported Jesus' ministry, began to eat at his conscience. He realized that according to the law, he was under a curse! For Deuteronomy states, "Cursed is the one who takes a bribe to slay an innocent person" (Deut. 27:25). Judas had done just that. He stood cursed and condemned. *Darkness began to overwhelm his soul.*

Though regretful, he is not so much thinking about Jesus, as he is the fact that he "betrayed innocent blood." If he was truly repentant he would have said that he betrayed "the Messiah, the Son of the Living God!" If he was truly repentant he wouldn't have gone to the chief priests, but rather to the Great High Priest, Jesus. He would had elbowed his ways through the crowd before Pilate and shouted in an oath, "This man, Jesus, is the victim of my own unjust intrigue with the chief priests! He is innocent!" He would have fallen before Jesus begging His mercy, for he had heard Jesus say, "Anyone who speaks a word against the Son of Man, it will be forgiven him" (Matt. 12:32). He would have "wept bitterly" like Peter did, and placed his faith in one of Christ's promises. Judas had seen many sinners forgiven throughout Jesus' ministry. He had even seen capital offenses forgiven—like the woman who was caught in the very act of adultery (John 8:11). But, even though he had seen Jesus forgive those sins, he did not seek out Jesus. In fact, as we will see, in many ways his treachery was partially a result of a rejection of Christ's kingdom and way of *"justifying the ungodly" (Rom. 4:5)*.

It is best to describe Judas as being remorseful. Matthew uses a different Greek word than the one normally used for repent. This word carries the idea of *regretting the consequences of your action, but not actually seeking pardon*. After committing this heinous act, Judas regretted it and realized it wasn't worth it. The *four months wages* he had acquired to get rid of the man who did not fit his messianic longings now felt like a millstone. He experienced "the sorrow of the world" that "produces death" (2 Cor. 7:10). So, he threw back the "blood money" and "hanged himself."

Luke gives a few more details about this hanging, "Now this man purchased a field with the wages of iniquity; and falling headlong, he burst open in the middle and all his entrails gushed out. And it became known to all those dwelling in Jerusalem; so that field is called in their own language, Akel Dama, that is, Field of Blood" (Acts 1:18-19). After Judas fled from the temple, he went out by the Potter's Gate, near the valley of Gehenna, and likely found a tree above a ravine. One can imagine after hanging for a time, the branch snapped, Judas hit some other obstruction, turned over head first, and made a big splash when he hit the ground. A terrible sight for anyone to see that day! *Though, not as terrible as the sight of Jesus on the cross just hours later.*

We've seen that Judas' treachery echoes the story of David (Day 1). At the end of his life, David began to unravel in many ways. He committed adultery with Bathsheba, he essentially sentenced Uriah to death, and he had issues with many of his sons, with his eldest son, Absalom, seeking to take the kingdom from him by force. Realizing how his kingdom was ending in shambles, David became truly contrite. He wept as he crossed the Kidron river to the Mount of Olives. *He knew he was not deserving of his kingdom.* While weeping, he learned one of his closet cabinet members and confidants, Ahithophel, had sided with Absalom. Why would Ahithophel do such a thing? Well, *Ahithophel was actually the grandfather of Bathsheba.* It appears he may have partially broke rank with David because he believed David was an *ungodly* and *wicked man* in doing what he did with his granddaughter and Uriah. He was not the sort of king Ahithophel wanted to follow. David *deserved* to have the kingdom stripped from him. Schilder writes that Ahithophel "cannot endure the Gospel of free grace, as it returns David…to the throne, and accompanies the return with a message that God justifies the ungodly—freely."[20]

In many ways this is the issue Judas had with Jesus. Not only was his heart moved with covetousness, but he had rejected the way Jesus, as the Messiah, came to save. He scoffed at the perfume being poured on Jesus for His *burial* (John 12:7). The first time Jesus calls Judas a "devil" is when Jesus rejected the crowd's attempt to *take Him by force and make Him king* (John 6:15). Judas, as the one apostle from Judah (the town of Kerioth), was likely more intent than even James and John at gaining a *prominent seat on a throne in Jerusalem* as Jesus wiped out the Romans. His heart was set on fleshly and material things. *It was a heart set against the spiritual kingdom, against the message of grace, against the justification of the ungodly.* Just as Ahithophel rejected the king that wore the badge of that message, so Judas rejected Jesus. Ahithophel "hanged himself", just like Judas (2 Sam. 17:23). *We all hang ourselves when we reject the message that God justifies the ungodly.*

Though Judas threw the thirty pieces of silver back to the chief priests, they wanted nothing do with that "blood money." In a similar way, we will see how Pilate wanted nothing to do with the trial of Jesus, and tried to "wash his hands" of Christ's blood. In the story of the Passion it is those who try to *remove* the blood, throw it way, and wash it off who ultimately are doomed. In contrast, it is those who *receive* Jesus' blood (like the thief on the cross) who ultimately have their robes washed clean in that blood (Rev. 7:14). *Everyone must deal with the blood.* It either becomes what we place our trust in, or we reject and push it away to our own destruction and perdition, judging ourselves "unworthy of eternal life" like the Jews in Pisidian Antioch (Acts 13:46).

Matthew says the priests buying a field with the blood money "fulfilled what was spoken by Jeremiah the prophet." His quote combines material from Jeremiah and Zechariah, and primarily comes from Zechariah. He wrote, "the LORD said to me, 'Throw it to the potter'—that princely price they set on me. So I took the thirty pieces of silver and threw them into the house of the LORD" (Zech. 11:13). They counted God, *the One of Infinite Worth*, for the price of a slave (Ex. 21:32). With Christ's blood they bought a field for sojourners (Matt. 27:7). For the foreigners who came to Jerusalem and died. Many early church fathers, including Augustine and Chrysostom, said "the field" was "the world" just like it is in one of Jesus' parables (Matt. 13:13). In this sense one sees *a picture of the blood of Jesus purchasing an eternal resting place for the whole world—Jews and Gentiles.* Ludolph of Saxony wrote, "by his blood Christ has bought perpetual rest and the joys of Paradise for us sojourners."[21]

Lord Jesus, may my tears always be tears of repentance like Peter, rather than tears of worldly regret like Judas. Judas should have accepted Your substituted death of hanging on a tree instead of hanging himself on a tree out of remorse. You said, "It would have been good for that man if he had not been born" (Matt. 26:24). When we don't accept Your free gift of grace and justification, we are only left with torment in this life & the life to come.

DAY 13
Delivered to Pontius Pilate
(Matthew 27:1-2, 11-14; Mark 15:1-5; Luke 23:1-2; John 18:28-32)

The gold from the temple precinct began to sparkle as the first rays of sunlight broke over Jerusalem. Our Lord had been in the custody of the chief priests all night. His face and body would have been covered in the dried *spit* of his accusers and dried *blood* from their beating. Bruising began to appear from the symbolic stoning He endured, and His body was primed to experience pain to the fullest extent. John says it was "early morning" when the chief priests led Jesus bound to the Praetorium—a place associated with a praetor—a leading Roman general or official. Any place the 'praetor' occupied was known as 'the Praetorium.'

Before Jesus entered Jerusalem on Palm Sunday He prophesied that the chief priests would "deliver Him to Gentiles to mock to scourge and to crucify" (Matt. 20:19). That prophecy was now being fulfilled. Matthew informs us that the chief priests and elders "delivered Him to Pontius Pilate the governor" (Matt. 27:2). Jesus was delivered over to the leading Gentile in Judea. Interestingly, the first time a 'governor' is mentioned in the Gospels it refers not to Pilate, but to Jesus Himself. Speaking of Bethlehem, the prophet Micah wrote, "out of thee shall come a Governor, that shall rule my people Israel" (Matt. 2:6, KJV). Though Jesus stood before a governor, the highest ruling official in the land, He ultimately was the Governor and the Judge over Israel. The Governor was about to be governed. The Judge was about to be judged. In His providence, He willed it to be.

Who is Pontius Pilate? 'Pontius' is his nomen (representing his tribe) and 'Pilate' is his cognomen (representing his family). His praenomen (personal name) is not preserved for us, though tradition says it was Lucius. Tradition also says that his wife was Claudia—a daughter of Caesar Augustus, and that is one reason why Pilate received the post he did in Judea. Regardless of his personal background, it is an established historical fact that Pontius Pilate served as the governor in Judea from AD 26-36.

At the beginning of his term in AD 26 Pilate came to a quick realization of the zealous nature of the people he was governing. He brought iconic standards with a bust of Caesar (who was considered a living god) attached to them into Jerusalem. The Jews interpreted this act as one of *gross idolatry* and protested the standards for six days, even willing to die for the sake of their removal. Pilate finally realized he wasn't going to win that battle, and wisely removed the standards. A little further into his reign Pilate took money from the temple treasury to build an aqueduct into Jerusalem. This caused a riot with large numbers of Jews being beaten and some dying as a result. An even more *egregious act* by Pilate is recorded in Scripture by Luke. Jesus reminds His audience "about the Galileans whose blood Pilate had mingled with their sacrifices" (Luke 13:1). Apparently Pilate killed a bunch of Galilean pilgrims while they were offering sacrifices in Jerusalem! Why? We are not told, but it probably had to do with some sort of civil disruption. Whatever the case, this incident could have been part of the reason Herod and Pilate were not friendly at the time of Jesus' trial—as Herod had jurisdiction over the Galileans (Luke 23:12).

While Pilate normally dwelt in a magnificent palace on the shore of the Mediterranean in Caesarea, for the Jewish feasts he would come to Jerusalem to maintain the peace. He most likely stayed in the Fortress Antonia—the largest palace/fortress in the city built by Herod the Great. It was replete with baths, courtyards, and was perfectly positioned to view the temple precinct during the festivals. It is here the chief priests and elders dragged the chained Jesus—a walk of about five minutes—to deliver Him over to crucifixion and death.

These white-washed sepulchres followed a vain tradition that said they could not enter into the homes of Gentiles. This was nonsense according to the Old Testament, and certainly was contrary to the heart of God. Acquiescing to their tradition, Pilate came out of the Praetorium to meet them on ground where they were comfortable. He addressed them, "What accusation do you bring against this Man?" (John 18:29) After a little hemming and hawing, the chief priests ended up pinning three accusations on Jesus. Luke gives the best summary of them, writing, "they began to accuse Him, saying, 'We found this fellow perverting the nation, and forbidding to pay taxes to Caesar, saying that He Himself is Christ, a King" (Luke 23:2).

The first two accusations were patently false. The third was misleading. Concerning the first accusation, Jesus had done the opposite of "perverting" or "subverting" the nation. In His most *prominent* and *public* sermon He taught His followers concerning Roman officers, "whoever compels you to go one mile, go with him two", and "love your enemies, bless those who curse you, do good to those who hate you, and pray for those who spitefully use you and persecute you" (Matt. 5:41-44). This was preached before thousands! A well-documented sermon that He told His disciples to shout from the rooftops throughout Israel (Matt. 10:27). Concerning, "forbidding to pay taxes to Caesar", that very week in Jerusalem Jesus had publicly told the Pharisees and Herodians, "Render to Caesar the things that are Caesar's"

(Mark 12:17). He had also chosen a tax collector working for Rome to be one of His chief apostles, and had spent time preaching the kingdom of God to tax collectors (Matt. 9:9-13).

Though the first two accusations were meant to pique Pilate's interest, the last accusation was really what the Jewish leaders were staking everything on—*Jesus' claim to be the Messiah.* They added the term 'king', wanting to give the impression to Pilate that Jesus was *mounting a coup* against Rome. This, of course, was far from Jesus' mind! He had *already resisted every militaristic attempt at kingship.* After feeding the five-thousand the crowd wanted to "take Him by force to make Him king", but "He departed again to the mountain by Himself" (John 6:15). He would not allow it! That was not the type of King He would be. We've already seen how in the garden of Gethsemane Jesus commanded Peter to put away his sword (Matt. 26:52). Nothing about Jesus' ministry spoke of "subverting" the nation in a political sense, telling us to not pay taxes, or making Himself a king in a sense that spoke of militaristic revolution. Though these pernicious lies of the Jewish leaders would ultimately fall flat, Pilate would still struggle with how to properly handle the situation, as we shall soon see.

Lord Jesus, You were falsely accused of aligning Yourself against Rome and Caesar. Amazingly, in time You still did 'conquer' Caesar. Just not in the way You were being accused of. You conquered his heart! At that time Rome began to mount crosses on churches all throughout their land. They began to confess You as Lord and God! Caesars and many mighty kings began to bow, not through the force of arms, but by perceiving Your almighty and loving reign in Heaven at the right hand of the Power (Matt. 26:64). Help me to more fully perceive Your reign. Conquer my heart fully by Your almighty love as I confess that You suffered under Pontius Pilate for ME. Help me to see You as the ultimate Governor and authority over my life so that whatever I do in word or deed, I will do it all in Your name, Lord Jesus (Col. 3:17).

DAY 14
Christ's 'Good Confession'
(Matthew 27:11; Mark 15:2; Luke 23:3-5; John 18:33-38; 1 Timothy 6:13-16)

After the chief priests maligned Jesus with *three false accusations,* Pilate left them outside and entered the Praetorium. Throughout this section of the Passion we will see Pilate enter and exit the Praetorium multiple times. While inside the Praetorium he has private conversations with Jesus, and then exits to speak with the chief priests who believed they would be unclean if they stepped foot in the fortress. After calling Jesus to stand before him in private conference, all four Gospels record Pilate privately asking Jesus, "Are You the King of the Jews?" This was the third accusation that the chief priests had made, and Pilate knew the first two accusations could be wrapped within this one—so he cuts right to the chase with one straightforward question.

Was Jesus committing high-treason? Was He like one of the other Jewish pretender-kings that had surfaced after Herod the Great? People like Judas of Galilee, Theudas, or the later Simon bar Kokhba? Did Jesus have ambitions to start an uprising similar to the Maccabees? Was he like the Yeshua of old, that great military commander, Joshua, who had conquered the land of Canaan? Though direct, there was likely some sarcasm in this question. Pilate knew the chief priests had not come with pure motives. Governors would have been very aware of seditious leaders within their territories who had been gaining followers in order to enact a *rebellion.* This son of a carpenter from Nazareth certainly didn't fit that bill. But, knowing it was Passover, and knowing a riot was not good for his career, he pressed the question to Jesus anyway—"Are you the King of the Jews?"

Summarizing Pilate and Jesus' conversation, Matthew, Mark, and Luke have Jesus respond, "It is as you say." Short and to the point. John gives a much fuller record of everything that was said between them. From John's narrative we learn that it is in the middle of the conversation that Jesus says, "You say rightly that I am king." Hence, all four Gospels have Jesus answer in the affirmative. He would not shy away from His identity as King! (Although, as we will see later in John, Jesus certainly did want Pilate to understand the *true nature* of His kingdom.)

This affirmative answer became known to early Christians as Christ's 'good confession.' At the end of Paul's letter to Timothy he encouraged Timothy, saying, "Fight the good fight of faith, lay hold on eternal life, to which you were also called and have confessed the good confession in the presence of many witnesses" (1 Tim. 6:12). The 'good confession' that Timothy and other Christians confessed was simply the same confession Christ made, as Paul goes on to say that Christ Jesus "witnessed the good confession before Pontus Pilate" (1 Tim. 6:13).

The good confession is acknowledging Jesus is King. The fact it is "good" has to do with its content and spirit. The content of Christ's confession is "good" in the sense that it is the very core of the Christian faith. *The Christian life begins with a confession that Jesus is 'Lord/King', and a switch of allegiance to worship and follow Him alone.* Paul writes, "if you confess with your mouth the Lord Jesus and believe in your heart that God has raised Him from the dead, you will be saved" (Rom. 10:9). A confession that should be followed with baptism as one publicly makes known their life is no longer their own. It is also "good" in spirit. Christ was not timid, embarrassed, or frightened in telling the representative of Caesar exactly who He was. There was *no ulterior motive* and *no hidden agenda* that might stain the character of the confession. This "good" spirit should also characterize the confession of His followers. His was a pure, genuine, *supremely good* confession.

Before confessing He was King, John lets us know that He first made clear to Pilate that His kingdom was of a whole different order. He said, "My kingdom is not of this world. If My kingdom were of this world, My servants would fight, so that I should not be delivered to the Jews; but now My kingdom is not from here" (John 18:36). Jesus made clear that the accusation of the chief priests—high treason—was false. Yes, He was a King, just not a seditious one. His citizens were dual citizens—citizens of heaven and earth (Phil. 3:20). Those who were "born from above" would enter the kingdom of heaven while remaining good citizens on earth (John 3:3-5). His kingdom is one that is "within you" (Luke 17:21). His subjects are to bear witness to this kingdom through a transformed life that includes obeying and praying for the civil leaders of their world (Rom. 13:1; 1 Tim. 2:1-2). His disciples are those who are in the world, but not "of it" (John 17:11-14). Meaning, they are not stained by its influence. Rather, they are the light of the world that "shine as stars amidst a wicked and perverse generation" (Phil. 2:15, NIV).

After confessing He is indeed King, though of a much higher order, Jesus tells Pilate that He came into the world in order to "bear witness to the truth." Pilate's response? "What is truth?" (John 18:37-38) Pilate is not asking a genuine question here. In fact, he leaves the room as he is saying it. Rather, it is a derisive remark that is soaked with sarcasm. Pilate belonged to the class of men that view the search for truth as a frivolous activity. Men who think, "Truth? Objective, absolute truth? I've lived long enough to know that search is pointless!" Pilate had a worldly cynicism about him, thinking that the philosophic endeavor for truth served little to no purpose to society or his life. Why waste your time on questions of 'truth'?

The irony of course is that Truth is standing right before Pilate! Jesus had declared the prior evening, "I am the way, the truth, and the life. No one comes to the Father except through Me" (John 14:6). Truth certainly does matter. It is objective. And truth finds its source, grounding, beginning and end in Jesus of Nazareth. To be confronted with Jesus is to be confronted with the Answer to life's most *important* and *difficult* questions. Though Pilate *rejected* the truth Jesus bore witness to, he still quickly came to understand that Jesus was no threat, and that the accusations of the chief priests were groundless. So, after Pilate's philosophic scoff, "he went out again to the Jews, and said to them, 'I find no fault in Him at all'" (John 18:38). At that point, according to Roman law, Jesus should have been released, but out of fear of the Jews, Pilate kept Him a little longer. Everything that happens after this proclamation is both illegal and unjust on Rome's end.

Lord Jesus, thank you for making the "good confession" before Pontius Pilate. May I be like Timothy and live in a way that truly honors Your confession. You are the "only Potentate, the King of kings and Lord of lords" (1 Tim. 6:15). In light of the fact that Your kingdom is not of this world I choose to strive for the supernatural. I desire Your kingdom to come, and Your will to be done, on earth, and in my life, as it is in Heaven. Help me to realign my priorities with a 'heavenly kingdom' focus. Your Word says, "If then you were raised with Christ, seek those things which are above, where Christ is, sitting at the right hand of God. Set your mind on things above, not on things on the earth. For you died, and your life is hidden with Christ in God" (Col. 3:1-3). I desire Your ways and kingdom life to be replicated in me! May the world perceive that You are the King of my heart and life!

DAY 15
Before Herod Antipas
(Luke 23:6-12)

Pilate had just come out of the Praetorium after his private conference with Jesus and announced Jesus' innocence. Such a declaration made the chief priests exceedingly angry. They couldn't let this 'blasphemer' get away unscathed! Luke tells us "they were the more fierce saying, 'He stirs up the people, teaching throughout all Judea, beginning from Galilee to this place'" (Luke 23:5). Pilate's heart likely jumped the moment he heard Jesus was from Galilee. Maybe he could rid himself of this wretched situation!? So upon learning that Jesus was indeed a Galilean, "he sent Him to Herod" (Luke 23:7). This was the beginning of Pilate's guilt as he should have set Jesus free.

Herod was in Jerusalem to observe Passover. He would have been residing at the Hasmonean palace. The Hasmoneans were a dynasty that ruled over the Jews from the time of the Maccabees in 140 BC to the time of Herod the Great in 37 BC. The palace was about four hundred yards from the Praetorium, only a five minute walk for Jesus and the angry priestly mob. Upon arriving at Herod's residence we are told that Herod was quite excited. He thought Jesus might be able to give them some holiday entertainment! Though he had never met Jesus before, he had heard rumors of His miracles and wanted to see if Jesus would do something 'magical' for his family and friends.

Who exactly is Herod? This is not "Herod the Great"—the Herod that slaughtered the infants in Bethlehem at the beginning of Matthew's Gospel (Matt. 2:1-18). Though, this is *that Herod's son.* Following Herod the Great's death, his kingdom was divided between his three sons—Herod Archelaus, Herod Philip II, and Herod Antipas. Herod Archelaus reigned as an ethnarch over Judea, Samaria, and Idumea until AD 6. We meet him when Mary, Joseph, and Jesus return from Egypt (Matt. 2:22). Herod Philip II reigned as tetrarch over Iturea, Trachonitis, and Batanea on the East side of the Sea of Galilee (Luke 3:19). Philip II was the first husband of the infamous Herodias before his brother, Herod Antipas, swept her into his arms (Matt. 14:3). Herod Antipas, the Herod Jesus was standing before, reigned as tetrarch over Galilee and Perea. This is the Herod who plays an important part in the Passion narrative.

As the tetrarch over Galilee Herod Antipas had jurisdiction over Jesus. In fact, though Herod likely had never seen Jesus before, it is very possible Jesus often saw him from a distance growing up. For Herod rebuilt the town of Sepphoris—a large Galilean town three miles from Nazareth where Herod moved his capital for the first twenty years of Jesus' life. It is very possible that the bulk of Joseph's work was done in Sepphoris, as it was a much larger town than Nazareth, and that Jesus would have visited Sepphoris often to go to the market and engage in work with Joseph. It is almost certain he saw the pompous Antipas from time to time.

Antipas showed his loyalty to the Roman Emperor, Tiberius, by building a city called 'Tiberius' on the western shores of the Sea of Galilee over an old cemetery. Jesus likely did not visit this city in His ministry as there is no record of a visit in the Gospels, as well as the fact that many Jews considered it *unclean*. Though Antipas was a *great builder* like his father, what the New Testament focuses on is his moral failings. If Jesus' family was 'the holy family' in Israel, the Herodians were 'the unholy family.' Antipas had taken his niece and sister-in-law, Herodias, as his wife. This outraged John the Baptist! He told Antipas, "It is not lawful for you to have her" (Matt. 14:4), and he "rebuked" Antipas "for all the evils" he had done (Luke 3:19). These incidents angered Herodias even more than Antipas, and after having her daughter dance scantily before her husband and his friends she was able to get Antipas to behead John on her behalf (Matt. 14:1-12).

Later Antipas heard about the miracles happening under Jesus' ministry. Some were even saying Jesus was "John risen from the dead" and that "Elijah had appeared." This perplexed Herod so much that "he sought to see Him" (Luke 9:7-9). He must have not sought very hard though, for he never did end up meeting Jesus. Toward the end of Jesus' ministry some Pharisees told Jesus that Antipas wanted to kill Him. Whether that was true information or not, Jesus responded, "Go, tell that fox, 'Behold I cast out demons and perform cures today and tomorrow, and the third day I shall be perfected'" (Luke 13:32). He gave Herod a riddle about His resurrection. Something that Herod would have disregarded as ridiculous, seeing he was a Sadducee. He also called him a 'fox.' Foxes in the Bible are destructive (Judg. 15:5; Song 2:15). *An apt descriptor for this wicked ruler who murdered the greatest old covenant prophet to have ever lived (Matt. 11:11).*

As Jesus stood before that 'fox' bound, disfigured, and disgraced in Jerusalem, Herod Antipas began to question Him at length. Would Jesus entertain him and his household? The answer, of course, is "no." Jesus "answered him nothing" (Luke 23:9). He would not be their play thing. An evil and perverse generation seeks a sign, and the only sign they would get was the sign of Jonah (Matt. 12:39). After Herod's lengthy questioning, the chief priests grew impatient. They began to "vehemently accuse" Jesus, likely bringing up what He had said that night about being the Divine Son of Man. This accusation from the shouting priests gave Herod at least one more chance at some fun. He probably said something like, "A divine king, huh? Fetch me a gorgeous robe! Let's give this peasant carpenter obeisance!" They clothed Jesus in a splendid, sparkling, likely white robe. And after mocking Jesus to his heart's delight, Herod told the priestly mob to take Jesus back to Pilate. Jesus was "mocked" by the Sanhedrin, Herod's court, and later by the soldiers in the Praetorium, the chief priests and scribes at the cross, and even the two men He was crucified with. He had prophesied, "they will mock Him" (Mark 10:34). His Passion is a "stumbling block" to Jews and "foolishness" to Greeks (1 Cor. 1:23). Jesus endured the mocking, ridicule, and scandal of His Passion for the world's salvation. Ultimately, the One who would get the last "laugh" against these wicked rulers was God (Ps. 2:4).

Luke writes, "That very day Pilate and Herod became friends with each other, for previously they had been at enmity with each other" (Luke 23:12). Ideological enemies will unite around their shared hatred of Christ. Peter prayed, "For truly against Your holy Servant Jesus, whom You anointed, both Herod and Pontius Pilate, with the Gentiles and the people of Israel, were gathered together to do whatever Your hand and Your purpose determined before to be done" (Acts 4:27-28). Herod and Pilate meant it for evil. Yet, ultimately, God purposed it for good.

Lord Jesus, You are the King of the Universe. You reign over all things seen and unseen. You came from Heaven to earth to bear witness to the truth. As You stood before Herod, that 'fox' who simply wanted to see a magic show, You did not consent. Help me to not simply follow or love You for the sake of signs and wonders. I do desire for Your power to be at work through me, but more than that, I desire to know and love You for Your own sake. As I grow to love and know You, I know that signs will follow my life that will give You all the glory and praise! (John 14:12; Mark 16:17-18)

DAY 16
We Want Barabbas!
(Matt 27:15-26; Mark 15:6-15; Luke 23:13-25; John 18:39-40)

The chief priests, frustrated at the lack of concern Herod showed for Jesus' 'blasphemy', led Jesus back to Pilate. No matter what it took, they would convince Pilate to put Jesus to death. They would have Jesus publicly shamed and cursed by hanging on a tree, even if it meant forcing Pilate's hand. After Pilate received Jesus from the enraged mob of the chief priests, he made a second declaration of Jesus' innocence. He proclaimed, "having examined Him in your presence, I have found no fault in this Man concerning those things of which you accuse Him" (Luke 23:14). He then adds that the second civil magistrate who had jurisdiction over Jesus arrived at the same conclusion, "neither did Herod" (Luke 23:15). In light of Jesus' innocence Pilate promised to "release Him", "for it was necessary for him to release one to them at the feast" (Luke 23:16-17).

Though Pilate should have released Jesus strictly because He was innocent, he instead decided to attempt to release Jesus on the basis of a pardon. There was a custom during the Passover that one political prisoner would be set free each year. Pilate was likely thinking that releasing Jesus by this means would be good for public relations. He would show himself as merciful as well as avoid *embarrassing* his buddy Caiaphas—if Jesus was acquitted by the crowd, Pilate wouldn't have to shame Caiaphas publicly by going against his wishes for Christ's death. We know they were friends and politically aligned because Pilate had appointed Caiaphas as high priest for seven straight years.

Pilate cried out to the crowd, "You have a custom that I should release someone to you at the Passover. Do you therefore want me to release to you the King of the Jews?" (John 18:39). Luke gives this response from the crowd, "they all cried out at once, saying, 'Away with this Man, and release to us Barabbas'—who had been thrown into prison for a certain rebellion made in the city, and for murder" (Luke 23:18-19).

This stunned Pilate! He had every expectation they would choose Jesus. He didn't realize the chief priests and elders had gathered people to the Praetorium *who would do their bidding and had convinced other bystanders of their cause.* Matthew writes, "the chief priests and elders persuaded the multitudes that they should ask for Barabbas and destroy Jesus" (Matt. 27:20). Pilate was flustered. His wife had just sent him a message about a dream she had, saying, "Have nothing to do with that just Man" (Matt. 27:19). So, "wishing to release Jesus, again [Pilate] called out to them" (Luke 23:20). Did his pleading for the release of Christ work? No. Instead their cries became far more intense, "they shouted, saying 'Crucify Him, crucify Him!'" (Luke 23:21). The Greek word for "shout" had previously been used by Luke only for the shouting of those who were demon-possessed (Luke 4:22, 8:28). This is a demon-frenzied crowd! When Pilate asks, "Why, what evil has He done", Mark says, "they cried out all the more, 'Crucify Him!'" (Mark 15:14). A mob is a playground for demons, and when cries get louder and louder without recourse to sound reason, all sorts of evil can take place (cf. Acts 19:34).

Pilate was beside himself. He said, "Why, what evil has He done? I have found no reason for death in Him" (Luke 23:22). Do they respond by answering his question? No. They simply continue to shout! They have no desire to reason with Pilate. Luke writes, "they were insistent, demanding with loud voices that He be crucified" (Luke 23:23). How does the most powerful civil magistrate in the country respond? Does he release Barabbas for the Passover pardon and release Jesus because He was innocent in the sight of the law? No. Rather, "the voices of these men and of the chief priests prevailed" (Luke 23:23). So, after going through a symbolic hand washing ceremony, desiring to prevent a riot, he handed the innocent Man over to begin the crucifixion process by scourging. Pilate was both a coward and unjust—even though the chief priests had "the greater sin" (John 19:11).

While Jesus began the process of crucifixion, Barabbas was *unchained* and *set free*. Who was Barabbas? He is called a "robber" as well as a rebel who "had committed murder in the rebellion" (John 18:40; Mark 15:7). We are told he was "notorious", and the fact that he is named, unlike the two criminals crucified next to Jesus, shows how significant a character he is. Most scholars understand that he was most likely a "freedom fighter" of the zealot class. The Greek term used is 'lestai' which is the word Josephus uses to describe political revolutionaries. He was in prison and sentenced to death for the very same crime the chief priests were trying to pin on Jesus! Jesus suffered as the central 'lestai' between two other 'lestai' (Matt. 27:38). *He suffered as the 'chief sinner' in place of the real 'chief sinner' in that Jerusalem prison.*

The name Barabbas is an Aramaic patronymic (name of one's father) similar to Barnabas, Bartholomew, or Bartimaeus. "Bar" is Hebrew for "son of." Barabbas means "son of Abba." Abba was a popular Hebrew first name for men during the time of Jesus. Sometimes in Scripture one's praenomen (personal name) is combined with their patronymic. For instance, Peter is called "Simon Bar-Jonah" by Jesus (Matt. 16:17). Was Barabbas' praenomen preserved? Well, many scholars believe the original reading of Matthew and best manuscripts do preserve his name.

So the NIV, NRSV, and NET all say his name was "Jesus Barabbas" (Matt. 27:16). Thus, standing before Pilate were two men named Jesus Bar-Abba! For the Father in heaven had twice thundered from heaven about Jesus, "This is my beloved Son" (Matt. 3:17, 17:5). Abba means "father."

The eternal "Son of the Father", who came down from Heaven, as the "only begotten Son" of God, takes the place of a "son of the father" who was a murderer on death row (John 3:14-17). *The truth is, we are all Barabbas.* All of humanity is on death row. "The wages of sin is death" (Gen. 2:17; Rom. 6:23). "All have sinned and fallen short of the glory of God" (Rom. 3:23). But on Passover, a spotless Lamb of God has taken our place! On this Lamb was placed the sin of the whole world (John 1:29; 1 John 2:2). What Jesus Barabbas needed to do was not rejoice at the pardon of Pilate, but rather rejoice that He had been pardoned by the Heavenly Father through the merit of the Substitute who was about to die the death he deserved. If Jesus Barabbas received *that Pardon* he would no longer have simply been the son of Abba, but he also would have been the adopted son of the Almighty Heavenly Abba! (Rom. 8:15; Gal. 3:26) He would have passed from spiritual death into spiritual life (John 5:24; 1 John 3:14; Acts 26:18). That is the greatest pardon, eternal freedom!

Lord Jesus, You did not deserve to die. Both Pontius Pilate and Herod Antipas declared that You were innocent. In Hebrews You are described as "holy, innocent, [and] undefiled" (Heb. 7:26, NASB). By taking the place of 'Jesus Barabbas' as 'Jesus Barabbas' You have shown us that You are a perfect substitutional representative for every man. You have assumed our very identity and climbed the tree for our salvation. By being my representative it is as if I was on the tree. It is as if I died. It is as if I rose again. Thank you for taking my place, standing condemned in my stead, pardoning me, setting me free, and making me a child of the Father in Heaven!

DAY 17
The Just for the Unjust
(Matt 27:19, 24-26; Mark 15:15; Luke 23:13-16, 24-25; John 18:38, 19:16)

The search for guilt in Christ had been *extensive* and *lengthy*. All night and morning there was an inquisition of the Holy One. Three *earthly tribunals* had been set up to pass judgment on the Heavenly Judge who held them in His hands. The Sanhedrin, *the Supreme Court of the Jewish world*, could find no corroborating witnesses to sentence Him. In their desperation, they resorted to an unjust charge of 'blasphemy'—a charge they refused to investigate. Speaking of these Jewish leaders, Paul said, "though they found no cause for death in Him, they asked Pilate that He should be put to death" (Acts 13:28). Pilate, *the representative of the Roman world*, attempted on six different occasions to release Jesus (John 18:31, 38, 39, 19:1-4, 5-6, 12-14). He said, "I find no fault in Him at all" (John 18:38), "I find no fault in Him" (John 19:6), and "what evil has He done?" (Matt. 27:23). In the third tribunal Herod Antipas, *the tetrarch over Galilee*, "found no fault" in Jesus (Luke 23:14). The three highest tribunals in the religious and civil world of Israel could find *nothing* in Jesus worthy of death!

Besides the religious and civil leaders, we see multiple attestations to Jesus' innocence and perfect righteousness from other characters in the Passion narrative. Judas testified that he betrayed "innocent blood" (Matt. 27:3). After a supernatural dream, Pilate's wife proclaimed Jesus to be "just/righteous" (Matt. 27:19). Once Jesus is hanging on the cross the thief crucified next to Him will proclaim, "this Man has done nothing wrong" (Luke 23:41). Even the Roman centurion overseeing the crucifixion understood they were dealing with a just Man. He declared, "Certainly this was a righteous Man!" (Luke 23:47) The Passion narrative is screaming at us from beginning to end that Jesus was perfectly sinless and just.

The sinlessness of Jesus is very important. Remember, Jesus is crucified on Passover. Paul calls Him "our Passover lamb" (1 Cor. 5:7, ESV), and it was required that the lamb "be without blemish" (Ex. 12:5). John wrote, "in Him was no sin" (1 John 3:5). John was the apostle who *appealed to the seat of one's affections,* so he spoke of the sinless nature of Jesus at the depth of the heart. Paul wrote, "He knew no sin" (2 Cor. 5:21). Paul was the apostle who *appealed to the intellect,* so he spoke of the sinless nature of Jesus at the depth of the mind and will. Peter wrote, "who committed no sin" (1 Pet. 2:22). Peter was the apostle who *appealed to action,* so he spoke of the sinless nature of Jesus in word and deed. Jesus was stained by sin at no level. He never sinned in thought, motivation, desire, or act. He was like Adam in the beginning—unstained inside and out. A picture of what man was always meant to be.

When Paul described *the matters of first importance* the first thing he wrote was, "Christ died for our sins according to the Scriptures" (1 Cor. 15:3). In the same letter, in chapter one, he wrote, "the message of the cross...is the power of God" (1 Cor. 1:18). In chapter fifteen Paul makes clear "the message of the cross" *is* "Christ died for our sins." Meaning, the message of the cross is sacrificial in nature. *It is a sin and guilt offering.* Paul gives some of the divine logic for Christ's sacrifice in Romans: "God presented Christ as a sacrifice of atonement, through the shedding of his blood—to be received by faith. He did this to demonstrate his righteousness, because in his forbearance he had left the sins committed beforehand unpunished" (Rom. 3:25, NIV)

The Bible is clear that God is both merciful and righteous. In order to satisfy both His mercy and righteousness God came to earth in the person of the Son. *He would satisfy the claims of justice against sin by dying on the cross.* In this way God proved He was righteous for passing over the sins of those in the pre-cross world —for their sins were punished and paid for at Calvary. *He would also satisfy His heart of mercy by taking the punishment we deserved in our place as our representative.* Sin is an abhorrent evil with dire consequence—requiring the death of the Son of God. Only the blood of the sacrifice of Christ on the cross could 'propitiate' God's wrath and fully 'atone' for sin. (See Appendix B for more.)

The story of Barabbas is a great example of what Peter says about Christ's sacrifice. He writes, "Christ also suffered once for sins, the just for the unjust, that He might bring us to God" (1 Pet. 3:18). The just suffered *for* the unjust. Who are the unjust? Everyone. Why did He suffer *for* everyone? So that we might be brought to God. God is not willing that any perish, but that all come to repentance (2 Pet. 3:9). *Come to Jesus and receive life! See Him on the cross as the Just One bearing your sin!* This 'atoning sacrifice' for sin is a demonstration of Almighty Love that has the wooing power to 'draw all mankind' to Himself (John 12:32).

Speaking of the Barabbas event to the leaders at the temple, Peter said, "You disowned the Holy and Righteous One and asked that a murderer be released to you. You killed the author of life, but God raised him from the dead. We are witnesses of this" (Acts 3:14-15, NIV). He then called them to faith and repentance so that their "sins may be blotted out" and "times of refreshing may come from the presence of the Lord" (Acts 3:19). The Holy and Righteous One, the Author of Life, took the place of Barabbas. It is essential that we see ourselves in Barabbas' shoes. When we truly come to grips with our sin we realize we deserve nothing but death. *Yet, out of exceedingly great love, Someone stepped in and exchanged places with us.* He bore the punishment, curse, and death we deserved. Isaiah prophesied, "He was numbered with the transgressors, and He bore the sin of many" (Is. 53:12). Paul put it like this, "He made Him who knew no sin to be sin for us, that we might become the righteousness of God in Him" (2 Cor. 5:21). Christ died *for* our sins. This is the Gospel.

Speaking of the 'sweet exchange' Jesus endured for mankind's salvation, the author of the second century document, *The Epistle to Diognetus*, wrote, "The holy one for the lawless, the guiltless for the guilty, the just for the unjust, the incorruptible for the corruptible, the immortal for the mortal...O the sweet exchange, O the incomprehensible work of God, O the unexpected blessings."[22] The late medieval Christian, Thomas à Kempis, said, "The lamb is exchanged for the wolf; the Saint for the criminal; the best for the worst; the deadly sinner escapes in the place of the true God. Darkness is preferred to light; vice to virtue; death to life; clay to gold; the shell to the pearl; the infamous to the honorable!"[23] The Just, for the unjust. Amen.

Lord Jesus, You suffered as the Just One in my place in order to bring me to God. In one sense, what took place was outrageously wicked—we killed the Author of Life. Yet, You turned that wicked act into good by becoming a sin and guilt offering for us (Is. 53). Like the scapegoat that had the entire yearly sin of the nation transferred to it each Day of Atonement, so were You in Your Passion (Lev. 16:10), except You bore the sin of all history. The sin You carried was like a mountain compared to the sin of Barabbas which was like a grain of sand. In the rite of cleansing lepers (a leper picturing sin which eats away and leads to death), one bird was killed while another was dipped in the blood of the slain bird and released—flying, wings crimson red, as the sign of its redeemed freedom (Lev. 14:6-7). For who the Son sets free, is free indeed! Help me spread my wings and fly in Your freedom!

DAY 18
The Roman Scourging
(Matt 27:26; Mark 15:15; Luke 23:16; John 19:1)

After Barabbas was set free, Matthew and Mark give a short summary of what happened next. In Matthew's words, "when he had scourged Jesus, he delivered Him to be crucified" (Matt. 27:26). John records that much still occurred between the scourging and crucifixion. (See Days 19-21.) Though all four Gospels refer to His scourging and chastisement, none of the Gospels give any details about this brutal beating. Our understanding of what the scourging entailed must be gathered from any hints the rest of the Passion narrative gives, what Old Testament prophecy indicates, and secondarily what Roman historical descriptions of scourging detail and what the photographic images of the burial cloth of Jesus portray.[24]

The original readers of the Gospels would not have needed the *gruesome details* of scourging, for many of them had seen Roman scourging with their own eyes. It was a common form of Roman punishment enforced in every city and village across the empire. To simply read that Jesus was "scourged" would have made the stomachs of many early readers churn! The mere threat of scourging from a Roman officer could calm a crowd and straighten out a rebel, for the torture inflicted in scourging was so immense it at times would leave the victim dead.

In Luke and John it is made clear that Pilate scourged Jesus with the intention of being able to release Him. Because this was his last attempt to release Christ, he would have ordered the scourging to be *more grave than normal*—as He wanted the sight of

Jesus' bloodied and torn body to satiate the frenzied anger of the chief priests and elders. Maybe the sight of a half-dead man would stir their hearts to say "enough", or at least postpone the crucifixion like they were supposed to by law. Speaking of the horror of scourging and crucifixion, the Roman senator Seneca, wrote, "Would anyone willingly choose to be fastened to that cursed tree, especially after the beating that left him deathly weak, deformed, swelling with vicious welts on shoulders and chest, and struggling to draw every last, agonizing breath?"[25] We can assume Jesus' scourging would have been even worse than this description as Pilate was attempting to garner sympathy from the Jewish leaders. The fact that Jesus couldn't carry His crossbeam all the way to Golgotha also indicates that His scourging was very severe.

We can hear an *echo of Christ* in "the plowers plowed on my back; they made their furrows long" (Psalm 129:3). Isaiah prophesied the Suffering Servant would be "marred more than any man" (Is. 52:14), and, "He was wounded for our transgressions, He was bruised for our iniquities; the chastisement for our peace was upon Him, and by His stripes we are healed" (Is. 53:5). The word "stripes" is actually singular in Hebrew. It can be translated as "stripe", "wound", or "bruise." Peter quotes this verse in his first letter, "who Himself bore our sins in His own body on the tree, that we, having died to sins, might live for righteousness— by whose stripes you were healed" (1 Pet. 2:24). He also uses the singular tense, but in Greek. The *Englishman's Greek New Testament* translates it, "by whose bruise ye were healed."

Were there multiple "wounds" from Jesus' scourging? Of course! But the infliction of these wounds was so intense, and the blood flowed so freely, that an onlooker would have seen one giant crimson streak across the front and back of His body. The fact that His affliction can be understood as a "bruise" directs us to the first Messianic prophecy in Scripture. God told the serpent concerning the Messianic Seed of Eve, "He shall bruise your head, and you shall bruise His heel" (Gen. 3:15). The devil "bruised" Jesus with his venomous bite that day in Jerusalem. *But the scourging and crucifixion would ultimately be the beginning of the devil's own demise.* Like Haman, he would hang on his own gallows (Esther 7:10). The "lifting up" of Jesus on the cross was how the "prince of the world" would be "cast out" (John 12:31). The "blood of the lamb" and "word of testimony" about that blood is how Christians "overcome" the diabolical dragon in their own lives (Rev. 12:11). We join the serpent crushers of old like Jael and the woman of Thebez (Judges 4:21, 9:53; Rom. 16:20).

When Jesus healed sick multitudes, Matthew quoted Isaiah 53:5 as being fulfilled (Matt. 8:16-17). Earlier in His ministry Jesus spoke to a leading Pharisee and member of the Sanhedrin—Nicodemus. He told Nicodemus, "as Moses lifted up the serpent in the wilderness, even so must the Son of Man be lifted up, that whoever believes in Him should not perish but have eternal life" (John 3:14-15). *In these two stories we see the crucifixion linked to the bruising of the serpent* and *healing of both body and soul.* Jesus was referring to a passage in Numbers when the Israelites began to grumble about God's miraculous provision of angel bread (Ps. 78:25). They called it 'worthless.' In their bitterness God allowed serpents to come into the camp and bite. Sadly, many died. *Yet, in their distress the people asked Moses to pray for them.* He did, and God gave him a construction project—"so Moses made a bronze serpent, and put it on a pole; and so it was, if a serpent had bitten anyone, when he looked at the bronze serpent, he lived" (Num. 21:4-9). *The serpent is a symbol of the devil (Rev. 12:9). Bronze is a symbol of judgment (Deut. 28:23). God gave them a prophetic picture of Jesus Christ—the One who would be bitten by Satan and bear the curse and judgment on their behalf. Those that looked at their Sin and Sickness Bearer, would live.* In that moment every Israelite had a choice of what they were going to fix their eyes on. The same is true for all of us today who are bound by sin, sickness, bitterness, and the enemy. We must look to Jesus! "By faith" Moses was able to see "Him who is invisible" (Heb. 11:27). So can we. We can perceive the Lamb with all His covenantal markings who sits at the right hand of God (Rev. 5:6). The One who bore our sin and sickness, bruised the devil's head, and now reigns with all power and authority. Inner and outward healing still flows from Him today!

Concerning the scourging, the Romans would strip the victim naked, tie them to a pole, and usually two soldiers would take turns striking the back of the victim with as many lashes as they pleased. They would then flip the victim over and do the same to their front. There were three primary tools used to scourge—a virga, a flagrum, and a flagellum. While we can't know with absolute certainty which instruments were used to torture Jesus, the images from the Shroud of Turin indicate the Man of the shroud was intensely beaten by both a virga and flagrum. (See *Appendix A* for more information on these instruments and the wounds they inflicted.) Well over 350 wounds, with bits of flesh torn from His body, appear on the burial shroud. He was one large wound—disfigured beyond recognition (Is. 52:14).

Lord Jesus, You were stripped naked to cover my nakedness. You were put to public shame to cover my shame. With each lash of the flagrum, as Your body was bruised, and bits of Your flesh were torn from Your body, You thought of ME. Though the suffering was unjust, You willingly submitted to it in my stead in order to fulfill all righteousness. As immense pain surged through Your body, You mercifully carried my pain (Is. 53:4). The chastisement for my peace, my shalom, my wholeness, was on You (Is. 53:5). Thank you that by Your stripe(s) I am healed and made whole!

DAY 19
Crowned with Thorns
(Matt 27:27-31; Mark 15:16-20; John 19:2-3)

After the scourging, where Jesus was beaten to a bloody pulp, He was led back into the Praetorium. There He was surrounded by a whole band of soldiers—six-hundred armed men. Seeing this half-dead man who claimed to be King of the Jews, they proceeded to mock Him. First they clothed Him in a robe that had both crimson and purple hues to it. Symbolizing to them mock royalty (purple), but at a spiritual level their parody pointed to the truth that our King took upon Himself our sins (red). Next, they twisted a crown of thorns on His head. It would likely not have been a carefully woven wreath, but rather closer to a bushy cap that would have covered his whole head as the thorns would have been dangerous to handle and weave. After placing this 'crown' on Him, they placed one of their rods into His hand as a mock scepter. Then they began to "salute" Him, and "bowing the knee, they worshiped Him" (Mark 15:19).

This, of course, was all for a laugh. Immediately after their mock obeisance they rose up, grabbed the rod from His hand, and "struck Him on the head" (Matt. 27:30)—pounding the large thorns deep into that Sacred Head. The scalp is one of the most sensitive parts of the body with *multitudes of nerve endings* and more blood vessels than any other body part. Shockwaves of pain would have coursed through His body and blood would have flowed freely as they took turns spitting on Him and fiercely pounding the crown into Him. The coloration of His face would have begun to fade as His life force was being drained away.

Later, after Pilate showed Jesus to the crowd, they ripped the robe off of Him (allowing the wounds to flow again), and put His own bloodied clothes back on Him. This likely entailed *removing the crown* and then *beating it back in* for He was wearing a seamless robe which only had an opening *at the top* (John 19:23). Tradition says that as they *pounded the crown* back into His scalp, one of the thorns pierced through one of His eyes. Whatever the case, there was extensive pain surging through our Lord's Body.

What was the spiritual significance of Jesus being crowned with thorns? *It is immense.* In fact, in 1879 a Passionist Father wrote *The Mystery of the Crown of Thorns* which is over 300 pages long. The core of the spiritual significance is that 'thorns' are one of the primary signs of *the consequence of sin* and are attached to *the curse God gave for sin* (Gen. 3:17-19). Throughout scripture sinners are compared with thorn bushes (Judg. 9:14-15; Matt. 7:16). For Jesus to be crowned with thorns means He bore the penalty for our sin and took the curse upon Himself! *Jesus was the doubly cursed One that day—crowned with thorns and hung on a tree* (Deut. 21:23; Gal. 3:13). He fully took the penalty for humanity's sin on Himself. He is *the Greater Bronze Serpent*, the cursed One bringing life and healing to all who would believe on Him! (John 3:14-17)

Paul wrote, "Christ has redeemed us from the curse of the law, having become a curse for us" (Gal. 3:13). Read Deuteronomy 28 to get a handle on the curse of the law and what Christ has redeemed us from. Part of the curse of the law has to do with plagues and sickness. It says, "Also every sickness and every plague, which is not written in this Book of the Law, will the LORD bring upon you until you are destroyed" (Deut. 28:61). Every single sickness man has ever known is part of the curse of the law. But Jesus became that curse for us in order to deliver us from it. By His wounds we are healed, body and soul!

Another important aspect of the crown is understanding it in light of both Palm Sunday and the Binding of Isaac. On Palm Sunday Jesus rode on a donkey into Jerusalem fulfilling the Messianic prophecy of Zechariah 9. The crowds excitedly began to shout the 'Hillel Psalms' that were traditionally shouted as pilgrims entered the city. The crescendo of the Hillel Psalms is the end of Psalm 118, "Save now, I pray, O LORD" (Psalm 118:25). "Save now" is simply the word Hosanna. As the crowds shouted "hosanna" they were likely thinking something like, "Our Messiah has arrived! He is going to drive out the Romans! He is going to reign as king on David's throne! This is what we have spent centuries waiting for! 'Save us now!' 'Save us now!' 'Hosanna in the highest!'"

What the crowds didn't understand was that the 'hosanna' of Psalm 118 was meant to be a 'hosanna' *to the Lamb*. They didn't understand that the One who came in the name of Yahweh in verse 25 was *the same One* as the Sacrifice of verse 27 who needed to be bound to the altar! "God is Yahweh, and He has given us light; bind the sacrifice with cords to the horns of the altar" (Ps. 118:27). A better translation is, "Bind the sacrifice in thickets." The Hebrew term literally refers to 'branches of trees or bushes.' It could read, "Bind the sacrifice in branches of trees." Talk about Palm Sunday resonances. The crowds were strewing the streets with tree branches from the surrounding area (Matt. 21:8). Jesus, the Sacrifice, was literally caught in thickets!

First mention is important. The first time something is 'bound in thickets' in Scripture is in Genesis 22. In this story Isaac ascends Mt. Moriah with his father to offer a sacrifice. Rabbinic tradition says Isaac was 30 years old and that it happened on the 14th of Nisan, Passover. Regardless if he was 30 like Jesus, he was robust enough to carry wood up a mountain. What Isaac didn't know was that he was supposed to *be* the sacrifice. That is, until God provided a substitute. After God prevented Abraham's hand from slaying Isaac we are told, "Abraham looked up and there in a thicket he saw a ram caught by its horns. He went over and took the ram and sacrificed it as a burnt offering instead of his son. So Abraham called that place Yahweh Will Provide. And to this day it is said, 'On the mountain of Yahweh it will be provided'" (Gen. 22:13-14).

The sacrifice 'caught in a thicket' in Psalm 118 is meant to point back to the substitute 'caught in a thicket' on Mt. Moriah, which pointed forward to the ultimate substitute 'caught in a thicket' God would one day provide on that same mountain. Where is Mt. Moriah? Chronicles tells us it is *the exact place* the temple was built (2 Chr. 3:1). When Jesus made His triumphant entry into Jerusalem at the beginning of the Passover Festival, and they were strewing Him with tree branches, we are meant to see Him as the *promised substitutional sacrifice* who is 'bound in thickets' on Mt. Moriah! And He was not just 'bound in thickets', but later, 'caught by the horns.' *Just as the substitutional ram was crowned with thorns on Mt. Moriah, so Jesus was crowned with thorns on Mt. Moriah!* Like Isaac, Jesus would carry wood on His back for a sacrifice, but instead of having a substitute for His life, He would lay down His own life as a substitute for all. *He is the Greater Isaac and the Greater Ram. He is Yahweh-Will-Provide becoming His own Provision.*

Lord Jesus, though You were mocked by the soldiers, with a crown of thorns beaten into Your head, in that moment You became the Promised Lamb caught by the horns in the thicket. Those who perceive the way You have truly saved stand "before the throne and before the Lamb, clothed with white robes, with palm branches in their hands" crying out, "Salvation belongs to our God who sits on the throne, and to the Lamb!" (Rev. 7:9-10) I join the 'hosannas' of those in heaven rather than the 'hosannas' of Palm Sunday. Thank you for saving me from the curse by being crowned with thorns and climbing Mt. Moriah to die in my place! Hosanna to the Lamb!

DAY 20
Behold The Man
(John 19:4-12)

After the band of soldiers finished mocking and beating Jesus, Pilate came out of the Praetorium to converse with the chief priests and angry mob. He proceeded to give an introduction speech for Jesus, saying, "Behold, I am bringing Him out to you, that you may know that I find no fault in Him" (John 19:4). After this, Jesus was paraded in front of the crowd wearing the mock crown and robe while Pilate declared, "Behold the Man!" (John 19:5) We can imagine the soldiers lifting the robe as they twirled Jesus around and showed everyone His mutilated body. Pilate certainly hoped the horrific sight, and calling Him 'man' rather than exasperating them further by calling Him 'king', would enable a peaceable release. Would they not see that if this 'man' ever had seditious aspirations like the chief priests claimed, those aspirations had now been sufficiently quashed?

But we know the accusation of kingship was not the real sticking point for the chief priests, even though Pilate was not aware of that yet. So they shouted again, "Crucify Him!" (John 19:6). Pilate was stunned! He responded by telling *them* to crucify Him because he had found no fault whatsoever in Jesus. If they want to crucify an innocent man, Pilate was just about prepared to permit it to prevent an insurrection, but he would not get his hands dirty. Finally, the chief priests revealed their real reason for delivering Jesus to Pilate. They said, "We have a law, and according to our law He ought to die, because He made Himself the Son of God" (John 19:7). This is what had made their blood boil—blasphemy. Ironically, though they appeal to the law as the reason Pilate needs to kill Jesus, they also shout for Jesus to be crucified. Yet, the law prescribes stoning for blasphemy (Lev. 24:16). They are simultaneously demanding their law be both followed and broken! *Their true intention for desiring crucifixion was that all the Jews would see Jesus as an imposter who was completely humiliated, defeated by Rome, and, most importantly, cursed by God!*

Once Pilate heard that Jesus claimed to be "the Son of God" we are told "he was the more afraid" (John 19:8). Pilate knew there was something extraordinarily different about Jesus. No one had ever not defended themselves before him, like Jesus. No one had ever claimed to have a kingdom that was not of this world, like Jesus. Now, all of a sudden he learns that Jesus also claimed to be a son of God!? This shook Pilate. He had just scourged this man to a bloody pulp! Was this man he had just unjustly beaten really more than a man? Was He really the son of a god?

One must remember that the Romans believed in a multitude of gods. At times these gods were said to take on human flesh and have kids. The most famous 'son of god' being Hercules—a son of Jupiter. Stories abounded in Pilate's day of misfortune that befell those who mistreated the gods and their children. In fact, part of the reason Paul and Barnabas were greeted as Zeus and Hermes, and were met with garlands by the priests of Zeus who wanted to sacrifice oxen for them in Lystra, is because the inhabitants of Lycaonia were extra cautious to show hospitality to anyone who might be a god in fleshly form (Acts 14:6-18). In his work *Metaphorpheses* the poet Ovid tells a story about Zeus and Hermes visiting Lyconia in fleshly form. Everyone in the town rejected them except one elderly couple. In response, Zeus and Hermes fried them all to smithereens! With the exception of the hospitable couple, of course. One can see why those who believed stories like that had deep devotion to those gods and their children. They didn't want to be fried!

The judgments of the many so-called 'gods' from the Roman pantheon were *very fierce*, keeping many a superstitious citizen of that day participating in their idolatrous worship. For instance, Groenings writes, "Jupiter threw thunderbolts upon his enemies, Apollo cast poisoned arrows that caused pestilential ulcers, Mars devastated the territory of an enemy with bloody war, Neptune caused the sea to overflow its limits, Vulcan opened the earth and exhaled fire. Pilate then, if he assaulted the son of a god, would not escape the ire and revenge of the older divinity."[26]

After hearing the real reason the chief priests brought Jesus to him, Pilate led Jesus, the one true Son of God, back into the Praetorium. He asked Him point blank, "Where are You from?" (John 19:9) Jesus was silent. Pilate had already brushed Jesus off earlier by sarcastically quipping "What is truth?" to Jesus' claim that He came to bear witness to truth. Attempting to goad Jesus into an answer, Pilate boasted that he had power to crucify Him. In response Jesus said, "You could have no power at all against Me unless it had been given you from above" (John 19:11). Hearing this, "Pilate sought to release Him" (John 19:12). Pilate had heard enough. Jesus had now said a couple things that a 'son of a god' could potentially say. Though he might not have been convinced Jesus actually was a 'son of a god', he knew he wanted to do everything possible to set Him free and get the whole messy affair off his hands.

One thread that runs throughout the Gospel of John is the heavenly origins of Jesus. The Gospel begins, "In the beginning was the Word, and the Word was with God, and the Word was God…And the Word became flesh and dwelt among us, and we beheld His glory, the glory as of the only begotten of the Father, full of grace and truth" (John 1:1, 14). Jesus goes on to say about Himself, "No one has ascended to heaven but He who came down from heaven, that is, the Son of Man who is in heaven" (John 3:13). He says, "I have come down from heaven, not to do My own will, but the will of Him who sent Me" (John 6:38). Statements akin to these can be multiplied. Toward the end of his Gospel, John tells us why he included the stories and sermons of Jesus that he did, writing, "these are written that you may believe that Jesus is the Christ, the Son of God, and that believing you may have life in His name" (John 20:31).

Pilate came close to considering this truth, *but not close enough*. He not only scourged Jesus, but we will see in tomorrow's devotion, he actually handed Jesus over to be crucified after the chief priests *pushed him to a breaking point*. They were the ones who had "the greater sin" by delivering Jesus to Pilate (John 19:11). They were doubly sinful, for they knew where their power came from, Pilate did not. Yet, *God permitted Pilate to sentence Jesus to death because Jesus was willingly laying down His life to take away our sins.*

Lord Jesus, Pontius Pilate declared in Latin, 'Ecce Homo!' ('Behold, the Man!'). He was calling on the crowd to 'behold' You in all Your wounds— bathed in Your own blood. The chief priests and crowd did not rightly behold. They did not 'perceive' the reason You endured that scourging. "We, however, shall attentively gaze upon the Ecce Homo and impress it deeply upon our hearts. Yea, may the Lord be ever before our eyes, as He, bleeding from a thousand wounds, with the crown of thorns on His head and the scarlet mantle about His shoulders, stands publicly, as it were, in a pillory."[27] Jesus, You are the only begotten Son of God. You are 'begotten', not made. Your 'begottenness' was not in time, but in eternity. To be 'begotten' of the Father means that whatever the Father is, You are. You are the very same 'stuff', absolutely one in being and godness. The Father is only eternally Father because You are eternally Son! To You belongs all glory and praise!

DAY 21
Forcing Pilate's Hand
(John 19:12-16)

Throughout the trial Pilate sought to release Jesus. He pronounced Him innocent, delivered Him to Herod, sought to get Him released by a special Passover amnesty, and had Him scourged with the intention of swaying the emotion of the crowd to call for His release—calling on everyone to "behold" Him in His brutalized state. *None of this worked.* Deeply frustrated, Pilate sought to release Jesus one last time. After fearing Jesus might have a supernatural origin, John tells us Pilate came out of the Praetorium and again "sought to release Him" (John 19:12).

At this point the Jewish leaders needed to come up with a new strategy. Their first three accusations had proved fruitless, and their latest accusation of 'blasphemy' made Pilate even more reticent than before. So now they decide the only thing that might work is a form of *blackmail.* They resort back to their main accusation that Christ claimed kingship and tell Pilate, "If you let this Man go, you are not Caesar's friend. Whoever makes himself a king speaks against Caesar" (John 19:12).

This was their trump card. Pilate's hand was being forced! They were essentially threatening Pilate and letting him know that if he released Jesus they would make sure the Roman Emperor, Tiberius, was informed of what Pilate had done. They would tell Tiberius that Pilate was soft on rebels and was part of some treasonous conspiracy with Jesus. The title "friend of Caesar" was a title of honor that was given to leading men throughout the Empire, and it is very likely Pilate held that title at that time.

What was Pilate's response? He conceded. His resolve to release Jesus melted away as he thought about saving his own life. He did not want the mob to turn into a bloody insurrection. He also wanted to be on good terms with Tiberius and save his career. A relationship that already was a little strained over the Jews going to Rome in AD 26 concerning the Roman standard incident. So, *Pilate put self-interest before Christ. He put self-interest before Truth. He put self-interest before Justice.* Yet, his career would still come to an end in three short years! Self-interest in place of truth rarely pays the dividends we expect. Also, any bloody revolt that might have occurred if Pilate acquitted Jesus would have paled in comparison to the million-bodied bloody destruction of Jerusalem thirty-seven years later. Pilate should have followed the truth and his conscience. We all should. The more we give into compromise, the more our conscience becomes seared. And the harder it is to untangle from the messes we create.

While mulling over this new threat from the chief priests Pilate was sitting on the judgment seat which rested on a raised pavement. ("Gabbatha" simply means "elevated place.") Jesus stood before him. Pilate was about to pronounce the final judgment of the long trial that morning. In deep frustration, and likely with some *contempt* at the chief priests who were essentially forcing his hand, he uttered, "Behold your King!" (John 19:14) This stirred the mob up again! Like they had shouted earlier when Barabbas was present with Jesus, in a frenzy they scream, "Away with Him, away with Him! Crucify Him!" Egging them on with more contempt, Pilate responds, "Shall I crucify your King?" Boiling in rage at the idea of Jesus as their king, the chief priests cry, "We have no king but Caesar!" (John 19:15)

With those words the leaders of the people essentially committed apostasy. One of the foundational beliefs of the Scriptures is that there is one king—Yahweh. The King of kings and Lord of lords. David wrote, "Yahweh is King forever and ever" (Ps. 10:16). The sons of Korah sang, "For Yahweh Most High is awesome; He is a great King over all the earth" (Ps. 47:2). When the Israelites wanted Gideon to rule over them as king he responded, "I will not rule over you, nor shall my son rule over you; Yahweh shall rule over you" (Judg. 8:23). When the people finally did get their first king, Saul, God told the prophet Samuel, "they have rejected Me, that I should not reign over them" (1 Sam. 8:7). That is essentially what happened all over again before Pilate. The chief priests were rejecting God as their King and saying their full and sole allegiance was to Caesar!

The fact that the chief priests rejected Jesus and His Father as King before Pilate and the all the Jews that Passover morning *did not surprise Jesus*. That week He had spoken a parable against the chief priests about them being wicked vineyard dressers who would kill the son of the owner of the vineyard to gain power for themselves. At the end of the parable Jesus said, "Therefore I say to you, the kingdom of God will be taken from you and given to a nation bearing the fruits of it" (Matt. 21:41). That 'nation' or 'people group' would be *the church*—Jews and Gentiles from all over the world who would be disciples of King Jesus. The Jewish leaders would cease to function as leaders in God's Kingdom, unless they bowed their knees to Jesus.

After the chief priests shouted their allegiance to Caesar, Pilate handed Jesus over to them to be crucified. John also notes that "it was the Preparation Day of the Passover, and about the sixth hour" (John 19:14). Interestingly, Mark mentions that Jesus was crucified at "the third hour" (Mark 15:25). John and Mark were following a popular method of keeping time that split the day and night into four parts. The "third hour" would have been any time between 9AM-12PM. *It was 'the third hour', but also 'about the sixth hour.' So, sometime very close to 12PM.* Well, on Nisan 14th, the Jews would cease working around 12PM. At that time all leaven in their home "was to be solemnly destroyed, either by burning, immersing in water, or scattering it to the winds."[28] Their lamb was then taken and led to the temple to be sacrificed at 3PM. *At the very same time, the Lamb of God was handed over to be led to His execution site. A site where the leaven of the world's sin would be destroyed!*

The Passover theme throughout the Passion narrative is especially prominent in John's Gospel. When Jesus initially enters the narrative John the Baptist points at Him and declares, "Behold! The Lamb of God who takes away the sin of the world!" (John 1:29) There are four Passovers that Jesus attends in John which is the basis for our understanding that Jesus' earthly ministry was likely three and a half years long (John 2:13, 5:1, 6:4, 13:1). The second half of John, commonly referred to as 'the book of glory', begins by saying, "And the Passover of the Jews was near, and many went from the country up to Jerusalem before the Passover, to purify themselves" (John 11:55). A purity that pointed ultimately to what Christ would do for them. We will see how John alone also mentions "hyssop" at the cross (John 19:29) and that "not one bone of Jesus was broken" (John 19:36). Both Passover themes.

King Jesus, Pilate's failure began when he turned his back on You after You declared that You came into the world to bear witness to the truth. Whenever I turn my back on You, and Your word of truth, I too make sinful decisions. Ultimately, I know You were handed over to crucifixion for MY sin. As the lambs were being led to the temple, You were the Lamb of God who was led to the cross for ME. I join all the creatures surrounding Your throne in Heaven and declare, "Blessing and honor and glory and power be to Him who sits on the throne, and to the Lamb, forever and ever!" (Rev. 5:13)

DAY 22
The Via Dolorosa
(Matt. 27:31-32; Mark 15:20-21; Luke 23:26-27, 32; John 19:16-17)

As the lambs were being *led* into the temple to be slaughtered for the Passover, the Lamb of God began to be *led* outside the city to be crucified. In fact, all four Gospels mention that He was "led" to be crucified. He was fulfilling the *seven-hundred year old prophecy* —"he was led like a lamb to the slaughter" (Is. 53:7). Instead of His blood being spilled over the four horns of the bronze altar like the temple sacrifices, it would be spilled on the four corners of an accursed tree. What did this procession to Golgotha look like? A procession Christians in the medieval period began to call *the Via Dolorosa*. Meaning, *the Way of Suffering*.

The Gospel writers would have assumed their audience was familiar with the general process of crucifixion, so their description of the journey is not very extensive. Yet, there are still a few details one can glean when comparing the Gospels. It is clear Jesus began the procession by bearing the cross, that sometime during the procession a man named Simon was commandeered into carrying the cross for Jesus, that a great multitude followed Jesus, that He spoke to a group of mourning women, and that the two other criminals that were crucified next to Him were led with Him to the execution site.

Let's first settle in our imagination the added thoughts that likely went through the minds of *the first readers of the Gospels*. Generally, a Roman crucifixion procession would have a trumpeter at the forefront announcing the names of the criminals being led to crucifixion. Usually their crimes were on placards hung around their necks. These placards were generally whitewashed boards with red or black paint. We know Jesus' placard was hung above Him once crucified (Matt. 27:37). Each criminal would also have four soldiers assigned to carry out their crucifixion (as is the case with Jesus—the *four soldiers* who crucified Him split His clothing as their reward). There also would be a centurion on horseback overseeing the entire event as well as extra soldiers to make sure the populace didn't get out of hand. In order to instill as much fear in the populace as possible, the centurion would generally not take a straight route to the crucifixion site, but rather take a winding way down the most populated streets. They wanted *everyone* to see the wrath that awaited seditious traitors of Rome!

These tactics worked in the case of Jesus for Luke mentions that "a great multitude" followed Him (Luke 23:27). After He had risen from the dead Cleopas said, "Are You the only stranger in Jerusalem, and have You not known the things which happened there in these days?" (Luke 24:18) There is an assumption in this statement that everyone in Jerusalem either saw or heard of the crucifixion of Jesus. Later in the book of Acts Paul tells King Agrippa, "I am convinced that none of these things escapes his attention, since this thing was not done in a corner" (Acts 26:26). *The crucifixion of Jesus was a very public historical event that caused a great stir and was made widely known. Virtually no historians dispute this.*

It is John who tells us that Jesus began the procession "bearing His cross" (John 19:17). The word 'cross' here is a word that was used for the crossbeam of a Roman cross—the patibulum. This beam weighed anywhere between 30-125 pounds. Crucified victims would have the patibulum placed across their neck like a yoke and their hands would then be tied behind the beam with ropes as they journeyed to the crucifixion site. We can imagine the scourged, bled-out, and exhausted Jesus having His hands tied behind that heavy beam, buckling under its weight. Yet, that cross was not the heaviest thing that laid upon Jesus. For, "the LORD has laid on Him the iniquity of us all" (Is. 53:6). The weight of the rugged cross *crushed Him on the outside*, causing Him to slouch over as shockwaves of pain surged throughout His body, irritating His open wounds. Even greater, the weight of our sin *crushed Him on the inside*, experiencing the horror and deep darkness of all of the world's heinous evil and treason against God! While walking face down toward the city gate, on uneven cobble-stone roads, it is highly probable Jesus fell. In fact, tradition maintains that He fell three times.

While we can't say for certain that He fell, it would make sense of why Simon eventually was compelled to carry the cross. All crucified victims were supposed to carry their own cross. *The only reason Simon would be commandeered to take it from Jesus is that Jesus became physically incapable of carrying it.* Interestingly, the Shroud of Turin shows unique excoriations on the knees which scientists say look like were caused by a fall. The Shroud also shows the man with a broken nose. Remember, Jesus couldn't brace from a fall, seeing His hands were tied behind the cross. *He would have landed knee and nose first.* (A broken nose would not be an issue as the nose has no bones, just cartilage.) The Shroud also shows that His right shoulder was dislocated. This last detail likely is what led to Simon ultimately being commandeered, as *it is physically impossible for one with a dislocated shoulder to carry a cross.*

Concerning Simon, Luke says, "they laid hold of a certain man, Simon a Cyrenian, who was coming from the country, and on him they laid the cross that he might bear it after Jesus" (Luke 23:26). Romans could compel their subjects to carry burdens up to one mile. Referring to this practice, Jesus told His followers, "whoever compels you to go one mile, go with him two" (Matt. 5:41). So much for Jesus being an insurrectionist! This word 'compel' is only used again by Matthew *once*—referring to what the Roman soldiers do to Simon (Matt. 27:32). Though Simon was compelled to follow Jesus with a cross, ultimately Jesus wants *all* of His disciples to follow Him with a cross. He taught, "If anyone desires to come after Me, let him deny himself, and take up his cross daily, and follow Me" (Luke 9:23). *Jesus calls His disciples to daily self-denial, sacrificial living, and an imitation of His greatest act of love.* Isaiah prophesied "the government will be upon His shoulder" (Is. 9:6). *The cross is Christ's government and law for His people.* We are called to be a "living sacrifice" (Rom. 12:1). Only as our lives are surrendered at the feet of Jesus are we truly alive! Only as we 'die daily' to self, do we begin to emit the glow of resurrection power! The old man *must* be crucified. Our own agendas and egos *must decrease* so Christ can *increase* (John 3:30).

Mark, whose Gospel was originally sent to Rome, tells us Simon was "the father of Alexander and Rufus" (Mark 15:21). His original audience knew who those men were. Probably leading Christians in their community. In fact, in Romans Paul writes, "Greet Rufus, chosen in the Lord" (Rom. 16:13). Is this the same Rufus? Many think so. Ponder then the usefulness of carrying the cross. It leads to the conversion of not just the cross bearer, Simon, but also his family. In fact, the city of Cyrene had a very strong Christian community that sent out many missionaries (Acts 11:20). Was this due to Simon's influence? Quite possibly!

Lord Jesus, You carried the cross until You were physically incapable of carrying it one inch farther. At that point Simon carried it on Your behalf. He followed in Your footsteps. Help me be like Simon. To die to myself daily, pick up the cross, and follow You. Help me keep my eyes fixed on You as I hold Your symbol of love and redemption high for all to see. Paradoxically, it is only when I am carrying a cross that I am fully alive and fully free!

DAY 23
The Weeping Women
(Luke 23:27-31)

Right after Simon picks up the heavy crossbeam for Jesus we are given a glimpse into the crowds that followed Jesus' procession through Jerusalem. After being face down the entire walk from the weight of that beam, Christ finally is able to be more upright and look at His surroundings. Upon inspection He takes special notice of a group of women who were weeping over His great suffering. In one last act of public teaching before ascending the cross, He turns to these women and says, "Daughters of Jerusalem, do not weep for Me, but weep for yourselves and for your children" (Luke 23:28).

Why not weep at the sight of Christ's sufferings? Well, if one weeps for the anguish Christ experienced, rather than for what was the cause of that anguish, *their sin*, then their weeping is in vain. Christ *willed to suffer and die* on our behalf, and in this way. When we see Christ willingly pick up the cross our hearts should be flooded with joy! Luther said of this passage, "He wants us to rejoice, to glorify God, to thank Him for His mercy, to praise, to extol and to confess Him, because His going to the cross has brought to us the grace of God, freed us from sin and death, and made us God's dear children."[29] Matthew Henry adds that His death "was his victory and triumph over his enemies; it was our deliverance, and the purchase of eternal life" therefore we should weep over "the miseries we shall bring upon ourselves, if we slight his love, and reject his grace."[30] To rightly behold Christ in His Passion is to be in a posture of adoration and thanksgiving, rather than one of sorrow for a poor man from Nazareth. The man walking to Golgotha was none other than the God-Man bearing our sins! Rejoice, again I say, rejoice!

Though we rejoice at Christ's death, and the eternal blessings it accrues, Christ does not say our tears are without use. He directs the women to weep for their sin and for all the temporal consequences that will result from those sins unless they find refuge in Him. These women were like those who constantly bemoan the faults and pains of others, but never look inwardly. Jesus wants those who are simply onlookers, simply 'women of Jerusalem', simply 'people of the world', to experience "godly sorrow" that leads to life (2 Cor. 7:10). By giving this very direct word, in the midst of His great suffering, Jesus was being loving (Lev. 19:17-18). He desired them to view His Passion, and their own dire predicament as a sinful nation, with clear vision.

When Jesus entered Jerusalem on Palm Sunday He "wept over" the city and all its inhabitants (Luke 19:41). He was now calling on them to *weep like He had wept*. He told Jerusalem the Romans would "build an embankment around you, surround you and close you in on every side, and level you, and your children within you, to the ground" (Luke 19:43-44). This was no laughing matter. They did not know the ways that make for peace. Jesus did not desire Jerusalem's destruction. In fact, earlier in His ministry He declared, "O Jerusalem, Jerusalem, the one who kills the prophets and stones those who are sent to her! How often I wanted to gather your children together, as a hen gathers her brood under her wings, but you were not willing! See! Your house is left to you desolate" (Luke 13:34-35). The fact that they killed the prophets, and would even kill apostles Christ would send them, meant that all the blood shed from the foundation of the world would be required of their generation (Luke 11:49-50).

They would undergo "the days of vengeance" (Luke 21:22). For this reason, and their refusal to come to Him, Jesus *wept*, and called for them to *join in His weeping.*

Jesus continued His sermon to the women, saying, "For indeed the days are coming in which they will say, 'Blessed are the barren, wombs that never bore, and breasts which never nursed!' Then they will begin 'to say to the mountains, "Fall on us!" and to the hills, "Cover us!"'" (Luke 23:29-30). No Jewish woman of that day envied women who were childless. Only in the most extreme of disasters would that be the case. This prophetic utterance of Jesus, like everything He said about it in His Olivet Discourse, was literally fulfilled in AD 70. During the siege by Rome we know that many families in Jerusalem began to die of starvation. Josephus records the details of a woman who roasted her own child, ate half, and then saved the rest for murderers who broke into her house looking for food.[31] During the siege Jerusalem was littered with thousands of crosses (not necessarily just for adult men), and the Romans desired to crucify more Jews, but they couldn't because they ran out of wood.

This type of horror, that would have especially impacted women and children, was not new in Israel's history. In fact, when Jerusalem and its temple was destroyed by the Babylonians, the Jews experienced a very similar fate. Jeremiah wrote about this calamity, "The tongue of the infant clings to the roof of its mouth for thirst; the young children ask for bread, but no one breaks it for them" (Lam. 4:4). Jesus was calling for the women of Jerusalem to realize that their nation was headed down a similar path. That their children would experience a similar fate. He was a *Greater Weeping Jeremiah.* What the women needed to do was place their faith in Him, rejoice in His redemptive suffering, and then take heed to His teaching to flee to the hills before the

Roman siege would begin so they could be spared that judgment (Matt. 24:16-20). *God truly desires to deliver us from evil (Matt. 6:13).*

Jesus' speech to the women ends with a somewhat cryptic statement. He says, "For if they do these things in the green wood, what will be done in the dry?" (Luke 23:31) There are a lot of different interpretations as to exactly what Jesus meant here, but the gist of it certainly ties into the destruction He had just prophesied would come on the women and their children. Whatever suffering He was experiencing ('in the green wood') would be much worse for them ('in the dry'). The Jews at this time were still largely under the good graces of Rome ('green wood'), but once they went into full blown rebellion, Rome would put their thumb down ('dry wood'). The scholar, Raymond Brown, believes the most probable meaning of Jesus' statement is something like this, "If they (the Jewish leaders and people) treat me like this in a favorable time (when they are not forced by the Romans), how much the worse will they be treated in an unfavorable time (when the Romans suppress them)."[32]

In the hour of Jesus' greatest suffering, as He had just buckled under the weight of His crossbeam because of the extensive scourging He had endured, *He was still thinking of others.* And His thoughts were not simply for the mourning women watching Him on the Via Dolorosa. His thoughts were for *you.* He desires *you* to correctly perceive His Passion. He desires for *you* to mourn not for Him but rather *your* paths that do not make for peace. He desires *you* to take refuge in Him!

Lord Jesus, You desire for the world to rightly perceive why You picked up the cross and marched to Golgotha. You desire the world to see that You did it for the joy that was set before You (Heb. 12:2). Open my eyes wider to perceive that truth. May my weeping be in union with Yours—a weeping for those who neither know You nor properly discern the sins of their life and nation.

DAY 24
The Crucified King
(Matt. 27:33-35; Mark 15:22-24; Luke 23:33; John 19:17-18)

Jesus arrived outside the city gate in a state of extreme pain, exhaustion, and shock. The amount of blood and bodily fluids He had lost, the scourging He had endured, the lack of any sleep all night, and the potential falls during the trek to Golgotha had physically incapacitated Him from being able to carry the cross the entire half mile from the Praetorium. Yet, with every last ounce of strength, Jesus pressed forward! Deeply desiring to be "lifted up" on that most torturous instrument of death for all the world to see. He would not be denied His glory. He would not be denied this shameful death. For paradoxically it would be the greatest act of love the world has ever seen. By this act He would cast out the prince of the world (the devil), judge the wicked systems of the world, draw all men to Himself, cancel the debt of our sin, bring us into the presence of God, break down the barriers between people groups, and reconcile all things to Himself! (John 12:32; Col. 2:14; Eph. 2:11-16; Col. 1:20)

All four Gospels mention Jesus was crucified at a place called 'the Skull', and three of them mention the name 'Golgotha.' Golgotha is Hebrew for *skull*. Some suggest the site got its name because it looks like a skull. Others suggest it might have gotten the name from Goliath of Gath—Gol(iath)gath. One thousand years earlier *David of Bethlehem* had defeated that *giant Philistine*, cut off his head, and taken it to the city of Jerusalem (1 Sam. 17:54). David is a type of Jesus. Goliath is a type of Satan. If

Golgotha was the site where David buried the skull of Goliath, then we see a picture of *the Greater David* crushing the serpent's head (Gen. 3:15). Those united with Christ, and crucified with Him, will also see Satan crushed under their feet (Rom 16:20). Another tradition in the church is that "the place of the skull" is where the *skull of Adam* was buried. This is why many Orthodox icons have a skull in their images of the crucifixion. The Last Adam brings the tree of life to the First Adam though His death on a tree. Though this is certainly theologically true, the idea of Goliath's skull in Jerusalem makes far more sense than the skull of Adam. Of course, even if Christ wasn't crucified at the exact spot Goliath's head was buried, the theological truth remains.

Upon arriving Jesus is offered wine laced with myrrh and gall. There is dispute as to whether this was an act of charity by some of the women to numb the pains of Jesus, or an act of torture by the soldiers. Large amounts of myrrh would make the drink a thirst-quencher—like drinking gasoline. While others suggest that a little myrrh in the wine might have a numbing effect. Whatever the case, Jesus has just a small "taste" and then turns away from it. The only cup He will drink to the dregs is the cup of wrath for our sins (Matt. 26:39). The offer of "gall" and "vinegar" is also a prophetic fulfillment of Psalm 69. There a righteous sufferer is hated "without cause", covered with "shame", reproached and made a byword, and ultimately given "gall for my food" and "vinegar to drink" (Ps. 69:21). Alongside of Psalm 22, Psalm 69 is one of the great prophetic psalms of Jesus' innocent sufferings on the cross for His people.

After the small taste and refusal of the drink we are told that Jesus was "crucified." It is remarkable how little detail is given about the manner in which He was crucified. The only detail we are given is that He was in the middle of the two criminals who were led to Golgotha with Him. Because a little later a drink has to be offered to Him on an extended reed, it is likely Jesus was crucified in the crux sublimis position. This would have been about two feet higher than the average cross which was crux humilis. *Jesus was positioned as the chief criminal, slightly higher than the others, at the cross-section of a busy road for the world to see!*

In a Roman crucifixion the four soldiers tasked with the duty would all have specific assignments during the crucifixion process. Two soldiers would hold down the victim's arms, a third would restrain the legs, and the fourth would either nail or tie the victim to the wood. The soldiers were most certainly shocked when it came to crucifying Christ. He would not have needed to be forcibly held down. Rather, He was the ultimate *Governor* and *General* in charge. He was *willingly* laying down His own life (John 10:18). Like His distant ancestor, Isaac, before Him, He would have *obediently laid upon the altar of sacrifice* (Gen. 22:9). He embraced the cross, preparing to turn that instrument of utmost horror, death, and shame, into the symbol most recognized in the world today for peace, life, and love. *Certainly, there was excruciating pain as He was fixed to the cross, but there was no struggle.*

While the four narratives of the crucifixion don't mention Jesus being *nailed* to the cross, many other Scriptures make it clear He was. Thomas said, "Unless I see in His hands the print of the nails, and put my finger into the print of the nails…I will not believe" (John 20:25). The psalm of the cross, Psalm 22, says, "They pierced My hands and My feet" (Ps. 22:16). Zechariah prophesied, "they will look on Me whom they pierced" (Zech. 12:10). The word "hand" in Greek and Hebrew refers to the hand and forearm. The word "foot" refers to the foot and lower leg. Most likely the piercing of the "hand" was through Christ's wrists. This way the hand would not tear from the weight of the body. The Shroud of Turin also indicates the wrist was indeed the place Jesus was nailed. Also, though many artistic depictions of Christ have Jesus with one nail through both feet, it is more likely that each foot was nailed separately at the ankle. That is what all the early artistic depictions of the cross of Christ show, and it was far easier for the soldiers—not needing to pound in a much larger stake through two feet. Four nail wounds in all. As each appendage of Jesus was hammered into the wood, and blood splattered onto the arms of the soldiers, and shockwaves of pain surged through Jesus' body, *He was thinking of you.* He was facing a torturous and certain death because the weight of *your sin* was on Him. While the nails were the physical instrument to hold Him there, He was the Son of God. If He wanted to, He could have come down at any moment. *What was truly holding Christ to the cross was His eternal love for you, indeed, for the whole world.*

While the type of cross varied greatly in the ancient world from anything from a stake, to a tree, to a T-shape, to a t-shape, it seems most likely that the traditional t-shape is correct. For the sign of Jesus' 'crime' was hung above His head (Matt. 27:37). With arms outstretched Jesus was inviting the world to find shelter in Him. He was inviting the world to see both the seriousness of their sin and the pledge of His love. Stretched up to heaven, down to hell, and side-to-side to all creation, God in Christ was reconciling "all things to Himself, by Him, whether things on earth or things in heaven, having made peace through the blood of His cross" (Col. 1:20).

Lord Jesus, You embraced the Cross as the climax of Your mission and sign of Your glory. At Golgotha, You not only defeated the spiritual enemy, Satan, but You also reconciled ME to God though I was an enemy. Your Word says, "When we were enemies we were reconciled to God through the death of His Son" (Rom. 5:10). Help me to love my enemies like You have loved me!

DAY 25
Gambling God's Garments
(Matt. 27:35-38; Mark 15:24-28; Luke 23:34, 38; John 19:19-24)

Immediately after lifting the cross into place the soldiers relaxed, sat down, and began to divide their spoil. They had stripped Christ of *all* His clothes. Though crowds in Israel once clamored to Jesus so they might simply "touch the hem" of His garment and receive healing (Mark 6:56), conquerors now divided those once sought after clothes amongst themselves. They left *nothing* to Christ. While most artistic depictions of the cross have Jesus wearing a loincloth, it is almost certain He hung on that accursed tree *completely naked*.

Nakedness was one aspect of the "shame" that accompanied the cross (1 Cor. 1:18, 23; Heb. 12:2). The early church depictions of Jesus, even some dating back to the late-first or second century on gemstones, all depict Christ naked. The nakedness of Jesus seems to be a consensus of the church fathers as well. One mid-second century Christian bishop from Turkey, Melito of Sardis, had this to say about Christ's Passion, "He who hung the earth [in its place] hangs there, he who fixed the heavens is fixed there, he who made all things fast is made fast upon the tree, the Master has been insulted, God has been murdered…O strange murder, strange crime! The Master has been treated in unseemly fashion, his body naked, and not even deemed worthy of a covering, that [his nakedness] might not be seen. Therefore the lights turned away, and the day darkened, that it might hide him who was stripped upon the cross."[33] The medieval priest, John

Tauler, wrote, "See, how the King of glory, Who clotheth and covereth all things, the heaven with clouds, the trees with leaves, the earth with grass and flowers, is Himself stripped of all clothing even to the skin."[34] Another medieval writer, Thomas à Kempis, thought upon Christ's nakedness like this, "as the first Adam, when placed in Paradise, walked, before his fall, in naked liberty; so didst Thou in like manner ascend the Cross naked, to regain the lost home of peace."[35]

As the bludgeoned Savior hung on the cross naked with His four limbs stretched out, *darkness was about to descend* on the land. The sun was created by the Man on the tree and would not dare to shine its light in an unseemly way upon its Creator. But before that physical darkness commenced, the spiritually dark hearts of the soldiers began to gamble for who would get the best cut of Christ's prized garments. As the placard above Christ's head indicated, they were gambling for *king's clothes*. After each solider secured his own part, they gambled for the most prized possession—*the seamless robe*. As Matthew and John point out, this was done to fulfill the prophecy of Psalm 22.

A seamless robe was very valuable as the skill to weave one was not common. It was likely worth more than all the rest of His garments together, and if the soldiers had torn the robe in four, its value would have been completely *cancelled*. Yet, though it was valuable in the material sense, its true value to Christ was what it represented spiritually. *Josephus tells us that the high priests of that day also wore robes that were seamless.* The Jews who initially read the Gospels likely thought about that connection. *That the One being stripped and offered on the cross was none other than the true High Priest of Israel.* This High Priest "has no daily need, like those high priests, to offer up sacrifices, first for His own sins and then for the sins of the people, because He did this once for all time when He offered up Himself" (Heb. 7:27). The High Priest was stripped of His garments to offer Himself once for all. As Hebrews goes on to say, "this Man, after He had offered one sacrifice for sins forever, sat down at the right hand of God" (Heb. 10:12). Jesus has come on the clouds to the Ancient of Days, and sits at the right hand of God in an eternal reign, never needing to sacrifice again. The Sacrifice of His own life is *eternally sufficient.*

The robe is described as being "without seam, woven from the top in one piece" (John 19:23). It is a picture of what Christ's body, the church, is meant to be. Christ desires that we have a *seamless unity* that starts from the top down. A God-created unity based in the Spirit, rather than a man-created unity based in institutions and fleshly coercion. The psalmist declared, "Behold, how good and how pleasant it is for brethren to dwell together in unity! It is like the precious oil upon the head, running down on the beard, the beard of Aaron, running down on the edge of his garments" (Ps. 133:1-2). The night before Jesus was stripped of His seamless garment He prayed to the Father for everyone who would come to believe in Him. He prayed, "I in them, and You in Me; that they may be made perfect in one, and that the world may know that You have sent Me, and have loved them as You have loved Me" (John 17:23). Christ desires His church to be a seamless, loving, Spirit-created unity from the top-down.

Above Christ hung the titulus Pilate had written. It was normal for the judicial authority to write out the crime the man was being crucified for and have it hung around their neck as they carried their cross to the crucifixion site. What is unique about Jesus' titulus is that once Jesus arrived at Golgotha it was nailed above His head. This is the only recorded instance of that in history. On top of that, usually a titulus was only written in multiple languages for highly important men who were being crucified, so Jesus is being singled out as *very significant*. Latin was the official language of Rome. Greek was the universal language, the lingua franca. Hebrew the language of the Jews. Everyone who passed by that main highway near the city gate would see and know the one hanging on the cross was "the King of the Jews." This, of course, infuriated the chief priests! They sent a delegation back to Pilate to demand that he change the titulus to read, "He said, 'I am the King of the Jews'" (John 19:21). Pilate wouldn't budge, likely getting back at them for forcing his hand.

The Jewish German scholar, Schalom Ben-Chorin, writes that the Hebrew text most likely read, "Yeshu Hanorzri Wumelek Hayehudimi."[36] What is interesting about this is that when the first letter of each word is put next to each other it spells the divine name—YHWH. Some have suggested that this was yet one more reason for the frantic bemoaning of the chief priests. Ironically, YHWH truly *was* on that cross. The Maker of all things seen and unseen *was* exposed in His Son for the world to see. The Alpha and Omega who holds time and eternity in His hands *was* held by Roman nails. The One who had been stripped, whose clothes had been gambled, who was half dead in excruciating pain, *is* none other than the Eternal One. Paul reminds us that the rulers "crucified the Lord of glory" (1 Cor. 2:8). He encourages the elders in Ephesus "to shepherd the church of God which He purchased with His own blood" (Acts 20:28). Yes, Jesus of Nazareth, 'the King of the Jews', is none other than YHWH, the King of the Universe!

King Jesus, You were completely stripped of Your clothing to deal with MY shame. The titulus that hung above You was written in the three most popular languages of Jerusalem so everyone would know exactly who hung on the cross for their salvation. You desire the entire world, every tribe and tongue, to know You reigned as King from a cross. May Your church be filled with a greater Spirit-led unity and glorify You as King and God over all!

DAY 26
Shamed and Ridiculed
(Matt. 27:39-44; Mark 15:29-32; Luke 23:35-37)

As we ponder the Passion it is important to put ourselves in first-century shoes. What would the average first-century person have thought about when seeing a crucified man or hearing the Gospel message of 'Christ crucified'? For them crucifixion was not a message of love. Most had no understanding of the *biblical* or *theological* framework undergirding it. Rather, crucifixion to them was simply the most cruel form of torture ever devised. This torture was *invented* by Persians, *advanced* by Carthaginians and Greeks, and *perfected* by Romans. Because of its heinous nature, crucifixion was seldom discussed in polite company or written about at length. The Roman historian, Tacitus, referred to crucifixion as "the most obscene type of death."[37] The famed orator, Cicero, called it "the most cruel and disgusting penalty"[38] and said "[the] very word cross should be forbidden in the presence of a Roman citizen. Romans shouldn't have to think of a cross, see a cross, or hear the miserable word."[39]

Who wants to think of a naked man nailed or tied to a tree bleeding-out in intense pain while shouting profanities, starving, and many times surrounded by beasts of prey preparing to swoop down or pounce on their half-dead carcass at any moment? While there were some who had a sadistic desire to see such penalties (for instance in Pompeii there is an ancient advertisement preserved for a show that would feature both gladiatorial fights and crucifixions), the majority of the public did not go rushing to see such shameful abuse. That sight was largely meant to deter foreign armies, put fear into the slave population, and flex the might of those in power.

Many of the subjected people in Rome had personally witnessed crucifixion or heard of mass crucifixions of the past. Concerning these mass crucifixions, King Darius I of Persia had 3,000 political enemies crucified simultaneously in 519 BC. A few centuries later Alexander the Great littered a stretch of the shore of the great Mediterranean power Tyre with 2,000 crosses of men he had conquered. The Jews experienced this mass form of torture when their king, Alexander Jannaeus, crucified 800 Pharisees in front of the entire city at the turn of the second century BC. Around that same time, the slave and gladiator, Spartacus, was leading his uprising against Rome. Though his army grew to 120,000 men they were squashed by the Romans, and the 6,000 soldiers who remained to the end were crucified along the main highway into Rome. Crosses stretched for 120 miles—a sign that *no one* should dare rebel against Rome's might!

This form of torture continued into the Christian era. The crazed emperor, Nero, blamed Christians for a large fire he had started in Rome. After shifting blame to them he ordered many of them to be crucified, or burned alive as human torches for his nighttime entertainment. A couple of years after this incident, when Jerusalem was destroyed by a Roman army, Josephus tells us, "In time, soldiers ran out of wood for crosses. But it didn't matter because they had run out of room for crosses even if they had found more wood."[40] The Christian historian, Eusebius, writes of the last great Christian persecution known as the Diocletian persecution. He says Christians "were nailed to the cross upside down and then kept alive until they starved to death."[41] To the ancient mind, the cross spoke of *absolute horror.*

Cicero referred to crucifixion as the "extreme and ultimate penalty for a slave."[42] It was called the *supplicium servile*, meaning, "the slave's death." Jesus was the Suffering Servant/Slave prophesied about in Isaiah. Reflecting on the extreme humility that Christ undertook as God in our midst, Paul wrote that He "emptied Himself, by taking the form of a slave" and "humbled Himself by becoming obedient to the point of death, even death on a cross." In light of this Slave's vindication in resurrection and exaltation to the Ancient of Days every tongue will confess "that Jesus Christ is LORD, to the glory of God the Father" (Phil. 2:7-11, LSB). *The shameful death of the Slave, who became the exalted Lord over all things, and is confessed as One who bears the Divine Name, was foolishness to the Greek, and a stumbling block to the Jew. But to the one who believes? The very power of God! (1 Cor. 1:23-25)*

The practice of crucifixion was put into the dust bin of history by the first Christian Emperor—Constantine. From that time forward the cross began to be placed on public buildings. It became a symbol that spoke the opposite of what it originally signified. A symbol of love, grace, and self-sacrifice. Nailing a man naked to a large wooden plank in public after being brutally scourged is now unthinkable in much of the modern world. The Bill of Rights forbids "cruel and unusual punishment" as did the English Bill of Rights before it. These sentiments primarily find their roots in one historical event—the crucifixion of Jesus.

In light of the utter shame and horror of crucifixion one can understand why those passing by Jesus "wagged their heads", "mocked", "reviled", "sneered", and made jest of Him. This sort of heckling was common for crucified victims hanging on main street. The Gospels record the chief priests, scribes, elders, soldiers, common people passing by, and even the two men crucified with Jesus engaging in this public ridicule. The religious leaders say, "He saved others; Himself He cannot save…let Him now come down from the cross, and we will believe" (Matt. 27:42). They issue the temptation to Jesus the devil had offered at the beginning of His ministry in the wilderness—a call on Jesus to achieve victory through the means of a public spectacle (Luke 4:9). They sought a sign, but no sign would be given to them except the sign of Jonah (Mark 12:38-42). Jesus had already performed multitudes of miracles, yet they had hardened their hearts. Ironically, His greatest miracle was being performed before their own eyes. He was bearing their sin and offering them eternal life! The great irony of the crowds call for Jesus to come down and "save Himself" was that if He did "save Himself", the world would never be saved.

The mockers also shouted, "Aha! You who destroy the temple and build it in three days, save Yourself, and come down from the cross!" (Mark 15:29). Ironically yet again, what Jesus really said was that *they* would "destroy" the temple (John 2:19). They were fulfilling that prophecy for all to see by destroying Jesus who is *the tabernacled presence of God* (John 1:14; John 2:21; Col. 2:9). Their mocking was simply the slanderous rephrasing of the "prophecy" that was presented at Jesus' trial that morning (Mark 14:58). We will see in the next devotion how our Savior responded to this shameful crucifixion and mocking. His heart was not full of *vengeance*, but rather, *love*. So, He silently endured their ranting and raving. *As this scene transpired yet one more element of the great prophecy of the cross, Psalm 22, was being fulfilled:* "All those who see Me ridicule Me; they shoot out the lip, they shake the head, saying, 'He trusted in the Lord, let Him rescue Him; let Him deliver Him, since He delights in Him!'" (Ps. 22:7-8).

Jesus, because You were put to shame, "Whoever believes on You will not be put to shame!" (Rom. 10:11) You transformed the most dreadful symbol in history into the most beautiful, gracious, and loving symbol. Thank you!

DAY 27
The First Word—Forgive
(Luke 23:34)

Jesus had just been nailed to the cross. The jeering and ridicule had begun. As He was being lifted up from the earth, tongue cleaving to the top of His mouth, blood dripping as His body was experiencing *extreme shock*, what was on His heart and mind? Displeasure? Anger? Revenge? No. *Instead, His heart was full of love, forgiveness, mercy, and grace.* As Jesus hung on the cross for the next three hours, He uttered seven final statements. Three right at the beginning as He was being lifted up and just before the sun turned dark, and four right at the end before He died and the earth shook. It was a deathbed sermon. These were the final words He desired the world to hear. Jesus had preached from a boat, a mountaintop, and even the temple precincts, but there was never a pulpit like the cross. Bellarmine wrote about this *final sermon*, "He preached to us words few in number, but burning with love, most useful and efficacious, and in every way worthy to be engraven on the heart of every Christian, to be preserved there, meditated upon, and fulfilled literally and in deed."[43]

The first word Christ uttered was *overflowing with grace*. Man was at his worst. They had "crucified the Lord of glory" (1 Cor. 2:8). And it wasn't just the soldiers, or Judas, or the chief priests, or Pilate who were responsible. Rather, every man was responsible. We have *all* sinned. And the only way our debt could be paid, justice could be satisfied, and we could be made righteous, was for Jesus to ascend the cross in our stead. Amazingly, as the nails pierced through the flesh of Jesus, the world was unaware they had punctured Love itself! They punctured One who had willingly fixed Himself upon that tree. And what oozed from this Eternal Love? *Forgiveness.* As Jesus' cross was slotted into place, and He gazed over a sea of ferocious faces while being lifted up, He forced His dry mouth open and cried, "Father, forgive them, for they do not know what they do" (Luke 23:34).

At this moment Jesus was fulfilling the prophecy of Isaiah—"He...made intercession for the transgressors" (Is. 53:12). He also was living out what He had taught in His sermon on the plain, "bless those who curse you, and pray for those who spitefully use you" (Luke 6:28). As well as His sermon on the mount, "love your enemies" (Matt. 5:44). Jesus' refusal to return insult for insult became an ethic code that both Peter and Paul taught the church to abide by. Peter wrote that Christ "was leaving an example for us" upon the cross. Part of that example being "when He was reviled, did not revile in return" (1 Pet. 2:21-22). Paul said of his ministry, "Being reviled, we bless" (1 Cor. 4:12). The prayer for forgiveness uttered by Jesus to His enemies has been *repeated* by many Christian martyrs, beginning with the first martyr—Stephen. As he was being stoned he cried with a loud voice, "Lord, do not charge them with this sin" (Acts 7:60). *Radical forgiveness is the way of Christ and His Church.*

Fr. Ignatius wrote, "The thought of the eternal perdition of the souls of His crucifiers is a greater source of suffering to Jesus than His own most bitter Passion!"[44] Quite true. Is there anything more horrifying than creatures created in God's image and likeness barred from eternal glory and bliss in heaven? Is there anything worse than being separated from one's Maker and Redeemer? Jesus laid down His life to provide forgiveness for every soul dead in trespasses and sin. This forgiveness could only be secured through the shedding of His blood (Heb. 9:22; Col. 1:14). For the blood spoke of His perfect *life* being poured out in place of our *life* (Lev. 17:14). If we confess our sin, the Bible assures us God will "forgive us our sins" and "cleanse us from all unrighteousness." This forgiveness and cleansing is effective solely because of "the blood of Jesus" (1 John 1:7-9). *The prayer of forgiveness uttered from Jesus' lips was mingled with His own blood, assuring us this forgiveness is indeed available and secure!*

God is righteous and cannot deny Himself. In order to satisfy His own righteousness, He became man to pay a debt to sin we could never pay—death. *As His life poured out, and He looked out at the sea of humanity bound in sin and ignorance, forgiveness was 'the first word' that thundered from His heart! It went straight to the throne and has reverberated through all human history! It is the very heart of God open and on display!* Can you hear it echoing in the halls of eternity? Even more, have you embraced this priceless gift? Paul traveled over land and sea to the Gentile nations because Christ sent him "that they may receive forgiveness of sins and an inheritance among those who are sanctified by faith" (Acts 26:18). Just as the Crucified Christ thundered forgiveness, the Resurrected Christ continues to thunder this same message through His people— imploring everyone to freely receive the forgiveness of sins.

Those in Christ have come to "the heavenly Jerusalem" and "to the blood of sprinkling that speaks better things than that of Abel" (Heb. 12:22-24). Abel's blood cried out for vengeance, as the blood of all martyrs do (Rev. 6:10), and God certainly does avenge that blood. Yet, those who have found their refuge in Christ, have come under the covering of blood that speaks a 'better' word. *The word of forgiveness.* Just as the Israelites sprinkled the blood of the Lamb over their doorposts on Passover, so the Christian has the blood of Christ sprinkled over their lives. Their debt has been paid, their sins, though mountainous, have been wiped away and forgiven! The blood of Jesus, the very life of God poured out for you, truly cleanses *any* and *every* sin!

Jesus once preached a parable about an *unforgiving servant* (Matt. 18:21-35). In this parable a servant owed a debt to the king that could never be paid in many lifetimes—ten thousand talents. Think of it as equivalent to the national debt. After begging his master for mercy, "the master of that servant was moved with compassion, released him, and forgave him the debt." What a powerful picture of salvation—being freed from a debt we could never pay! But, what did the forgiven servant do? He went and found a fellow servant who owed him about four months wages and "took him by the throat, saying, 'Pay me what you owe!'" His friend begged for mercy, but was granted none, and instead was thrown in prison until he could pay the debt. Upon hearing about this action by his servant, the king was furious and said, "Should you not also have had compassion on your fellow servant, just as I had pity on you?" This is the question that stands before all of us in light of receiving salvation in Christ. We have had a debt paid that we could never pay on our own. Will we extend that same compassion and forgiveness to others? Will we "be kind to one another, tenderhearted, forgiving one another, even as God in Christ forgave [us]" (Eph. 4:32)?

Lord Jesus, the soldiers crucifying You did not know they were crucifying the Lord of glory. In one sense, whenever we sin, we do not fully understand the magnitude of what we have done. Yet, Your first word from the cross still stands. You told Jonah, "should I not pity Nineveh, that great city, in which are more than one hundred and twenty thousand persons who cannot discern between their right hand and their left—and much livestock?" (Jonah 4:11) Just as You pitied the wicked Ninevites in their ignorance, and offered forgiveness, so You pity the whole world, holding out Your forgiveness grounded in Your blood for all who will receive. Ludolph of Saxony aptly stated, "O, how sweet was the melody of that prayer sung by Christ to the accompaniment of the hammers, and how many thousands have been converted by this harmony!"[45] May Your Song of forgiveness be my Song.

DAY 28
The Second Word—Paradise
(Luke 23:39-43)

Jesus had just spoken an astonishing prayer to the Father upon being lifted up—a word of forgiveness to the world that had crucified Him. As the soldiers began to divide His clothes, and the crowds hurled insults, Matthew and Mark both record that the two revolutionaries who were crucified on either side of Jesus *joined in the mocking.* Mark wrote, "Even those who were crucified with Him reviled Him" (Mark 15:32). These men were hardened sinners. With only hours left to live they weren't thinking upon eternal things, rather, they sought to distract themselves from their own pain as they joined the jest of others. How sad that men, even in the greatest of suffering, at times aren't humbled. Yet, *suddenly,* something miraculous took place! Whether touched by the silence of Jesus, the title above His head, or the word of forgiveness He just thundered over those who crucified and blasphemed Him, one of the thieves became contrite. He began to enter into a state of *retrospection,* his heart was *softened,* and in that moment of heartfelt repentance, *faith* welled up within him!

Turning his head toward the blaspheming thief who continued to join the jest against Jesus, the newly contrite thief "rebuked him, saying, 'Do you not even fear God, seeing you are under the same condemnation? And we indeed justly, for we receive the due reward of our deeds; but this Man has done nothing wrong'" (Luke 23:40-41). Earlier we learned that Barabbas was "chained with his fellow rebels; they had committed murder in the rebellion" (Mark 15:7). These two men were likely Barabbas' co-conspirators, with Barabbas having been the ringleader. They would have been zealous Jews who were attempting to bring back the glory of Israel by force. As Jesus took the place of their ringleader, one of the rebels began to realize he had been deeply misguided, and truly was suffering justice upon the cross. He reminds the other rebel that they will soon face a *heavenly tribunal*. He calls on him to *come to grips* with the sin they had committed. In fact, he makes a double confession of sin saying he suffered "justly" and was receiving the "due reward" for his deeds. This is the essence of repentance. To repent is to have a *change of mind and heart* that then leads to *a change in action*. It is to view sin the way God views it, and then declare it as so. The Greek word for confess is "homologeo" which literally means "same word." It means to say the same thing as God says, to come to grips that we have missed the mark, are out of line, and deserve justice. Here on the cross was a powerful display of true repentance.

Yet, this rebel was not simply repenting of his sin, He also *turned in faith* toward Christ. After his exhortation to the other rebel he turned to Jesus and said, "Lord, remember me when You come into Your kingdom" (Luke 23:41). He had a revelation that Jesus was King! He had a revelation that Jesus was the Messiah! His heart was *supernaturally opened* to understand the mystery of the cross that even Jesus' disciples had yet to understand. He knew he didn't deserve blessing in the world to come, yet, he still humbly asks the Lord to be "remembered" as He would come on the clouds to the Ancient of Days. This is *faith*. The rebel does not give a list of reasons why he *deserves* to be remembered, but simply stakes *everything* on what Jesus can do on his behalf!

Jesus responds to this man with His second word. He says, "Assuredly, I say to you, today you will be with Me in Paradise" (Luke 23:43). This is the only time Jesus responds to someone who speaks to Him at the cross. And it is a word of superabundant grace. A word of *blessing* and *assurance* to a robber and murderer. A word that reminds us of Jesus' first beatitude, "Blessed are the poor in spirit, for theirs is the kingdom of heaven" (Matt. 5:3). If one ever begins to doubt that salvation is by *grace alone*, through *faith alone*, they only ever need meditate on this second word of Jesus from the cross. For this man had led a life worthy of hell. He had no time for good deeds. As he was crucified to that tree he could run no errands and give no alms. All he could do was offer his heart to Jesus, with the only member of his body he still could move freely—his tongue!

As long as one is still breathing, they can give their heart to Jesus. It is never too late to come to Him and find rest for our souls (Matt. 11:28). One of the most wicked and heinous sinners in the Old Testament was a king named Manasseh. He was worse than all the kings of the pagan nations who lived in the Promised Land before him—even engaging in mass child sacrifice (2 Chr. 33:9). Yet, after suffering in bronze fetters in Babylon, his heart became contrite like the murderer on the cross. As his life was waning away he humbled himself, repented, prayed, and the Lord restored him to life (2 Chr. 33:12-13). The point of Manasseh's story is that it is never too late for even the most wicked, Hitleresque, chief of sinners to come to Jesus. Christ's blood is sufficient for all! Paul wrote, "This is a faithful saying and worthy of all acceptance, that Christ Jesus came into the world to save sinners, of whom I am chief" (1 Tim. 1:15).

Salvation can come *at the eleventh hour* (Matt. 20:1-16). It can come *on the death bed*. We must never minimize the abundance of God's mercy and grace. In the parable of the eleventh hour workers, the owner who gave every worker the same reward said to the workers who complained that they worked longer, "Are you envious because I am generous?" (Matt. 20:15, NIV) Let us never complain about God's gift of salvation to those we believe don't deserve it. He died for all! He is generous! Praise the Lord!

Notice the three aspects of the gift: *today, with me, paradise*. The contrite murderer needed no 'purgatory'—*he entered into life that very day*—as all believers do. Jesus' sacrifice was sufficient for all his sin. The second aspect of Jesus' Promise was the best. The murderer would be *with* Jesus. This is the true glory of eternity. Not paradise *in and of itself*, but rather being *with Jesus* in paradise. "To be absent from the body is to be present with the Lord" (2 Cor. 5:8). Paul did not long to go to paradise, but rather, "to depart to be with Christ" (Phil. 1:23). Paradise is creation imbued with the Spirit and raised to a glorious wonder far beyond anything we can possibly imagine. Grass as soft as pillows yet that sparkle like emeralds, air that exudes freshness, water that flows musically, and fruit that rejoices the heart. Yet, all of this pales in comparison to seeing Christ face-to-face, and being "with Him" for eternity. The thief went from the height of torturous pain to the undying rest of Paradise and "eternal weight of glory" (2 Cor. 4:17). Why? Solely because of the promise of Jesus and His redemptive work on the cross!

Lord Jesus, I recognize that the only One who can promise Paradise is the Lord of Paradise. You are the One who formed Paradise at the beginning that we might forever be with You, and who opened its gates again through Your Sacrifice. At the cross You "show me the path of life; in Your presence is fullness of joy; at Your right hand are pleasures forevermore" (Ps. 16:11). The murderer asked only to be "remembered" and yet in Your great goodness and mercy You exceeded his expectations. You truly are One who gives "exceedingly, abundantly above, all that we ask or imagine" (Eph. 3:20, NIV), when we ask in faith. Let me never minimize Your generosity, let me always glory in Your grace, both for me and everyone around me.

DAY 29
The Third Word—Family
(John 19:25-27)

After speaking forgiveness to the world at large and promising paradise to a murderer who turned to Him in faith, Jesus set His eyes upon the family—both natural and spiritual. This *word* also happened near the beginning of His crucifixion—before the sun was darkened. John informs us that at the foot of the cross were three Marys—Jesus' mother, Mary the wife of Clopas, and Mary Magdalene. In Hebrew their name is Miriam. A name that means "sea of sorrow." There was never a more sorrowful day for Christ's disciples (not yet fully understanding the purpose of His death). Yet, their *sorrow* would soon be turned to *joy*—just like the first Miriam sang and danced after Israel's deliverance from Egypt (Ex. 15:20). Indeed, turned into "great joy" (Matt. 28:8).

When Mary had taken Jesus to the temple to be dedicated when He was born, Simeon prophesied over her, saying, "a sword will pierce through your own soul" (Luke 2:35). The One she had nursed, the One she lovingly raised and taught to walk and talk, was now suffering the height of torture and shame. As she gazed upon her son she was experiencing a *martyrdom of the heart*. Her soul, her very life force, was "pierced" as she watched the One whom her entire life revolved around in extreme anguish.

Mary had been with Jesus not simply from the moment of His conception as He began to take on human flesh, but also from the very beginning of His ministry. She was there at the wedding of Cana where Christ first began to "manifest His glory" (John 2:11). In that first miracle Jesus also addressed her as "woman" instead of "mother" when she asked Jesus to solve the issue of shame for the couple who had run out of wine (John 2:3-4). Jesus reminded her, "My hour has not yet come" (John 2:4)—referring to the redemptive "hour" of His Passion. Yet, He still obeyed His mother and turned 180 gallons of water into wine. This act was simply a proleptic sign of the abundant grace that would come when Jesus would shed His blood for us on the cross. *His blood would be the 'best wine' we drink—bringing us from sorrow to joy! It would be the life of God we imbibe as we celebrate our 'union' with Him, the end of our shame, and the gift of our new family—the church!*

The other character who "stood by the cross" with the three Marys and His aunt Salome, was "the disciple whom He loved" (John 19:26). This is the way that John describes himself multiple times throughout his Gospel (John 13:23; 19:26; 20:2; 21:7, 20). It was his core identity. Because John knew how loved he was, he was always near Jesus. The previous night he "was leaning on Jesus' bosom" as they were sharing supper (John 13:23). He is likely the "other disciple" who entered the courtyard of the high priest with Peter (John 18:15). Ultimately, he is the only apostle that went to Golgotha and was an eyewitness of the crucifixion.

It seems that John wanted to emphasize that his steadfastness to Jesus was not a result of how wonderful he was, but rather a consequence of the love he had received and internalized. After listening to Christ's heartbeat during the Supper it was as if *supernatural courage* was built into him where he would not only enter the high priest's courtyard after initially fleeing Him, but actually go and stand near the foot of the cross! This would have been a very dangerous place for him to be. Yet, the love of Christ compelled him to be there. Ultimately, "the disciple whom Jesus loved" is a picture *every believer*. Jesus told all of His disciples the previous night, "As the Father loved Me, I also have loved you; abide in My love" (John 15:9). There is no greater love than the love of the Father for the Son. It is with that *same exact love* that Jesus loves *all* His disciples! Jesus loves every single disciple with an eternal, immeasurable, inexhaustible, omnipotent love! This is why every disciple can be filled with *supernatural courage*. We can all deeply internalize the love of Jesus like John did. We can all 'stand near the cross' often and be in awe of Christ's extravagant display of love for the world!

As Jesus was looking at His mother, He said, "Woman, behold your son!" (John 19:26) Looking at John, He said, "Behold your mother!" (John 19:27) Jesus was making sure His mother was taken care of. As the LORD who gave the commandment, "honor your father and mother" (Ex. 20:12; Matt. 15:4), Jesus obeys His own command to the greatest extent. In the New Testament, when Paul is talking about care for widows, children are instructed to "repay their parents; for this is good and acceptable before God" (1 Tim. 5:4). Joseph was gone. Jesus' brothers at that point did not believe in Him (John 7:5). So Jesus made sure His mother would be taken care of and looked after. Mary's sister, Salome, was the mother of the beloved disciple (cf. Matt. 27:56; Mark 15:40; John 19:25). When Jesus commits His mother to the care of John, He is committing her to one who *knew her well as her nephew*, who was *from a family with financial means* as the fishing business of Zebedee had hired servants (Mark 1:20), and most importantly to someone who *had internalized His love and would share that love and care with His mother.*

Reading this story at a *spiritual* and *typological* level we can see that Mary is a picture of the church and the disciple whom Jesus loved is a picture of all believers. This is how John speaks of things in Revelation 12. There we see the "woman" give birth to Jesus. He is immediately persecuted by the devil, but ultimately is victorious and ascends to the right hand of God in heaven where He reigns with a rod of iron (Rev. 12:1-5). Though the dragon can no longer devour Christ, he does seek to devour the church. Yet, the dragon stands defeated by "the blood of the Lamb" and the word of the testimony of Christ's disciples in that blood (Rev. 12:11). The 'blood' stands for Christ's atoning sacrifice on the cross. Though defeated, the dragon still seeks to persecute "the woman" and "the rest of her offspring" (Rev. 12:17). The "woman" is a picture of the church. The "rest of her offspring" is a picture of disciples of Jesus—members of the church. Every disciple who is loved by Jesus must love the church. For to be joined to Jesus is to be joined to His body—the church. *To enter the church is to enter a new family—an eternal family.*

John's obedience to Jesus' instruction was immediate. He writes, "from that hour that disciple took her to his own home" (John 19:27). This is possibly why three hours later Jesus' mother is not mentioned among the women who are watching the crucifixion from a distance (Mk. 15:40; Mt. 27:55). The internal suffering Mary was experiencing at Golgotha was an immense internal martyrdom. She needed to be taken care of at home. *Ultimately, she would rise to be a great pillar of strength for the budding church at Pentecost.* One in fervent prayer in the upper room (Acts 1:14).

Jesus, You are my brother (Heb. 2:11; Mk. 3:34). You have given me Your Father and Your mother (Jn. 19:27; 20:17). You have brought me into Your family! As I meditate on Your Passion, it is a wonder to me that in the hour of Your greatest suffering You were only thinking of others. You thought of the world drowning in their sin and offered them the word of forgiveness. You were attentive to the murderer hanging next to You and offered Him eternal paradise. And You were attentive to Your mother who was experiencing a sword piercing through her soul. Thank you for my 'spiritual family'—the church. Thank you for taking care of me there until You receive me in glory.

DAY 30
The Fourth Word—Forsaken
(Matt. 27:45-47; Mark 15:33-35; Luke 23:44)

After Jesus' initial three words darkness covered "the land" of Israel for three hours from 12PM to 3PM. During these hours of Jesus' greatest suffering, while clothed in darkness, He remained *silent*. This was not a solar eclipse, as the moon was full for Passover, but rather a supernatural darkness. It was a sign of judgment, as the darkening of cosmic bodies is throughout the Old Testament (Is. 13:10; Ez. 32:7; Joel 3:15). Part of the curse of the Law included, "you shall grope at noonday, as a blind man gropes in darkness" (Deut. 28:29). God spoke of a prior judgment in this manner, "I will make the sun go down at noon, and I will darken the earth in broad daylight" (Amos 8:9). The darkness at Golgotha was a supernatural darkness like the one that clothed the land of Egypt for three days during the ninth plague—a "thick darkness" which "even may be felt" (Ex. 10:21-22). It was like the darkness that hovered over Egypt throughout the tenth plague *when the firstborn sons were put to death.*

What was happening on the cross was the Ultimate Passover. The only begotten Son of God is the firstborn Lamb slain so Death would "pass over" those who have His blood applied to their lives. The only begotten Son was taking the curse and judgment humanity deserved. The wages of our sin being death (Rom. 6:23)—both physical death and spiritual death in the "outer darkness" of hell (Matt. 8:12, 22:13, 25:30). Jesus was entering into that outer darkness and separation *on our behalf.* He was entering the state that 'the rich man' in His prior parable had experienced—"being in torments in Hades" with "a great gulf" between him and the serenity of the righteous in Abraham's bosom. This man cried out for just *one drop* of water, as Jesus will cry out for something to *quench* His thirst in His fifth word (Luke 16:19-26). The Son of God was experiencing the inner and outer torments our sins merited to the full! The Son of God was entering darkness, and the sun He created in the beginning ceased to give its light in solidarity with its Creator.

Toward the end of this darkness Jesus uttered His last four words right before He died. The first of these words was His fourth word, "My God, My God, why have You forsaken Me?" (Matt. 27:26; Mark 15:34). This is the only time Jesus spoke to His Father using the term 'God' instead of 'Father.' He was speaking in our stead, as our substitute, as one who had the momentary human sensory experience of being abandoned and separated from the Father's presence due to sin. (More on that in a bit.)

What Jesus was also doing by speaking this word was *intentionally* quoting the first line of Psalm 22. As He spoke this line, the part of the crowd who were Jews would have been struck in a similar manner to someone singing the first line of a popular song in our own day. Those familiar with the tune would have had the rest of the song play through their head. Well, all devout Jews had the psalms *memorized*, and as Psalm 22 played through their heads many would have realized that every verse of the psalm was being prophetically fulfilled right before their eyes!

Psalm 22 continues with Christ "crying out" simultaneously in the day and night (v. 2). He is forsaken because God "is holy" (v. 3). He trusts in God amidst forsakenness like the fathers (v. 4-5). He is a "worm" who is being "reproached" and "despised" (v. 6). He is "ridiculed" as people mock Him and call for God to deliver Him (v. 7-8). He is the fully 'faith-full' one from womb to tomb (v. 9-11). The religious leaders surround Him like the "bulls of Bashan"—raging with their vile blasphemies (v. 12-13). All of His bones are "out of joint" and His heart is "melted" (v. 14). His "tongue clings to His jaws" like we will see in His fifth word (v. 15). He says, "they pierced My hands and My feet"—a *graphic* depiction of crucifixion written hundreds of years before it was even devised (v. 16). With the tearing of flesh and drastic loss of fluids, He says, "I can count all my bones" (v. 17). "They divide My garments among them, and for My clothing they cast lots" (v. 18). As a result of this redemptive suffering, "All the ends of the world shall remember and turn to the LORD, and all the families of the nations shall worship before You" (v. 27).

While the physical sufferings described in this Psalm are great, *by far* the worst suffering is the spiritual suffering of forsakenness at the beginning of the Psalm that Jesus utters. *God is the perfection of holiness.* Before Him the seraphim veil their faces as they sing the thrice holy (Is. 6:5). God is "of purer eyes than to behold evil, and cannot look on wickedness" (Hab. 1:13). As Jesus "became sin" upon the cross He endured the worst of all punishments—a sense of utter separation and alienation from the Father (2 Cor. 5:21). He *rightly abhorred it,* and *trusted God through it,* in our stead.

Both John and Paul speak of Christ as the "propitiation" for our sin (1 John 2:2; Rom. 3:25). This means God's wrath toward sin is *satiated through justice being administered.* What is remarkable is that God is the One who "propitiates" Himself through taking on our sin! This is largely Paul's point in Romans 3:21-26. God gives Himself in the person of the Son, to pour out His blood, in order "to demonstrate His righteousness" and show He is "just and the justifier of the one who has faith in Jesus." God is not like an indulgent grandparent that simply lets sin go. No, sin is vile destructive brokenness that must be punished and ended. Because God is both the perfection of *love* and *holiness*, the cross is the means by which both of those perfections shine bright. For God neither overlooks sin, nor does He cease to show His merciful love for the most vile sinner. A. W. Pink wrote, "The Holy Scriptures leave it impossible to doubt that these words of unequaled grief were both the fullest manifestation of divine love and the most awe-inspiring display of God's inflexible justice."[46] (See *Appendix B* for a longer discussion of the sacrificial victim and the biblical case for penal-substitutionary atonement.)

At the cross the wrath of God was *satisfied* and the love of God was *magnified*. At the cross mercy and truth meet together and righteousness and peace kiss (Ps. 85:10). At the cross Christ was *forsaken* while we were *forgiven*. The Firstborn died in our place, in the darkness, so we could live! He was forsaken so that we will never be forsaken! Paul speaks of himself as "persecuted, but not forsaken" (2 Cor. 4:9), and in the light of Christ's substitutional death he declared, "neither death nor life, nor angels nor principalities nor powers, nor things present nor things to come, nor height nor depth, nor any other created thing, shall be able to separate us from the love of God which is in Christ Jesus our Lord" (Rom. 8:38-39).

Lord Jesus, You are perfectly righteous and perfectly loving. During Your Passion You were "pierced for MY transgressions" and "crushed for MY iniquities" (Is. 53:5). You who "never knew" or experienced sin were "made to be sin" for ME (2 Cor. 5:21). You "bore MY sins" in Your own body (1 Pet. 2:24). You truly are the "Passover Lamb" that was slain for ME (1 Cor. 5:7). The Firstborn slaughtered so that Your blood would propitiate the demands of Your justice and satisfy the longings of Your love. As You gave Your life as "a sacrifice to God for a sweet-smelling aroma" (Eph. 5:2), may my life be a "living sacrifice" of unceasing gratitude to You (Rom. 12:2).

DAY 31
The Fifth Word—Thirst
(Mark 15:36; Matt 27:48-49; John 19:28-29)

The fifth and sixth statements of Christ from the cross are both one word in Greek. The fifth word in Greek is sitio. Meaning, "I thirst." This word was part of His seven-point sermon from the pulpit of the cross—so it deserves our prolonged meditation as it is filled with pregnant meaning and profound truth. It was a word spoken immediately after His fourth word, and it too is connected with the crowds wondering (largely in a mocking way) if Elijah would come and save Jesus. These mockers, of course, did not know the 'coming of Elijah' had already been fulfilled typologically in the person of John the Baptist (Matt. 17:12).

Remarkably, Jesus' cry for thirst *is the only time He gives expression to His physical agony* throughout the entire Passion narrative. He had received no liquid since the Last Supper the prior evening. The sweat and blood lost in Gethsemane, combined with the beatings He received at the hands of the Sanhedrin and Pilate, combined with the blood that had been flowing freely for three hours from the cross, all contributed to His prophetic voice in the psalm, "My tongue clings to My jaws; You have brought Me to the dust of death" (Ps. 22:15). *There was an intense inner fire of suffering raging on the inside.* While some doctors in the 20th-century theorized that Christ died of asphyxiation, the leading hypothesis today is that He died of hypovolemic shock—a condition that has to do with the loss of liquid in the body. Extreme and total thirst.

The Fountain of Life, who became flesh for our salvation, was being drained of every fleshly fluid as He hung on the tree. John

Tauler said, "not only did He shed all His own Blood, and pour forth whatever He had of moisture by His tears, but the very marrow of His bones, and all His Heart's Blood, were consumed for our sakes by the heat and flame of His love."[47] While bringing deliverance to Israel, Samson killed a thousand Philistines with a jawbone, stacked the dead bodies up in heaps, and "became very thirsty" in the process (Judg. 15:18). So too, the Greater Samson, while disarming and bringing a deathblow to principalities and powers, and making a public spectacle of them at the cross (Col. 2:15), became "very thirsty" in His warfare for our salvation!

Yet, the primary reason Jesus said "I thirst" was not to complain about His physical suffering. Rather, it was spoken "that the Scripture might be fulfilled" (John 19:28). The Scripture Jesus was speaking of was likely Psalm 69:21. It states, "They also gave me gall for my food, and for my thirst they gave me vinegar to drink." Jesus came to fulfill every "jot and tittle" of Scripture (Matt. 5:18). He said, "My food is to do the will of Him who sent Me, and to finish His work" (John 4:34). His desire to accomplish even the smallest details of God's revealed will in Scripture is a lesson for all disciples. Man lives by "every word that proceeds from the mouth of God" (Matt. 4:4). Christians must be "doers of the word, and not hearers only" (James 1:22). We should "search the Scriptures daily" like the Bereans to see if there is anything about our life or mentality that is not in alignment with God's Heart—desiring His perfect will for our lives (Acts 17:11).

The reaction to Christ's cry was that a bystander—most likely one of the four soldiers guarding Him—"filled a sponge with sour wine, put it on hyssop, and put it to His mouth" (John 19:29). This was liquid from a "vessel full of soul wine" that was simply sitting near the cross. Likely the soldiers 'posca' that would keep their thirst sated the long day watching over the crucified victims. The mouth of these vessels would be plugged with a piece of sponge that served as a cork.[48] Because Christ was in a more exalted position, they couldn't lift the vessel to Him, but instead had to soak the sponge in the posca and lift it to Jesus at the end of a long reed.

While Matthew and Mark simply mention that the sponge was placed at the end of a "reed", John is more specific and makes sure we know the "reed" was actually "hyssop." This is very significant because hyssop is the plant that was dipped in the blood of the lambs on the night of the Passover in order to sprinkle the blood over the doorframes of all believing Israelites and Egyptians (Ex. 12:22). Raymond Brown writes, "As for the hyssop associated with Passover and sprinkling, most think of *Origanum Maru L.* or Syrian marjoram, a shrub that reaches about a yard in height, with a relatively large stem and branches with leaves and flowers that are highly absorptive and thus suitable for sprinkling (Lev 14:4-7; Numb 19:18)."[49]

By placing the hyssop on the bludgeoned Jesus, the soldier was dipping that sacred Passover plant into the blood of The Lamb! It is a picture that Christ's blood is to be sprinkled on believers who look to the cross in faith! In fact, Peter opens his first letter reminding his readers that they had been chosen "to be obedient to Jesus Christ and sprinkled with his blood" (1 Pet. 1:2, NIV). Because Christ has offered a perfect sacrifice on our behalf the author of Hebrews calls us to "draw near to God with a sincere heart and with the full assurance that faith brings, having our hearts sprinkled to cleanse us from a guilty conscience" (Heb. 10:22, NIV). He later reminds the church that they have come "to the blood of sprinkling that speaks better things than that of Abel" (Heb. 12:24). Look to the cross! See the hyssop smeared in the blood of the Lamb! Receive its 'better word' of new life!

The hyssop plant was not just used during Passover. It was also used to sprinkle the altar and the people with blood after the ratification of the old covenant at Mount Sinai (Heb. 9:19), and for the ritual for cleansing lepers and the unclean (Lev 14; Numb 19). Because of hyssop's association with *cleansing* and *purification*, David prayed in his deeply contrite prayer after committing adultery with Bathsheba, "Purge me with hyssop, and I shall be clean; wash me, and I shall be whiter than snow" (Ps. 51:7). David had *full assurance* in the cleansing power of the blood! The true hyssop that purges is, of course, the hyssop dipped in the blood of Jesus. A shower that makes one purified, clean, and without any lingering stains! (1 John 1:9; Is. 1:18)

The greatest thirst of Jesus on the cross was not physical, but rather *spiritual*. He thirsted for the souls of men! He does not desire that any perish, but that all come to repentance and faith (2 Pet. 3:9). He thirsted for *your* salvation. Even today Christ still thirsts for souls. He calls for His church to bring others to Him as the Living Fountain who thirsted so that no man need ever thirst again (John 4:14). In fact, living water currently flows from the Resurrected Christ to parch man's thirst for eternal life. We are assured there is "a pure river of water of life, clear as crystal, proceeding from the throne of God and of the Lamb" (Rev. 22:1). The Spirit and bride invite all who thirst to "come!" and "take the water of life freely" (Rev. 22:17).

Lord Jesus, the suffering You endured on the cross is far beyond any suffering I can imagine. As You were internally on fire from the lack of liquid, You only desired to drink the sour wine for the sake of fulfilling Scripture. You knew hyssop would be placed on You as a sign that I can receive the sprinkling of Your blood to cleanse my conscience and be purged from all sin. May I never minimize the cost of my salvation or Your love. May I have the same 'thirst' for Your prophetic word and for redeemed souls as You have always had, and always will have. A 'thirst' to see man fully alive and free!

DAY 32
The Sixth Word—Finished
(Matt 27:50; Mark 15:37; John 19:30)

Immediately after tasting the sour wine on the sponge Jesus shouted His sixth word, "It is finished!" (John 19:30). In Greek it is only one word—tetelestai. This Greek word is not in the *past* tense, but in something called the *perfect* tense. Meaning, though it has occurred in the past its effects and influence persist into the present.[50] *The emphasis is on present significance,* so it could be translated "it remains finished" or "it stands complete." Jesus was letting us know with this shout that the work the Father had sent Him to perform was *fully accomplished* and that nothing could ever reverse or annul its effect.

What is the "it" that is finished? In the immediate context we can say "it" is the fulfillment of all the prophetic texts that have to do with Christ's Passion. There are no loose ends to tie up, there is nothing that is needed to be done that was left undone. More specifically, we can say "it" stands for our redemption. The sins of humanity had been fully paid for by Christ's perfect sacrifice. Hebrews states, "every priest stands ministering daily and offering repeatedly the same sacrifices, which can never take away sins. But this Man, after He had offered one sacrifice for sins forever, sat down at the right hand of God…For by one offering He has perfected forever those who are being sanctified" (Heb. 10:11-12, 14). "It", redemption by sacrifice, *stands complete.*

No priest ever sat while performing their sacred duties. In fact, there was no furniture in the tabernacle or temple for priests to sit upon. They were constantly at work trimming wicks, taking care of the showbread, offering incense on the golden altar, or butchering sacrifices. Every one of them *stood* ministering daily. But something changed with the installation of Christ as High Priest. He no longer *stands* daily offering sacrifices for sin. Rather, He *sits* down. Meaning, there is no longer any sacrifices that need to be offered. For when He climbed on the cross for our salvation, and offered His blood on that altar, the sins of the entire world were atoned for once for all (1 Jn. 2:2; Heb. 10:10).

Jesus on the cross was the Sacrifice to end all sacrifices. No longer would man need to offer a turtledove, or a lamb, or a ram, or a goat, or a bull, for their sins. Instead, they simply offer their bodies as a *living sacrifice* in thanksgiving for Christ's final *deadly sacrifice*. Daniel had prophesied that the coming Messiah would "make an end of sin" and "shall bring an end to sacrifice and offering" (Dan. 9:24, 27). In fact, Daniel was very specific in saying that this would occur in the middle of the final "week" of years. Meaning, it would happen after three and a half years of the Messiah's ministry. According to the timeline of the Gospel of John, this is *exactly* when Jesus made an end of sin at the cross —three and a half years into His ministry!

The moment Christ cried "It is finished!" the *old covenant* became "obsolete" and its forms were ready "to vanish away" (Heb. 8:13). The veil of the temple was *immediately* torn, signifying that the temple's purpose had reached its *completion*. Its dispensation as a *shadow* of the *substance* of Christ had served its purpose. That moment it turned into a relic of the past that would soon be destroyed within *that generation* as Jesus prophesied—a prophecy that came to fulfillment in AD 70. The temple, and all the sacrificial system, has fully served its purpose. To build it again would be a defiant act against Christ, against the new covenant that He has brought, and against His *finished work* on the cross.

This, of course, does not mean that we do not continue to learn from the temple and the old covenant. All Scripture is "given by inspiration of God, and is profitable for doctrine, for reproof, for correction, for instruction in righteousness" (2 Tim. 3:16). We continue to 'receive the witness' of the Law, understand how it speaks of the glories of Christ's redemption and prefigures His Church, see the stories of Israel as an 'examples' for us, and thank the Lord that things like blood sacrifices and foreskins no longer pertain to what it means to be part of the people of God (Rom. 3:21, 31; 1 Cor. 9:9, 10:5; Gal. 5:6 etc.).

The word 'tetelestai' was used in the ancient world in a lot of interesting ways. When a prison sentence would come to a conclusion the jailor would write 'tetelestai' across the *certificate of debt* that was posted outside of their cell. The prisoner would leave having that document in hand as a testimony that their sentence *had been paid in full* and never needed to be paid again.[51] Another occasion the word 'tetelestai' was used was when a craftsman had completed a project. Upon surveying his work, and noticing every detail was just as it should be, they would exclaim, "It is finished!" In fact, it is very possible Jesus would say this after completing carpentry projects (Mk. 6:24).[52]

It is a glorious truth to know our eternal salvation has been fully secured by the work of another, and He is *fully satisfied* with His own work. The debt of our sin has been fully paid and never needs to be paid again (Col. 2:14). Being saved from sin, death, and hell is a gift from God. Paul writes, "by grace you have been saved through faith, and that not of yourselves; it is the gift of God, not of works, lest anyone should boast" (Eph 2:8-9). Grace is simply 'unmerited favor.' Faith is the instrument that receives this 'unmerited favor.' While we are to be people of "good works," our works are solely on the flip side of salvation—a fruit of our faith and salvation (Eph. 2:10). We work out the salvation that God has already graciously placed inside of us (Phil. 2:12). There is *nothing* we need to do to *earn* favor with God.

Though the work of redemption has been *accomplished* for all mankind, it still must be *applied* if its benefits are going to have an effect on our lives. And it is applied *by faith*. In other words, though salvation has been *given*, it still must be *received*. Paul says, "those who receive the abundance of grace and the free gift of righteousness reign in life through the one man Jesus Christ" (Rom. 5:17, ESV). On the road to Damascus, the Risen Lord spoke to Paul saying He was sending him to the Gentiles "to open their eyes, in order to turn them from darkness to light, and from the power of Satan to God, that they may receive forgiveness of sins and an inheritance among those who are sanctified by faith in Me" (Acts 26:18). Receive the forgiveness of sins! Be set apart to life by placing your faith in Jesus Christ! The work for your eternal salvation is *finished* and stands perfectly complete!

Lord Jesus, You are the One who declared "It is finished!" This means I never need to question it. For whatever You say I can fully rely on. Every type and shadow from the temple to the turtledove has found its fulfillment in You. There is not one aspect of Your work as my Great High Priest and Perfect Sacrifice that was left undone. That is why You are 'seated' at the right hand of the Majesty. Isaiah says that the Suffering Servant "shall see the labor of His soul, and be satisfied" (Is. 53:11). Thank you for looking upon Your work and being satisfied with me. Thank you for pouring out Your soul to death, bearing my sin, and making intercession for the transgressors (Is. 53:12). Help me to be satisfied with Your work in the same way that You are. May I fully understand I can never add anything to Your finished work, or secure any greater favor with You. I have rest for my soul knowing that Your finished work stands forever complete and secure (Matt. 11:28-30). I am saved by grace alone, through faith alone, in Christ alone (Rom. 3:28).

DAY 33
The Seventh Word—Commit
(Luke 23:46)

Luke is the only Gospel that records Christ's final word. He writes, "And when Jesus had cried out with a loud voice He said, 'Father into Your hands I commit My spirit.' Having said this, He breathed His last" (Luke 23:46). After shouting "It is finished!", Jesus immediately spoke a final word of *commitment* to the Father before bowing His head and giving up His spirit. There seems to be a great serenity in this final word. No longer is God spoken of as "God." No longer is there an agonizing cry of "forsakenness." No longer is there the physical pain implicit in the word "I thirst." Rather, the redemptive work of the cross stood complete, the darkness had lifted, the sense of alienation had dissipated, and the serene and tender word of "Father" was upon the Son's lips.

This was Jesus' last great act of trust. He had trusted the Father every moment of His life, and He would die no differently. In fact, when Jesus shouted "It is finished!", He had this final act of death that was about to occur seconds later on His mind. The death was included in His finished work. For His death was nothing less than a *substitutional death*. He died so that those who believe in Him never need to die. He earlier declared, "whoever lives and believes in Me shall never die" (John 11:26). Believers in Christ have "passed from death to life" (1 John 3:14). Though the bodies of believers are perishing, and will one day stop functioning, they are simply laid down in "sleep" until the day of resurrection (1 Cor. 15:51; Eph 5:14; 1 Thes. 4:14, 5:10). Though the body "sleeps" as seed, the inner man, sometimes referred to as the soul/spirit, immediately goes to be with the Father and Christ in heaven (2 Cor. 5:8; Phil. 1:23).

Throughout the Passion narrative Jesus has been in complete control. For instance, when He was arrested in the garden the soldiers *fell backwards* while He was *willingly bound*. The same control is present at His death. No one takes His life from Him. Not the soldiers, not the cross, not an unexpected heart attack, nothing. Rather, He lays it down of His own accord (John 10:18). His death was not a struggle, but an act of peaceful commitment into the Father's Hands.

Is there any place more secure in all heaven, earth, or under the earth, than the Father's Hands? Speaking to the Jewish leaders in Jerusalem at the Feast of Dedication, Jesus said, "My sheep hear My voice, and I know them, and they follow Me. And I give them eternal life, and they shall never perish; neither shall anyone snatch them out of My hand. My Father, who has given them to Me, is greater than all; and no one is able to snatch them out of My Father's hand. I and My Father are one" (John 10:27-30). When Jesus committed His human soul/spirit into the hands of the Father He was giving us an example to follow. *We are all called to commit our lives into the hands of God.* When we respond to the voice of our Good Shepherd, and place our faith in Him, our lives are secure in the Almighty Hands of the Father and Son. So secure, in fact, that no created spiritual or material power can pry us from their loving grasp (Rom. 8:38-39).

Every day the follower of Christ can wake up and recommit to being at rest in the Father's Hands. Every day they can wake up and say, "Thank you Father for having received my life. Thank you for securely holding on to me. Thank you that nothing can separate me from Your love. I choose to rest satisfied in Your life today." This sort of attitude should characterize our lives until the moment we lay upon our death bed, or are in the throes of persecution or battle, and we are called to utter these words with an even deeper sense of thanksgiving and trust. In fact, these were the words on the martyr Stephen's lips, "And they stoned Stephen as he was calling on God and saying, 'Lord Jesus, receive my spirit'" (Acts 7:59). Alfred Edersheim says these final words of Jesus have been the final words of many prominent Christians. He writes, "How many thousands have pillowed their heads on them when going to rest! They were the last words of a Polycarp, a Bernard, Huss, Luther, and Melanchton."[53]

Just as the fourth word is a direct quotation from Scripture, so this word is too. Psalm 31:5 says, "Into Your hand I commit my spirit." The context of this psalm is that God is a mighty fortress and rock of refuge. He is one that can be trusted to deliver us from evil and our enemies—the last enemy being death itself (1 Cor. 15:26; Rev. 20:14). The fact that Jesus was quoting Scripture to the Father throughout His greatest trial shows us that we also should have a deep reservoir of Scripture in our heart that we can make use of throughout our trials. We should pray Scripture. We should speak God's word back to Him. We should become familiar with the language of Zion. For to pray Scripture is to pray the perfect will of God.

Consider also how often the word "Father" was on the lips of Christ. His first recorded statement in Scripture is simply, "Did you not know that I must be about My Father's business?" (Luke 2:49) Jesus refers to God as "Father" over one hundred times in the Gospel of John alone. In His most famous sermon in Matthew, the Sermon on the Mount, He speaks of God as "Father" seventeen times. Jesus, as the Eternal Son of God incarnate, has a unique relationship with God as Father. He is the "only begotten Son of God", meaning, He is the Son of God according to His eternal essence/nature—the *eternally begotten One*. God has never not been Father because He has always had the eternal Son with Him. This is the mystery of the Trinity. The mystery of the Godhead. At the same time, God has made us His children by *adoption* and *grace*. John beautifully states, "Behold what manner of love the Father has bestowed on us, that we should be called children of God!" (1 John 3:1) Paul writes, "God sent forth His Son…that we might receive the adoption as sons. And because you are sons, God has sent forth the Spirit of His Son into your hearts, crying out, 'Abba, Father!'" (Gal. 4:4-6). Jesus is the eternal Son by *nature/essence*, we are sons by *grace*. This means we too should address God as our "Father." And when we understand who God is as our Father, there can be a greater sense of *commitment*. All of our ambitions, hopes, plans, desires, dreams, concerns, and fears can be fully entrusted into His hands. For He is a *Good Father* who *unreluctantly* gives "good things" to those who ask Him (Matt. 7:11).

The word 'commit' in Greek is paratithémi. Para means "right close beside." Tithemi means "to place, put." It means "to set right next to." Jesus was entrusting His life to the Father in a very up close and personal way. When Jesus 'committed' His spirit into the Father's Hands, it was done with absolute assurance and confidence. He died knowing His life was in very good hands.

Lord Jesus, thank you for laying down Your life willingly that I might live. As I think upon Your final word from the cross, I have a greater appreciation that nobody took Your life from You. Father, help me to live with a deeper dependence on You. I want my life to be a reflection of the sort of loving trust that Jesus exhibited in death. Holy Spirit, may my final words echo the final words of Jesus the day I'm received into unceasing glory and eternal rest.

DAY 34
The 7 Words As New Creation
(Genesis 1:1-2:4; John 1:1-17)

"In the beginning God created the heavens and the earth" (Gen. 1:1). Over the course of seven days God *spoke* in order to form and fill this creation. These seven days of creation are the foundation of much of the architecture of Scripture as well as the seven day weeks most cultures observe.[54] God in His infinite wisdom chose to create over the span of seven days, through the power of His Word, rather than create everything in an instant. One remarkable feature of the crucifixion is that the One who is hanging from the cross is the eternal Word who originally spoke everything into existence. The Word who became flesh in order to redeem us (John 1:1-14). The One hanging on the tree is the Lord of Glory, the Maker of all things seen and unseen. As He hung there in order to free mankind and all creation from sin and death, He spoke seven words that pair remarkable well with the seven days of creation. *What the Word was doing from the cross was nothing less than speaking 'new creation' into existence!*

On the First Day the Word of God said, "Let there be light" (Gen. 1:3). He saw that the light was "good" and separated it from the "darkness." Jesus' first word from the cross was, "Father, forgive them, for they do not know what they do" (Luke 23:34). Light and forgiveness are connected in Scripture. For instance, the Resurrected Lord told Saul to preach to the Gentiles in order "to turn them from darkness to light, and from the power of Satan to God, that they may receive forgiveness of sins" (Acts 26:18). To be in sin, *without forgiveness*, is to be in the kingdom of *darkness*. It is to be chaotic and without form. The Word of God spoke His merciful word of forgiveness to translate us from the kingdom of darkness into the kingdom of light of His dear Son (Col. 1:12-13). New creation life is founded on the free forgiveness that Jesus offers at the cross. Nothing more and nothing less. His shed blood is the shining bright light declaring a new day for humanity. All that one must do is "receive" it and His light of new creation life will shine in their heart (2 Cor. 4:6).

On the Second Day the Word of God created a firmament as a barrier between heaven and earth, and placed some of the created waters both above and below this firmament (Gen. 1:6-8). This is why there is a crystal sea before the throne of God in heaven. It is the heavenly water placed there on the Second Day (Rev. 4:6). The Word's second word from the cross was a promise to the crucified murderer who reached out to Him in faith. The Word said, "Assuredly, I say to you, today you will be with Me in Paradise" (Luke 23:43). This murderer was taken all the way up through the firmament, up to Paradise. Up to the throne of God and crystal sea. Why? Because the Word on the cross *spoke*, and it was done!

On the Third Day the Word of God separated the land from the seas (Gen. 1:9-10). The theme of this day is natural separations. The "land" throughout Scripture is used to speak of Israel. The "sea" throughout Scripture speaks of the Gentiles. The Word's third word from the cross was about breaking down barriers of natural separation. He told His mother, "Woman, behold your son!", and His beloved disciple, "Behold your mother!" (John 19:26-27). Jesus was showing us that in the new creation the family of God takes precedence over natural bonds and connections. There is something special, something eternal, about the family of God that isn't there with natural relations. At the cross God breaks down every barrier of separation that has separated people groups. There is neither Jew nor Greek, slave nor free, male nor female, for we are one in Christ (Gal. 3:28).

On the Fourth Day the Word of God spoke the sun, moon, and stars into existence for signs, seasons, days, and years. The greater light was to "rule" the day and the lesser light was to "rule" the night (Gen. 1:14-19). The Word's fourth word from the cross was the first word spoken after the sun was darkened. He cried, "My God, My God, why have You forsaken Me?" (Matt 27:46). As the ruler of the day went dark in a sign of judgment, the Son of God, the Eternal Ruler of all things, took the judgment of the world upon Himself. The Word hung there as our Substitute, our Representative, and our Sin-Bearer. The Judge was judged. The Eternal Light was clothed in darkness in order to suffer the outer darkness we deserved and bring us into new creation light.

On the Fifth Day the Word of God created all the sea creatures and birds of the air (Gen. 1:20-23). There is a special emphasis on "the great sea creatures" that would abound in "the waters." The Word's fifth word from the cross was "I thirst" (John 19:28). Jesus was yearning for water just like a fish needs water in order to survive. His greatest thirst was to catch many fish through the dragnet of the cross in order to bring them to the shores of new creation (John 12:32; Matt 13:47-15; Mark 1:16-17).

On the Sixth Day the Word of God made all the land animals, and afterwards made mankind in His own image and likeness (Gen. 1:24-31). At the end of the Sixth Day the narrator tells us "the heavens and the earth, and all the host of them, were finished' (Gen. 2:1). The Word's sixth word from the cross was "It is finished!" (John 19:30). In view of His full, sufficient, and redemptive sacrifice to bring us into new creation life, the Word of God shouted the same thing He did at the end of His initial creation. As He viewed His work upon the cross He likely said something like, "This is very good—a fully sufficient work!", in the same way that the Word called creation "very good" at the end of the Sixth Day (Gen. 1:31).

On the Seventh Day the Word of God "ended His work which He had done, and He rested on the seventh day from all His work which He had done" (Gen. 2:2). The Word's seventh word from the cross was "Father, into Your hands I commit My spirit" (Luke 23:46). He rested in the hands of the Father until He was raised from the grave on Sunday morning. The Word made flesh died on the *sixth* day (Good Friday), was laid to sleep in a garden tomb to rest on the *seventh* day (Holy Saturday), and rose again on the *eighth* day (Resurrection Sunday)—*the day of new creation.*

The first three days were about *forming.* The last three days about *filling.* Light and space on Day One corresponds with the Light Bearers on Day Four. The waters and the atmosphere on Day 2 correspond with the fish and birds on Day 5. The land on Day 3 corresponds with the land animals and man on Day 6. The first word from the cross corresponds with the fourth word in that we are forgiven because He was forsaken and died on our behalf. The second word from the cross corresponds with the fifth word in that just as the murderer is assured entrance into Paradise, so Christ's thirsts for many more souls to fully fill Paradise. The third word from the cross corresponds to the sixth word in that the finished work of the cross breaks down every barrier of separation and makes us into one new humanity!

Lord Jesus, thank you for being the Word made flesh in order to speak new creation life into existence and form me into a new creature (2 Cor. 5:17).

DAY 35
Eden's Gate Is Opened Wide
(Matt 27:51-53; Mark 15:38; Luke 23:44-46)

Immediately after Christ yielded His spirit to the Father, and bowed His head in death, we are told that all creation (heaven above, earth below, and even the underworld) responded to the death of their Creator. Matthew writes, "the veil of the temple was torn in two from top to bottom; and the earth quaked, and the rocks were split, and the graves were opened; and many bodies of the saints who had fallen asleep were raised; and coming out of the graves after His resurrection, they went into the holy city and appeared to many" (Matt. 27:51-53). What is of greatest significance here, and is something that Matthew, Mark, and Luke all mention, is that *the veil was torn.*

There is some debate as to whether this was the outer or inner veil of the temple. In my mind maybe all of the Gospel writers kept that point nebulous because they wanted us to see the significance of the tearing of both veils, as well as the veil of Christ's flesh (Heb. 10:20). Josephus lets us know that the outer veil of the temple—which was visible to everyone looking at the temple—was mostly blue and purple, 60-90 feet high, and had starry constellations woven into it. The people understood that when the priests entered God's House on their behalf they were entering into *the heavenly realm.* Further into the temple another zone, the Holy of Holies, was partitioned off by a second veil. This veil was about the same size as the outer veil, and had large cherubim guardians woven into it (Ex. 26:31). Only one person was permitted access past this veil once a year—the high priest on the Day of Atonement. He would enter with the blood of a bull and goat, sprinkle the blood on the mercy seat atop the ark of the covenant, and make atonement for Israel's sins.

Within the temple itself (i.e. between the two veils) the priests walked barefoot among Edenic symbolism. We are told that Solomon "carved all the walls of the temple all around, both the inner and outer sanctuaries, with carved figures of cherubim, palm trees, and open flowers. And the floor of the temple he overlaid with gold" (1 Kings 6:29-30). The doors were made of olive wood and also had the Edenic symbolism carved into them. God's home among the Israelites was like it was in the beginning —gardenesque. Yet, though God condescended and came closer to Israel than any of the other nations, *full access* to His presence *was not permitted*. Concerning the inner veil, Edersheim writes it was "of the thickness of the palm of the hand, and wrought in 72 squares, which were joined together; and these Veils were so heavy, that, in the exaggerated language of the time, it needed 300 priests to manipulate each. If the Veil was at all such as is described in the Talmud, it could not have been rent in twain by a mere earthquake."[55] The tearing necessitated *an act of God*.

The 72 squares makes one think of the nations of the world which is symbolically represented by both 70 and 72 in Scripture. The veil prevented access *to the whole world*. Only one thing could swing open that gate, relieve the guardian cherubim from duty, and grant access to every nation—the blood of Jesus. Matthew and Mark both record the veil was torn "from top to bottom" when Jesus died, indicating that the hand of God was the one tearing that thick veil from its 60+ foot height. Luke also indicates that it was torn "in the middle"—meaning that it was torn directly over the mercy seat of the ark. As Jesus died, and His remaining life force—*His blood*—was poured out, the blood was presented on the heavenly mercy seat, and the door to God's presence was swung wide! Though the Jews would *patch that veil,* and *rehang it in the temple* for the next 37 years, ultimately it was a relic of the old covenant that had passed away. It's destruction at the death of Christ was a birth-pang of the coming destruction of the temple as a whole. The temple was now a hollow shell of God's presence. *God moved out from His Home* like He did during the time of Ezekiel and the Babylonian captivity (Ezek. 10).

Another interesting fact is that there are only two times Mark uses the word "tear" in his Gospel—at the very beginning of Jesus' ministry and at the very end. While Matthew and Luke say the heavens were "opened" during the baptism of Jesus in the Jordan, Mark uses the stronger verb "torn" (Mark 1:10, ESV). What happened with the descent of the Spirit, and Jesus' entrance into public ministry, was nothing less than a *cosmic shaking event.* The same is true of His death—the climax of His ministry. Remember, the outer veil had a 'panorama of the heavens' woven into it. Just as the heaven was "torn open" at the Jordan, and the Spirit was poured out on Jesus, anointing Him for ministry, so at the cross the heavens were "torn open" to the world, and the Spirit has been poured out on all flesh!

After God's Room was torn open at the death of Christ, and the Spirit of God rushed out from that old covenant temple, those who received that Spirit into their hearts became "living stones" of God's new temple (1 Pet. 2:5). Fully fulfilling God's promise to "dwell in them" and "walk among them" (Lev. 26:12; 2 Cor. 6:16). Worship is no longer restricted to a physical building in Jerusalem. Jesus said, "The hour is coming when you will neither on this mountain, nor in Jerusalem, worship the Father…But the hour is coming, and now is, when the true worshipers will worship the Father in spirit and truth; for the Father is seeking such to worship Him" (John 4:21-23). That time is *now.*

In Luke, the earthquake and rending of the veil occur in the verse immediately after Jesus promises paradise to the murderer who had reached out to Him in faith. Luke wants us to see these two events as connected. It is also interesting that Matthew notes that "the graves were opened" and some saints had an *open door* to exit their tombs after Jesus exited His. This was a sign that Jesus' resurrection was simply the firstfruit of all resurrection life (1 Cor. 15:20). The fact that Matthew mentions this phenomena at the death of Jesus, rather than later in His resurrection narrative, shows us that it is the death of Jesus that slays death. Jesus took on flesh "that through death He might destroy him who had the power of death, that is, the devil" (Heb. 2:15).

As Jesus burst the bonds of death on resurrection morning, the saints burst the bonds of death with Him! They walked out of their open tombs! Imagine Zechariah, Elizabeth, Anna, and others strolling through the streets of Jerusalem shocking multiple people as they declare that Jesus had set them free. Many say that these saints ascended with Jesus into heaven as He left us in a "cloud"—not just a physical cloud but "a great cloud of witnesses" (Acts 1:9; Heb. 12:1). It wasn't just Jesus and the crucified murderer who strolled through the opened gates of Paradise, but all the other souls set free from Abraham's Bosom!

Lord Jesus, if stony rocks were split in view of Your redemptive work, certainly stony hearts can be softened in view it. All three zones of creation were shaken: heaven (symbolized by the tearing of the veil and the darkened sun), earth (by the rocks splitting), and the underworld (by the rolling back of the tomb stones). Your shed blood and finished work on the cross forever reshaped the contours of reality—of things in heaven, of things on earth, and of things under the earth. At Your Name every knee will bow "of those in heaven, and of those on earth, and of those under the earth" and confess You are Lord (Phil. 2:8-11). May I shake with holy fear and trembling at Your great salvation and ever more bow the knee of my heart and life!

DAY 36
Truly, This is the Son of God
(Matt 27:54-56; Mark 15:39-41; Luke 23:47-49)

In light of Jesus' final words, His death, the shaking of the earth, and the rending of the rocks and temple veil, there were many reactions from the crowd gathered around the cross. The primary reaction came from the centurion who was overseeing the entire crucifixion process. Matthew, Mark, and Luke all record the centurion making *a statement of faith*. What is interesting about Matthew's account is that it is not simply the centurion who makes the public profession, but also "those with him guarding Jesus" (presumably the twelve other soldiers responsible for crucifying the three men, and possibly other guards present for security). Matthew writes, "So when the centurion and those with him, who were guarding Jesus, saw the earthquake and the things that had happened, they feared greatly, saying, 'Truly this was the Son of God!'" (Matt 27:54)

This chorus of faith was the culminating factor of many things. These men had watched Jesus not revile back while they and others were reviling Him. They saw His care for His mother. They observed how He appeared to be in complete control of His life as He bowed His head and willingly gave up His spirit. They saw how the sun was darkened almost the entire time He was crucified. They witnessed creation mourn and *shake in travail* as He died. Even more important than what they saw was what they heard. The only thing they heard on His heart and lips was *grace*. They heard His word of *forgiveness* after they nailed Him to the cross. They heard His *promise of paradise* to the murderer crucified next to Him. They heard the *triumphant cry*, "It is finished." Bernard of Clairvaux said about the centurion, "He did not believe because of what he saw, but because of what he heard: *faith then comes by hearing, and hearing by the word of Christ.*"[56]

While the religious officials remained silent in view of the cosmic portents, the Gentile soldiers knew God was at work. They knew the Man crucified there must have been the King of the Jews. He must have been the Son of God, as they heard the Jewish leaders tell Pilate (John 19:7). Tradition says the centurion became a very devout Christian after the resurrection, and some believe the Gospel writers likely received part of their eyewitness testimony straight from him. It is interesting to note that Luke describes a second statement from the centurion besides the one recorded by Matthew and Mark. Luke writes, "So when the centurion saw what had happened, he glorified God, saying, 'Certainly this was a righteous Man!'" (Luke 23:47)

Luke lets us know that the centurion "glorified God." Other translations say he "began praising God." This was the first fruit of the promise of Psalm 22 that as a result of Christ's suffering on the cross "all the families of the nations shall worship before You" (Ps. 22:27). While praising God the centurion declared, "Certainly this was a righteous Man!" It is interesting to note who declares Jesus as "just", "innocent", and "righteous" over the course of His Passion. While Jesus is being taken to Pilate, remember that Judas confesses to some of the chief priests that he had betrayed "innocent blood" as he threw the thirty pieces of silver back at their feet (Matt. 27:4). Pilate says three times that Jesus was "without fault." Pilate's wife said she suffered in a dream because of this "just Man" (Matt. 27:19) In the narrative of Luke alone there are *seven* confessions of the innocence of Jesus (Luke 23:4, 14, 15 [twice], 22, 41). Luke wants us to know

Jesus suffered as the *completely* and *perfectly* innocent and faultless One. Part of the Gospel proclamation throughout Acts is that Jesus is the 'Righteous/Innocent One' and it stems ultimately from the Passion Narrative (Acts 3:14; 7:52; 22:14). He was the righteous for the unrighteous (i.e. the entire world) so that the world might be brought to God (1 Pet. 3:18, ESV).

The two people during the Passion who *profess faith* in Christ are the murderer next to Him and the Roman centurion overseeing His death. A morally repulsive figure who actually deserved death (according to his own evaluation), and a man who was literally in charge of overseeing the torturous death of Jesus. Both of these men received the grace that poured forth from the cross. Eugenia Constantinou writes, "With their physical eyes, both the thief and the centurion beheld a bloody and battered man dying as a condemned criminal. But with the eyes of faith, they recognized his divinity."[57] And in faith they reached out to the One who *died for the chief of sinners* (1 Tim. 1:15). The Son of God died for the murderer, for the centurion, *and even for a wretch like you*. May all have the courage to publicly profess faith like the murderer and the centurion, for it is upon *profession of faith* in Jesus that we are saved (Matt. 10:32; Rom. 10:10; Acts 4:12).

What are some other responses from the crowd surrounding the cross at the death of Jesus? Luke has an interesting detail that none of the other Gospels record. Right after reporting what the centurion said, he writes, "And the whole crowd who came together to that sight, seeing what had been done, beat their breasts and returned" (Luke 23:48). In light of the cosmic signs the onlookers realized something *dreadfully significant* happened. After fear, or remorse, or possibly even some contrition for what happened to Jesus, they began to beat their breasts and go home. It appears many onlookers had an awakening moment that the crucifixion of Jesus was extraordinarily unjust. They realized that the signs that were given were *heavenly signs*. This caused fear, and seemingly *regret*. I'm sure that when the apostles began to preach the Gospel in the streets of Jerusalem seven weeks later, some of these same people who were regretful at the death of Jesus, became thankful. They began to believe that His death was *redemptive*. They were "cut to heart" again, and this time instead of beating their breasts they received Christ's forgiveness in that state of having their heart reopened (Acts 2:37).

After narrating the reactions of the soldiers and crowds, three of the Gospels find it important to include that some of Jesus' close acquaintances were watching from a distance. And there is a special emphasis placed on the female disciples. Luke writes, "But all His acquaintances, and the women who followed Him from Galilee, stood at a distance, watching these things" (Luke 23:49). These women include Mary Magdalene, Salome, Mary the mother of James and Joseph, and others. Though in the background throughout most of the Gospel Narrative, these women serve as the key witnesses to Christ's death, burial, and resurrection. While the crowd "returns" to the city, these women stay put, see the entire burial process through, and come back Sunday morning with more burial spices. The women serve as a greater example of discipleship in the Passion Narrative than the men—fearlessly following Jesus no matter the danger or cost.

Lord Jesus, You came to Your own and Your own did not receive You, but as many as did receive You, You gave them the right to become children of God. A right for all who would believe in Your Name (John 1:11-12). Though Your own—the chief priests—mocked Your status as the 'Son of God', the Gentile centurion and soldiers believed and became Your children. May they serve as an example for me. A sinner who also contributed to Your death. May I courageously confess You as 'the Son of God' for all to hear and see!

DAY 37
The Lamb's Blood and Water
(John 19:31-37)

John tells us "it was the Preparation Day" for the Sabbath. Meaning, it was *Friday*. Shortly after Jesus died, as the sun inched toward the horizon, the Jewish leaders began to get nervous that three men were still hanging on crosses. These leaders did not want their land to be "defiled", so they asked Pilate to speed up the death of the crucified men before sundown (Deut. 21:23). Pilate consented, and the soldiers on duty broke the legs of the two criminals on either side of Jesus. This was a common practice *known as crurifragium*. Soldiers would take an iron mallet, or similar sort of club, and smash the legs of the crucified victim causing massive internal bleeding—three liters of blood from the femurs alone. The extreme loss of blood, combined with the prior loss of blood due to scourging and crucifixion, would quickly lead to hypovolemic shock as oxygen would no longer be able to circulate throughout the body to keep the victim alive. The Romans wanted to make the death quick, but they also still wanted it to be torturous, so rather than simply sticking a spear through the victim's heart they invented *crurifragium.*

After the two criminals legs were smashed and they were gasping for their last breaths in deep anguish, when the soldiers came to Jesus they saw "He was already dead", so "they did not break His legs" (John 19:33). John goes on to say, "these things were done that the Scripture should be fulfilled, 'Not one of His bones shall be broken'" (John 19:36). This prophecy likely refers to two different prophecies. The first being that of the righteous sufferer in Psalm 34 who "guards all his bones; not one of them is broken" (Ps. 34:20). The second being a reference to the Passover lamb. The Israelites were commanded, "nor shall you break one of its bones" (Ex. 12:46; Num. 9:12). For 1,500 years the Israelites had been careful to keep that command every Passover. Now, as the ultimate Passover Lamb had just been slain, He too would have none of His bones broken.

Not too much earlier the Gospel writers recorded that Jesus died at the ninth hour—3PM. *This was the exact time the Passover lambs in the temple precinct began to be sacrificed.* The Jewish men each brought a lamb there for their household, slaughtered it, and the blood of that lamb was gathered into silver and golden bowls by the priests who would pass the blood-filled bowls down a priestly line where the final priest splattered the blood at the base of the altar. Though there was a draining system to the Brook Kidron for the excess blood, the amount of blood from the thousands of lambs was so immense that the temple floors received thorough washing. After the sacrifice the lambs were hung up along the Great Court where they were flayed, their entrails were emptied, and their fat burned as an offering. Finally, the owner would take the remainder of the lamb to roast for their festive celebration.[58]

Each family at Passover would make a special dome-shaped oven where the lamb was placed upright on a spit and cooked. The early second century Christian apologist, Justin Martyr, describes the Jewish practice of his time like this, "For the lamb, which is roasted, is roasted and dressed up in the form of a cross. For one spit is transfixed right through, from the lower part up to the head, and one across the back, to which are attached the legs of the lamb."[59] These spits were always made of wood because a metal spit would cause the lamb to be cooked from the inside rather than solely roasted from the outside. The lamb literally hung on a mini-wooden cross as it endured the fires of suffering from the outside-in! A lamb that had shed its blood so death would pass over faithful participants, who did not have one of its bones broken, and who had been inspected for four days by the priests to make certain it was pure, spotless, and without defect!

Though the soldiers did not break the legs of Jesus, John observed as one of the soldiers "pierced His side with a spear" that "immediately blood and water came out" (John 19:34). This also fulfilled prophecy—"they shall look on Him whom they pierced" (John 19:37; Zech 12:10). This act affirmed beyond a shadow of a doubt that Jesus *truly died* on the cross. The pouring forth of blood and water powerfully pictured His life poured out for the world. Isaiah declared, "He poured out His soul unto death" (Is. 53:12). God made clear that "the life of the flesh is in the blood" (Lev. 17:11). Also, water is a symbol of the Holy Spirit throughout Scripture (John 7:37-39). When blood and water poured out, the entire life force of the Son of God flowed out as a gift to humanity. The blood *for our forgiveness*, and the water *for our immersion in the Spirit of life* (Matt. 26:28; John 4:14).

From a natural perspective it appears that what happened was the fluids in the pleural sac that surrounds the heart began to separate once Christ's body stopped circulating the blood. The heavier red blood cells settled at the bottom of this pool of liquid while the lighter plasma and water substance floated on the surface. Once the lance pierced Christ's side, where His heart was, the pleural sac was rent open and the red blood that had settled at the bottom poured forth first, after which the watery substance followed. This was a testimony that Christ truly did die and did not simply 'swoon' or 'faint' on the cross.

How does the *piercing of Christ's side* tie into Scripture's history? In the beginning Adam was put in a "deep sleep" in a garden, his "side" was opened, and a bride was formed from his side whom he called "woman" upon rising (Gen. 2:21-23). The Last Adam was put into a *deep sleep* on the cross, His side was *opened*, He was placed *in a garden*, and He called His new creation *bride* "woman" upon rising (John 20:15). Also, *after being redeemed by the Passover lambs*, the Israelites were without water in the wilderness. God told Moses, "I am going to stand there in front of you on the rock at Horeb; when you hit the rock, water will come out of it and the people will drink" (Ex. 17:6, CSB). Paul says "that Rock was Christ" (1 Cor. 10:4). *As the Divine Presence was struck with the rod of judgment, gracious water poured forth to revive the dying people.*

God's people were not to simply receive that water of life, but bring it to the nations. It began with the patriarchs digging *wells* (Gen. 26:18), moved to the bronze *laver* during the time of Moses (Ex. 30:18), then the larger bronze *sea* during the time of Solomon (1 Kgs 7:23). Finally, the sea was tipped over in Ezekiel and *the water flowed out as a river to the nations* (Ezek. 47:9). The "bronze" water-containers were a symbol that judgment had to come upon the water-container before the water was released. Once that judgment was received, merciful waters began to flow. The Bible ends with an invitation to receive from the crystal water of life that proceeds from the Lamb: "And the Spirit and the bride say, 'Come!' And let him who hears say, 'Come!' And let him who thirsts come. Whoever desires, let him take the water of life freely" (Rev. 22:1, 17). A free fountain of life for all!

Lord Jesus, You are the Lamb of God. Everything about Your Passion testifies to this truth. As You hung on the cross, not only were none of Your bones broken, but Your side was opened so that Your new creation bride, Your church, could be formed. How marvelous it is to know that I am one with You (Eph. 5:32). Since Your blood and water were poured out, I've received Your life and am one Spirit with You (1 Cor. 6:17). I'm cleansed, washed, refreshed, and made fully new by the fountain from Immanuel's veins!

DAY 38
The Sacred Heart of Christ
(John 19:34-37; John 20:27; Hebrews 10:19-22)

After describing how blood and water poured from Christ, John quoted Zechariah. He expected his readers to know the entire passage he was pulling from. The full context of the prophecy is, "And I will pour on the house of David and on the inhabitants of Jerusalem the Spirit of grace and supplication; then they will look on Me whom they pierced. Yes, they will mourn for Him as one mourns for his only son, and grieve for Him as one grieves for a firstborn" (Zech. 12:10). Notice how God is the speaker. God is pierced! The Divine Shepherd is struck (Zech. 13:7). The NKJV makes that very clear by capitalizing the pronouns. Even more striking is how the *mourning* for this *Pierced God* is compared to mourning for an "only son" and "a firstborn"—exactly who Jesus is as the eternal Son of God! This mourning is connected to God's pouring out "the Spirit of grace and supplication" on the *inhabitants of Jerusalem*. Something that is *symbolically portrayed* as water and blood pour forth from the pierced side and comes to full fruition at Pentecost when the enthroned Son pours the Spirit into the Upper Room in Jerusalem (Acts 2:1-21).

The last six chapters of Zechariah are a miniature Passion. Each chapter is either quoted or alluded to in one of the Gospel Passion narratives. The theme of the Spirit being *poured out* in chapter 12 continues into chapters 13 and 14. "In that day a fountain shall be opened for the house of David and for the inhabitants of Jerusalem, for sin and for uncleanness" (Zech. 13:1). Those who come to the streams of Living Water will rejoice that Yahweh is King over all the earth (Zech. 14:8-9).

One very rich tradition in the church based off this passage in Zechariah (as well as Hebrews 10:19-23), is to read the rending of Christ's Sacred Heart as an invitation to 'come' and 'dwell' there. The "torn veil" *is* His flesh (Heb. 10:20). His Heart *is* the very Holy of Holies. We draw near to God through Christ's Heart in order to have *sweet and intimate fellowship.* It is fitting that "the disciple whom Jesus loved", the one who reclined on Jesus' heart during the Last Supper, is the one who recorded the opening of that Heart on the cross. So, how has the church at large spoken of this 'invitation' into the Sacred Heart of Christ?

The *early church father*, Augustine, spoke of "the gate of life" being "thrown open" when Christ was pierced with the spear. He said that just as Noah was commanded to make a "door" in the side of the ark so that those who entered would not perish, so God made a "door" in the side of Christ so those in Christ would not perish, but enter into new creation life.[60] The *medieval church* developed these thoughts. Bernard of Clairvaux wrote, "Where can the weak find a safe and secure resting place, save in the wounds of the Savior?"[61] Thomas à Kempis added, "O great and precious wound of my Lord! To be tenderly loved above all wounds, deeply pierced and widely opened, that all the faithful may enter; marvelous in its flowing, abundantly blessed; last formed, but chief in note…Enter, O my soul, enter into the right side of thy crucified Lord. Enter, by this renowned wound, into the most loving heart of Jesus…For, where wilt thou be able to rest more securely, dwell more safely, and sleep more sweetly, than in the wounds of Jesus Christ, who was crucified for thee? …Where, when lukewarm, wilt thou be so effectually restored to the glow of love; where so quickly rescued from all turmoil?"[62] John Tauler sang, "Nothing hath He hidden in His Heart, which He hath not wholly given to us…Behold! He inviteth us into His sweet wounds, and into His loving and open side, even as into a rich wine-cellar flowing with all delights."[63] Ludolph of Saxony declared, "For our sake the heart of Christ was pierced with a wound of love so that by reciprocal love we could enter his heart through the door in his side and unite all our love with his divine love; there, glowing like iron in the fire, it may be rendered into one love."[64]

This line of thought continued in the *Protestant churches* after the *Reformation*. The English Reformer, Bible Translator, and Puritan, Myles Coverdale, wrote, "his gate is opened wide to all faithful believers: he that hides himself in this hole, is sure from all hurt and harm. Of this holy and godly fountain, who so drinks once, or takes a draught of the holy love, doth forthwith forget all his adversities and griefs, and shall be whole from all wicked heat of temporal lusts and bodily provocations: fervently shall he be kindled in love and desire of eternal things, and shall be replenished with the unspeakable goodness of the Holy Ghost." He continued, "Here are opened the conduits and well pipes of life, the way of our health, wherein we find rest unto our souls, and shadow for heat and travail: this fountain of grace is never dried up."[65] The Puritan, Joseph Hall, added, "O precious and sovereign wound, by which our souls are healed! Into this cleft of the rock let my dove fly and enter, and there safely hide herself from the talons of all the birds of prey."[66] Another Puritan, Isaac Ambrose, said of Jesus' wound, "O gates of heaven! O windows of paradise! O palace of refuge! O tower of strength! O sanctuary of the just! O flourishing bed of the spouse of Solomon! Methinks I see water and blood running out of his side, more freshly than these golden streams which ran out of the garden of Eden, and watered the whole world."[67]

The *Roman Catholics* have also written with great delight about the Sacred Heart of Jesus in this way. Fr. Ignatius said the pierced side of Christ was a door "through which we might enter, and behold the ever-living, ever-burning love of the Heart of Jesus…His Heart is a furnace of love, which not all the waters of the sea can ever extinguish…enter it frequently in spirit, and there your incredible hardness of heart will be softened, and your icy coldness warmed…Permit me, O my Jesus, to kiss Your wounded side, and to enter into Your Divine Heart, where you may destroy my malice in the flames of its charity, transform me totally into Yourself, and fill my soul with Your Divine love."[68] Groenings summed up many who went before him, saying, "Only what enters through this portal, shall be saved…The wound of the side is the golden gate of the true temple of the Lord wherein all the sick, all the beggars and all the needy obtain health and grace and mercy. It is the entrance to the true paradise, in which alone delight and peace are to be found… The Heart of Jesus is, indeed, the strength of the just, the consolation of the afflicted, the refuge of sinners. For the tempted soul, it is the cavern in the rock in which the timid dove hides itself from the hawk. To the soul which feels itself to be a parched soil, it is the fountain of living waters. To the sad and depressed soul, it is the spiritual wine-cellar in which the Divine Bridegroom gladdens His promised bride with heavenly delights. …With confidence, then, let us enter into the Sacred Heart of Jesus in all our needs. In it there is room for all men."[69]

Lord Jesus, Your Heart was the veil that was torn so that we can boldly come into God's Holy Presence. As I approach the Father in prayer, I come through Your burning Heart of love that poured forth blood and water to make me new. Just as You and the Father have come to reside in my heart by the Spirit (John 14:23), so I have also been brought into Your Heart by that same Spirit! Your Body never saw corruption. Thus, Your Sacred Heart is ever-flowing with love and grace! I receive from the abundance of that Grace! Thank you for sweet and intimate fellowship as I rest in Your love!

DAY 39
A Burial For A King
(Matt 27:57-61; Mark 15:42-47; Luke 23:50-56; John 19:38-42)

As the lifeless body of Jesus hung on the cross, head bowed to the ground and fully drained of blood, the women wept at a distance wondering what would happen next. Suddenly, there emerged a powerful, rich, and eminent man. One who had a *prominent seat* on the Sanhedrin. This man walked up to Christ's cross and began the process of taking Him down (as both Mark and Luke record). We can imagine this man, possibly with the help of some soldiers or even a servant, pulling the nails from the dead hands and feet of Christ. The One who holds all things in the palm of His hands was now held in the palms of this Jewish leader. Who was this man stained in the blood of Christ?

He was Joseph of Arimathea. Each Gospel takes significant space to describe his act of gaining possession of Jesus' body. From them we learn he was rich, a prominent member on the Sanhedrin, that he had not consented to the council's decision to put Jesus to death and hand Him over to Pilate, that he had been eagerly waiting for the kingdom of God, that he was a good and just man, and that he was a secret disciple of Jesus. Having the sort of clout he did as a wealthy and prominent member on the Sanhedrin, we are told that he approached Pilate and asked him for Jesus' body. Mark adds that he "took courage" in this act. To ask for the body of a man who had just been crucified for sedition was *risky*. On top of that, the fellow members of the Sanhedrin would have disowned Joseph for making such an act.

An honorable burial would have been *obscene* in their eyes! They had all declared Him a blasphemer and beat Him up that morning. Josephus says that blasphemers should be "buried ignominiously and in obscurity."[70] An early Christian work called *The Martyrdom of Polycarp* describes how the Jews were very active in opposing an honorable burial for Polycarp. So, by asking for the body of Jesus, and giving Him a burial akin to royalty, Joseph had everything to lose—his reputation, honor, wealth tied into various relationships, his seat on the Sanhedrin, and many other social connections. The chief priests surely wanted Jesus' body thrown in the cemetery designated for criminals with all the other cursed men who were hanged. But Joseph was able to make a deal with Pilate before they could get their way! This was to fulfill the prophecy of the Suffering Servant that He would be buried "with the rich at His death" (Is. 53:9).

The town of Arimathea is the town 'Ramathaim' in the Old Testament. The hometown of the prophet Samuel (1 Sam. 1:1). This is the prophet that raised David up from watching sheep and anointed him as king. It is interesting to note that many kings of Israel were buried in garden tombs. In fact, the book of Nehemiah tells us David himself was buried in a garden. The Septuagint states, "as far as the garden of David's sepulchre" (Neh. 3:16). This tomb was well known during the time of Jesus (Acts 2:29). We are also know the kings Amon and Manasseh were buried in the "garden of Uzza" (2 Kings 21:18, 26). When Jesus was buried by Joseph in an expensive "garden tomb", He was Israel's everlasting King, the promised Son of David, buried by a man who echoed David's own story (2 Sam. 7:16).

A few other details also point to Jesus' burial being that of a king. Matthew tells us Joseph "rolled a large stone against the door of the tomb" (Matt. 27:60). Sauter writes, "[of the] more than 900 Second Temple-period burial caves around Jerusalem examined by archaeologist Amos Kloner, only four have been discovered with disk-shaped blocking stones. These four elegant Jerusalem tombs belonged to the wealthiest—even royal—families, such as the tomb of Queen Helena of Adiabene."[71] Another detail that portrays a *kingly burial* is the amount of spices that were brought to bury Jesus. Concerning the great reformer king, Asa, we are told, "They buried him in his own tomb, which he had made for himself in the City of David; and they laid him in the bed which was filled with spices and various ingredients prepared in a mixture of ointments" (2 Chr. 16:14). Like King Asa, Jesus also had a tomb *filled with spices*. In fact, "a mixture of myrrh and aloes" that weighed "about a hundred pounds" (John 19:39). This was *immense*. Josephus speaks of one famous teacher of antiquity being buried with forty pounds of spices, as if that was extravagant. Jesus' burial was *far more extravagant*, even, *royal*.

Where did the funds for such an elaborate and expensive burial come from? Nicodemus (John 19:39). Like Joseph, Nicodemus also was a "secret" disciple. One who earlier met with Jesus at night and asked him questions (John 3:1-21). One who also protected Jesus from the fury of some of the Jewish leaders (John 7:45-52). One interesting fact about his night discussion is that Jesus told him, "Just as Moses lifted up the serpent on the pole, so the Son of man must be lifted up" (John 3:14). I imagine that conversation was going through Nicodemus' mind as he watched Jesus being lifted up on the cross! Maybe some of the prophecies of the Old Testament began to connect for Him. Whatever the case, he was an *extraordinarily wealthy* man like Joseph, Annas, and Caipahas. So he brought 100 pounds of myrrh and aloes. He was publicly making it very clear, just like Joseph, what He thought about Jesus. This action alone would likely have proved to be far more costly to him than even the cartload of spices!

Joseph and Nicodemus both "took the body of Jesus" (John 19:40), "wrapped it in a clean linen cloth" (Matt. 27:59), and then "bound it in strips of linen with the spices" (John 19:40). The linen strips were likely wrapped around his jaw, ankles, and a few other places to hold the corpse in place while rigor mortis would begin over the next few hours. By *touching* the *dead corpse* of Jesus they were making themselves ceremonially unclean (Num. 19:11). On the eve of Passover, no less! They would be unable to dress the lamb for the Passover feast that night, and participate in the meal, as *they opted instead to 'dress' the Ultimate Lamb of God.*

Jesus was *dressed in a 'clean linen shroud.'* (More on this in Appendix A.) One interesting facet about this is *linen garments* are what the priests in the temple would wear. The high priest would wear linen clothing when he went to sprinkle blood on the ark on Yom Kippur (Lev. 16:4). Also, just as Jesus was laid in a tomb out of "hewn rock" with a "large stone" rolled over the entrance, so the stones in the temple were *hewn* and *large* (1 Kgs. 5:17). As He was laid in the tomb, the women were very attentive to *where* He was laid (Mark 15:47). When they investigated the empty tomb on Sunday morning they were *very attentive to the fact that there were two angels exactly where His head and feet had lain* (John 20:12). A picture of the ark of covenant (Ex. 25:19). Jesus being laid to rest in the tomb is a picture of His *finished work.* He is the High Priest, who offered Himself, as a perfectly sufficient sacrifice! (Heb. 7-10)

Lord Jesus, help me follow the example of Joseph and Nicodemus. Help me to be courageous and take a stand for You even when it might be costly. Help me to know that even if I might lose some worldly privilege for being a public witness for You, that what I gain in return is far greater. May I handle You in a way that people understand that You truly are the Lamb of God who has offered a perfectly sufficient sacrifice for the sins of the world. Grant me a greater revelation of who You are as the crucified, buried, and risen King!

DAY 40
Love Stronger Than Death
(Matt 27:62-66; John 19:41)

The body of Jesus was wrapped in linen and lying in a dark tomb. A large stone had been rolled over the tomb's mouth. As the sun set Joseph, Nicodemus, and the women *scurried home* for the Sabbath. At this point one would think the Passion narrative was over. Not so! Matthew tells us there was a devious group of men who remained near the tomb. He writes, "On the next day, which followed the Day of Preparation, the chief priests and Pharisees gathered together to Pilate" (Matt. 27:62). The "next day" began at *sundown*. These men had been feverishly working for the last 24-hours to make sure Jesus was crucified and put to death. Though that deed had been accomplished, they knew that Jesus had made claims of resurrection. So, to prevent the disciples from stealing the body of Jesus, they watched the tomb and immediately asked Pilate to secure and seal it—assuring no such shenanigan would take place. Pilate responded, "make it as secure as you know how." So they *sealed the stone* and *set a guard*.

What 'dead man' needs to be surrounded by an army? Only the dead God-Man! Matthew implies *several guards* ran to the city to announce what happened resurrection morning (Matt. 28:11). There were not a couple of dimwits set around the tomb, but rather a guard large enough to repel a guerrilla attack from many brawny fishermen. Fishermen who were in *hiding* at that time and had *no faith* in the resurrection, let alone a desire to fake the resurrection! Besides the guard, there was the seal. The seal was likely set up with wax and ropes, and would have made very clear even the slightest of disturbances. For one to break that seal would mean death. An Old Testament example of a den having a large stone rolled over it with an official seal is the story of Daniel. After Daniel was thrown in the lion's den, "a stone was brought and laid on the mouth of the den, and the king sealed it with his own signet ring and with the signets of his lords" (Dan. 6:17). We know how that story ends. Daniel exits the den alive! Just as Jesus would rise out of death, the domain of the satanic roaring lion (1 Pet 5:8), *alive* forevermore!

Jesus prophesied several times that He would rise "on the third day" (Matt. 16:21, 17:23, 20:19; 1 Cor. 15:4). The first day of death was Friday, the second day began a few hours later at sundown, and the third day began Saturday at sundown. *I imagine the chief priests were thinking about running to the tomb the fourth day, having their servants drag out the body of a corrupting corpse, and putting it on display to show that Jesus of Nazareth was simply a great occult deceiver and failed messiah like they had claimed.* That did not happen. Instead, they were confronted with an empty tomb!

Though the soldiers did not see the Risen Christ, they did experience an earthquake, and possibly saw an angel. Yet, they still chose to take 'hush money' about the event rather than truly investigate whether that Jewish carpenter they were guarding might have been someone *more than* a carpenter (Matt. 28:15). But why did the Jewish leaders remain in unbelief? Well, they also were in unbelief when Lazarus was raised from the dead (John 11:45-53). In one of Jesus' parables a man in the tortures of hell pleaded to Abraham to resurrect a poor man so his brothers *could know the truth.* Abraham said, "If they do not hear Moses and the prophets, neither will they be persuaded though one rise from the dead" (Luke 16:31). *A prophetic foreboding of what would happen after Christ rose from the dead. Some simply refuse to believe.*

As Jesus' body lay in the tomb, what was His soul/spirit doing? Christians differ over this question. Some say He was *experiencing the glory* He had before His incarnation with the Father in the highest heaven, others that His soul was *asleep* with His body, others that He endured even *more sufferings* in hell as man's representative, and still others that He went to hell *as Victor* and led those in Abraham's bosom up to glory with Him upon His resurrection. The last option is the one that has been the traditional view, and I believe it is correct. It has been historically referred to as 'Christ's harrowing of hell.' In the Apostles' Creed Christians recite that Christ "descended to hell." The idea is He descended *as Victor.* In the words of Ludolph, "Then the gates of hell were thrown down. The Lord, dragging the great devil in chains, led the vast army of saints out of the underworld with great rejoicing, and, walking before them, he brought them into the great Paradise of delight and pleasure that lies to the east beyond the seas."[72] Just as the commander of David's guard, Benaiah, "had gone down and killed a lion in the midst of a pit on a snowy day" (2 Sam. 23:20), so Christ went down into the pit of a roaring lion and rendered him powerless! He went down already having been victorious on the cross, enforcing that victory, and preparing to lead the demonic principalities and powers in a public triumph upon resurrection! (Col. 2:15)

Regardless of all the details that took place after Jesus committed His spirit to the Father, Jesus ultimately burst forth from the tomb as "the firstborn from the dead" (Col. 1:18) after being laid in a tomb in which "no one had yet been laid" (John 19:41). He entered the world through a *virgin womb*, and re-entered the world through a *virgin tomb*. It was also a tomb that did not belong to Him. He was placed there as *a representative*. His death and burial would both be *on behalf of others*. This virgin tomb was also in a *garden*. What do people do in gardens? They plant seeds.

When Jesus was lowered into that hole in the garden He was the greatest Seed ever planted. In fact, just days before His death He declared, "The hour has come that the Son of Man should be glorified. Most assuredly, I say to you, unless a grain of wheat falls into the ground and dies, it remains alone; but if it dies, it produces much grain" (John 12:23-24). This Seed would not produce a thirty-fold harvest, nor a sixty-fold harvest, nor even a hundred-fold harvest. Rather, this one Seed would harvest billions upon billions of souls! A Seed that is still producing a great harvest today! Jesus spoke this word specifically to "the Greeks" who were in Jerusalem for Passover (John 12:20-21). Those who had previously been outsiders to the covenants and promises. But, by His death, they would become insiders! Jesus was thinking of *every single person* as He endured His Passion!

Though Rome, the Jewish authorities, and the devil himself did everything they could to hold Jesus in the grave, they could not succeed. For Jesus is the Resurrection and the Life (John 11:25). He said concerning His life, "I have power to lay it down, and I have power to take it again" (John 10:18). It was laid down for *you*. It was raised up for *you*. This is Eternal Love incarnate! A Love infinitely greater than anything we could possibly imagine or comprehend! A Love that rose again and declares from His throne at the right hand of the Majesty, "I am He who lives, and was dead, and behold, I am alive forevermore. Amen. And I have the keys of Hades and of Death" (Rev. 1:18).

Lord Jesus, thank you for planting Your Life as a Seed in Joseph's garden two-thousand years ago. With all the church I confess that You "died for our sins according to the Scriptures", that You were "buried", and that You "rose again the third day according to the Scriptures" (1 Cor. 15:3-4). You are my Risen and Reigning Lord and Savior! Your Passion is absolute proof of Your eternal, unwavering, unconquerable, infinite Love! (Rom. 5:8, 8:31-39)
All hail, King Jesus! All hail, the Savior of the world!

Appendix A
The Burial Shroud of Jesus

The burial cloths of Jesus play an important role in the Passion Narrative. All four Gospels reference Jesus being wrapped in a linen shroud before His burial. In Mark's words, "And Joseph bought a linen shroud, and taking him down, wrapped him in the linen shroud and laid him a tomb" (Mark 15:46, ESV). Two of the Gospel writers, Luke and John, also mention the burial cloths in their account of the resurrection. The witnesses who enter the tomb Easter morning see *three* things. First, that the tomb is empty. Second, Mary sees two angels sitting at the head and foot of where Jesus had lain—a theological message that Jesus' blood was spilled and accepted on the mercy seat of heaven. Third, the only physical objects that are seen are Jesus' burial cloths—His shroud, head covering, and likely some linen strips that held the shroud in place until rigor mortis set in (John 20:6-8; Luke 24:12).

Were the only physical artifacts in the tomb treated as insignificant by Peter, John, Mary, and the first witnesses? Were they simply viewed as dirty rags? Or, were they preserved? What's more, is it possible the resurrection—*the most powerful event in human history*—occurred in a manner that could have effected the shroud that wrapped Christ's body? Many Christians throughout the centuries have claimed that the burial cloths of Jesus *were indeed preserved*, and that His shroud currently resides in a chapel in the northern Italian city of Turin. Is this true? Or, is the Shroud of Turin simply the work of a medieval forger looking to strike it rich?

One thing to keep in mind is that this Shroud has only been in the possession of the Catholic Church since 1983. Before that it was owned either by private citizens or royalty. Regardless of who has possessed the Shroud, it is understandable *why many are skeptical of it.*

The relic industry in the medieval period was certainly corrupt and something that frustrated many Catholics and Reformers alike. Christians would pilgrimage to see objects such as a 'baby tooth of Christ' or 'a vile of milk from Mary's breast'. Luther sums up his frustration with the vast amount of fake relics in his day by saying, "What lies there are about relics! One claims to have a feather from the wing of the angel Gabriel, and the Bishop of Mainz has a flame from Moses' burning bush. And how does it happen that eighteen apostles are buried in Germany when Christ had only twelve?"[73]

Is the Shroud that resides in Turin a fake akin to 'Gabriel's feather'? Or, is it authentic? Something God providentially preserved in a similar manner to how He wanted some of the wilderness manna and Aaron's rod to be preserved? (Ex. 16:32-34; Numb. 17:10) Something akin to archaeological objects we possess like the ossuary of Caiaphas and sarcophagus of Herod the Great? For the past thirty-five years the claim for *authenticity* has fallen on difficult times. In 1988 a Carbon-14 test was conducted on a piece of the Shroud. The test came back with results that the flax for the linen was harvested sometime between AD 1260-1390 with a 95% confidence rate. At the press conference the man who oversaw the test, Oxford professor Edward Hall, declared the Shroud to be "a load of rubbish." The *New York Times'* headline of this momentous test simply read, "Fraud." *Time Magazine* would not be outdone and declared in their subtitle that the test "proved" the Shroud could not have been the burial cloth of Jesus. The following month, the headline for London's *Evening Standard* on August 26 read, "The Shroud of Turin is a Fake." To put a nail in the coffin, the international scientific journal *Nature* published an article in February of the following year with signatories of twenty-one names of those most closely associated with the radiocarbon test. It concluded, "These results therefore provide conclusive evidence that the linen of the shroud of Turin is medieval." For many people today, the only thing they know about the Shroud of Turin, if they know anything, is that it radiocarbon dated to the fourteenth century and is *undeniably a fraud.*

Is this true? Does it matter? What exactly is so unique about this Shroud and why would I include it in a devotional on the Passion of Christ? In the remainder of this appendix we will look at the physical properties of the Shroud, the history of the Shroud's whereabouts, and the many scientific tests which have been conducted on the Shroud the last 125 years. After reading, you will be able to decide for yourself whether the *New York Times* and *Time Magazine* were correct in their judgments on the Shroud. Remarkably, the Shroud is by far the most studied artifact in human history. Over 13,000 academic articles have been written on it. One can even get a postgraduate certificate in Shroud studies at the Pontifical Academy—a year long course that simply gets student's feet wet. Many of the top scientific minds of our day are baffled by this object. In fact, no one has ever been able to duplicate it or the image that mysteriously resides on its surface. Scientists from atheistic, agnostic, Jewish, and other religious and philosophical backgrounds have been converted to Christianity after investigating the Shroud for themselves. In fact, many have become *devout followers* of Christ. Why? Hasn't the C-14 test proved it is a medieval forgery?

Before we answer that question, what exactly is the Shroud of Turin? It is a 14'6" x 3'9" linen cloth with the lightness of a modern bed sheet. Using the Assyrian cubit, which was the measurement used in first-century Israel, it measures at an even 8-cubits long by 2-cubits wide—one of many of the Shroud's first-century Jewish features. The Shroud's weave is a herringbone Z-twist three-to-one twill pattern. This is a rare and expensive expert weave. In fact, there are no known linens from the medieval period with this same weave, and in ancient Egyptian times complex three-to-one patterns have largely been found in royal tombs. The man who was running the Carbon-14 dating project at the British Museum, Michael Tate, could not find a control sample from the Middle Ages because of the unique weave, size, and material of the Shroud. What is more, the closest example to a three-to-one Z-twist herringbone weave is a first-century woolen cloth that was found in a Roman fort in Egypt. The Shroud also has a stitch that runs three-inches from its edge down its entire eight-cubits length. In 1998 textile expert, Dr. Mechthile Flury-Lemberg, who was part of the team in charge of overseeing the removal of a backing cloth that had been sowed into the Shroud testified that in her forty-year career she had only observed a similar stitch pattern once in her life —in a cloth that dated to the first-century in Masada, Israel. On top of the unique first-century weave and stitch pattern, the size of the Shroud is larger than any linen tunic that was produced on a loom during the Middle Ages. Dr. Flury-Lemberg states, "Tapestries during the fourteenth and fifteenth centuries were very small—only between three and six feet high…If you find linen bed sheets from that time (which is rare), you will find a seam in the middle of the sheet. Two loom pieces will have been sewn together at their selvedges to make them wide enough for the bed."[74] The actual Shroud itself bears the weave, stitch, and size of a first-century Jewish linen cloth. If a forger truly concocted this in the fourteenth-century, they spared no expense getting the most minute details correct on the simple 'canvas' they would use.

As far as the known historical provenance of the Shroud of Turin, it can irrefutably be traced back to Lirey, France in 1355. This is 223 years before it came to reside in Turin, Italy in 1578. During its time in Lirey, it was simply known as the Shroud of Christ, or the Shroud of Lirey. Later we will see it was likely the same Shroud that was in Constantinople and Edessa known as the Shroud of Constantinople and Image of Edessa. The only reason the word "Turin" has been stuck to it is because that is where it has resided the last 455 years. While there are many historical documents that give testimony to the Shroud's public showings in Lirey, France, in 1855 a medallion commemorating these showings was found in Paris. This medallion has been dated between 1349-1356 and displays the full front and back image of

1355 Lirey Shroud Exhibit Medallion
Image part of Public Domain. Taken from Wikimedia Commons.

the naked body of Christ, the unique herringbone weave, and has the coat of arms of the family of Geoffrey de Charny on the left and the coat of arms of his wife on the right.

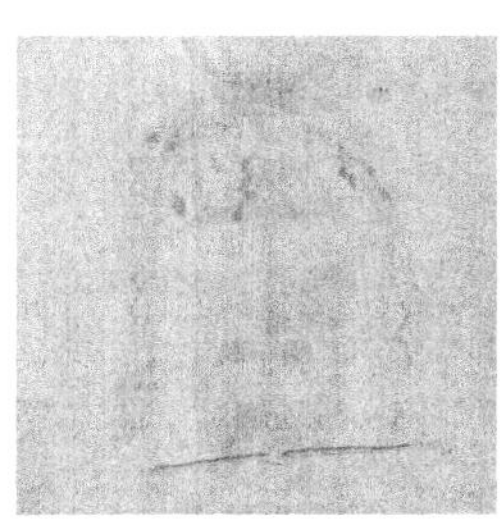

Shroud of Turin - Facial Image

Having now mentioned 'the body', what is most remarkable about the Shroud is not the linen cloth or weave, rather, it is the image of a crucified victim with bloodstains that reside within the very upper fibrils of the surface of the cloth. To the left is the facial image—the most famous and viewed part of the cloth throughout its history. But the cloth itself actually has the imprint of *the entire crucified man*. The following page is a full-length picture of the cloth complete with a description of what one is observing. The Shroud as it currently exists also contains eight diamond shaped burn marks from a fire it was rescued from in 1532 while residing in Chambery, France, visible water damage likely from how it was stored in a jar early in its history, and unique 'poker holes' from some mysterious past event. Yet, though battle scarred and nearly destroyed on multiple occasions, just about the entirety of the full body image, with its bloodstains, remain unscathed.

The faint image shown here is the only image that was seen for the vast majority of the Shroud's history. Though, we will see, this would all dramatically change in 1898. Before investigating the image on the Shroud and the scientific evidence related to the image that supports a first-century date, what is the historical evidence for the Shroud existing prior to 14th-century Europe? There have been many books written on this subject appealing to evidence from numismatics, iconography, and ecclesiastical history. Oxford trained art historian, Ian Wilson, has most famously chronicled a probable journey of the Shroud in his book *The Shroud —Fresh Light on the 2000-Year-Old Mystery*. Wilson, and others, relate an early tale of a disciple of Christ named Addai who travelled to Edessa, Turkey in order to respond to a letter that King Agbar V

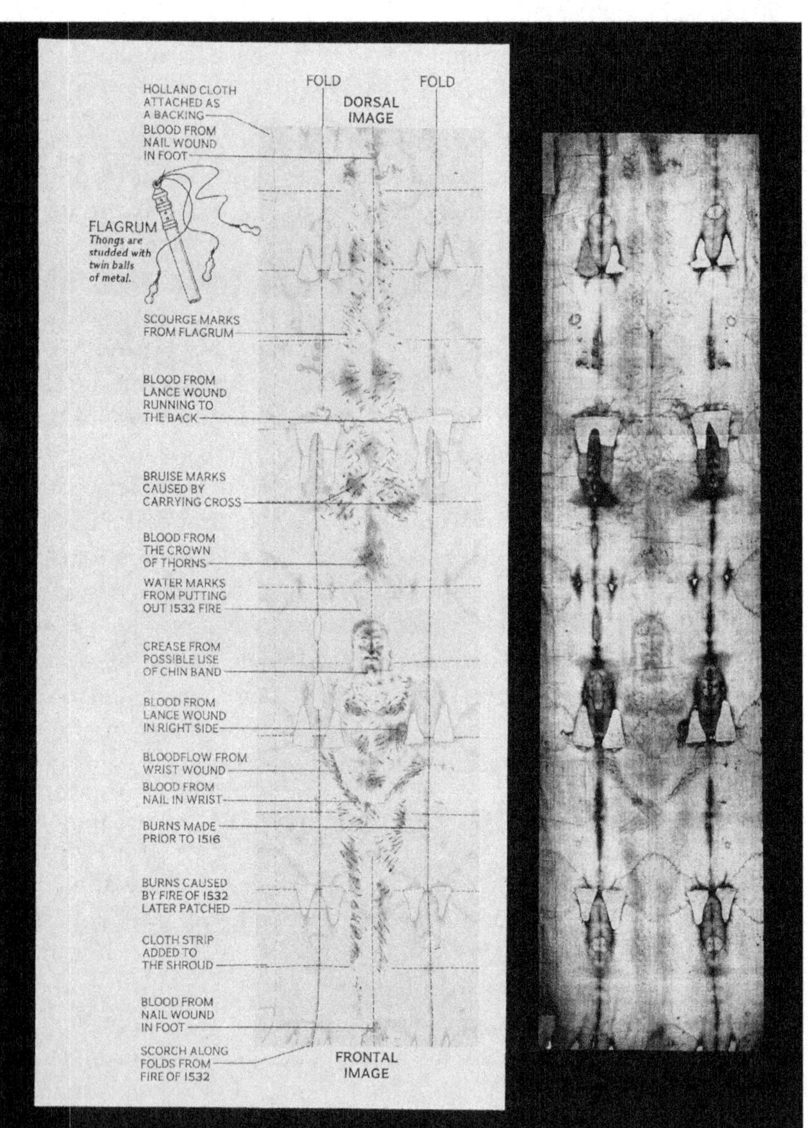

Full Body Image - Shroud of Turin

sent to Jesus. The story goes that Addai arrived with a message from Jesus and a cloth that bore His image. We have editions of this legend as far back as the fourth century historian Eusebius. An eighth-century Latin edition of the legend has Christ state in His supposed letter, "if you wish to see my face in the flesh, behold I send to you a linen, on which you will discover not only the features of my face, but a divinely copied configuration of my entire body."[75] Most certainly this letter is not an actual historical document written by Jesus, but many scholars do see in it a historical grain of truth. It appears the Edesssan legend developed from Christians seeking to explain how they came to be in possession of a linen cloth that bore the full body image of the crucified Christ. Someone likely inventing a story of Jesus washing His face with a linen cloth and sending it to King Abgar.

Regardless of whether Abgar V ever saw the linen cloth, or how long it might have been in Edessa in the early centuries, what is *certain* is that a linen cloth bearing an image of Jesus became prominent in that city in AD 544. It became known as the Image of Edessa and The Mandylion. During AD 544 a large Persian army surrounded Edessa's walls. The church historian Evagrius, who was a student in Edessa at the time of this attack, records that at the moment when all seemed lost to the citizens of the city, "[the Edessans] brought the divinely created Image, which human hands had not made, the one that Christ the God sent to Abgar when he yearned to see him."[76] The result was that the wooden siege ramp built by the Persians caught fire and they were defeated. The Edessans attributed this victory to Christ and His Image. The Image of Edessa from that moment forward *dramatically grew in popularity and began to have a profound impact on Christian art.* While it is possible the Image was hidden in Edessa for 500 years like some legends claim, a more likely history is that it spent time in both Antioch, Syria and Ravenna, Italy before ending up in Edessa sometime before AD 540 when Ravenna was conquered by the Byzantine Empire. In support of the Shroud spending some time in Antioch, at the second council of Nicea in AD 787 a sermon attributed to the fourth-century church father, Athanasius, was read. The sermon stated that in the year AD 68 an "image of our Lord and Savior at full length" was taken from Jerusalem and moved to Syria.[77] The sermon goes on to state that this image remained in Antioch to the author's own day. Stephen E. Jones suggests that Shroud was removed from Antioch around AD 380 when the Arian Christians were expelled from that city and eventually found a safe haven in Ravenna—a city friendly toward Arians. The primary reason Ravenna was the likely home of the image is because of a mosaic in the Sant' Apollinare Nuovo church called 'Christ Enthroned' that reliably dates to AD 505-526. Based on the amount of artistic overlay between the mosaic and the Shroud, "the artist must have worked directly from the Shroud, not from a copy of it."[78]

What we know for certain is that the linen ended up in Edessa before AD 544 and during this period it became the most famous relic in the Christian World, known as 'the divinely created image', and especially, 'the image made without hands'—in Greek one word, *acheiropoietos*. Knowledge of an 'image' on the burial shroud of Jesus was widespread at this time. For instance, the AD 589 Mozarabic Rite, a Spanish liturgy, states during its offertory on the first Saturday after Easter, "Peter ran with John to the tomb and saw the recent imprints (vestigia) of the dead and risen man on the linens."[79] Sometime during the sixth or seventh century the Image of Edessa began to be described as 'tetradiplon' in the *Acts of Thaddaeus*. Tetradiplon simply means 'doubled in four' and it appears to have been uniquely coined by the author for the distinct way the Image of Edessa was folded. Remarkably, if one doubles the Shroud of Turin four times they get the most important part of the image (the face) in a dimension that is easy to display and transport. The Shroud of Turin doubled four times looks like this…

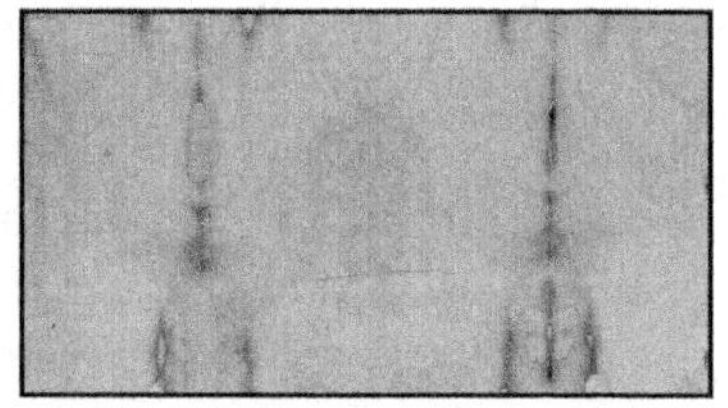

Shroud of Turin when it is Tetradiplon
© Vernon Miller, 1978.

While some referred to the Image of Edessa as being an image of an entire body, most only knew of the Image bearing the face. Why? Because it was tetradiplon during most of its history—something the *fold marks* on the Shroud of Turin testify to even today! Remarkably, at the time of the reemergence of this image in Edessa a total transformation of Christian iconography began. The first five centuries of Christianity was replete with many very different images for Christ. Most which were Roman in appearance of a man who was young with a clean-shaven face and short hair. In the sixth-century that dramatically changed. From that point forward the images of Christ all seemed to follow a strictly set pattern of a Semitic looking man with long hair, a beard, a mustache, hair-covered ears, a longer and more pronounced nose, an enlarged left nostril, a raised right eyebrow, deeply set almost 'owlish' eyes, and many other such common features. In 1962 the oldest such icon was discovered in Saint Catherine's Monastery in the Sinai desert. It dates to AD 550 and has become known as 'Christ Pantocrator.' Why, only six years after we know the *Image of Edessa* began to become prominent in Edessa as the Image that saved Edessa from Persian invasion does the iconography of the Christian world completely change?

The most reasonable explanation is the Image of Edessa was considered to be the genuine face of Christ that was inexplicably 'not made with human hands', but rather in some way *made by Christ Himself.* The iconographers would view themselves as duty bound to follow this 'Divine Blueprint.' What has interested many historians is how much these 'Divine Blueprint' icons from the 6th-14th century have in common with the Shroud of Turin. This is one reason many believe the Shroud of Turin *is* the Image of Edessa. Interest in the remarkable connections between Byzantine icons, the Image of Edessa, and the Shroud of Turin has especially waxed strong the past 125 years. In 1985 Dr. Alan Whanger took the comparative study of these images to new technological heights when he developed something called Polarized Image Overlay technique which is used to find points of congruence between

'Christ Enthroned'
6th Cent. Mosaic
Image part of Public Domain. Taken
from Wikimedia Commons.

'Shroud of Turin'
© Vernon Miller, 1978.

'Christ Pantocrator'
6th Cent. Icon
Image part of Public Domain. Taken
from Wikimedia Commons.

'Justinian II Gold Solidus'
7th Cent. Coin
Image part of Public Domain.
Taken from Wikimedia Commons.

images. In a court of law 45 to 60 points of congruence are enough to declare faces to be the same. Using Polarized Image Overlay, Dr. Whanger discovered that the Shroud of Turin and the Pantocrator icon have 250 points of congruence. Fives times the needed amount!

What is just as remarkable as the Christian art radically shifting in the sixth-century with the prominent display of the Image of Edessa, is the change in Christian coinage. In fact, Shroud expert Giulio Fanti recently wrote a large book on the subject in 2021 called *Byzantine Coins Influenced by the Shroud of Christ*. One of the early famous coins is the AD 692 gold solidus of Justinian II. Giulio Fanti and Pierandrea Malfi "performed a statistical evaluation on the whole set of 'coincidences' and report in their study that their statistical calculations returned a certainty greater than 99.99% that the Shroud was the model for Justinian's 692 gold solidus coin."[80] On top this, coins minted in AD 969-976 during the reign of John I Tzimiskes have even stronger resemblances to the Shroud.

While the Mandylion resided in Edessa, its significance was well known across the Christian world. In AD 769 Pope Stephen III gave a sermon in which he stated that Christ "stretched his whole body on a cloth, white as snow, on which the glorious image of the Lord's face and the length of his whole body was so divinely transformed that it was sufficient for those who could not see the Lord bodily in the flesh to see the transfiguration made on the cloth."[81] A clearly recognizable reference to the Mandylion (i.e., the

Shroud of Turin). Though Edessa eventually went through a season where it was ruled by Muslims, Christians were still given liberty and the Mandylion remained safe. But, in AD 943 a Byzantine army of 80,000 men showed up at Edessa's gates. More than enough to obliterate the city. Astonishingly, the army was willing to allow Edessa to remain unharmed and free if the authorities would simply grant one request—hand over the Mandylion. Because this was one of the most sacred objects in the world, the Muslim leaders of Edessa actually had to think about it! Eventually, they agreed, and the Mandylion was handed over to the army after which it was marched 700 miles west to the Byzantine capital, Constantinople.

After a 400+ year stay in Edessa, the Mandylion finally arrived in Constantinople in AD 944. It was paraded into the city and a grand ceremony was held. In fact, a Feast Day was established to commemorate the arrival of the Mandylion in Constantinople every year—August 16th, 944. This Feast Day is still observed by the Eastern Orthodox Church even though they lost possession of the Mandylion in AD 1204. Upon its arrival the Emperor, Constantine VII Porphyrogennetos, even commissioned for its official story to be told for historical record in a document titled *The Story of the Image of Edessa*. A story we still possess with manuscripts that date back to the 10th century. While the Story likely got much of the Edessan history correct, it is also likely that it was infused with legend when speaking of the Image's early years—especially the legend of Jesus' supposed letter to Abgar V.

What took place the 260 years the Mandylion was displayed in a grand chapel in the most illustrious city in all of Medieval Europe? A highly likely event would have been the arrival of a Hungarian artist who viewed the Shroud/Mandylion. One thing we know for certain is that an image in the *Hungarian Pray Codex* is an exact replica of the Shroud of Turin, and it reliably dates to AD 1192-1195! This codex is the first book ever written and bound in the Hungarian language. Within it are four drawings depicting the death and burial of Jesus. Experts believe the images are possibly replicas of a more elaborate artistic rendering from the turn of the

11th century. Whatever the case, we know what was drawn preserves key details about what the Shroud looked like *at the very latest* in AD 1195. In 1993, Prof. Jerome Lejeune, published a list of nine common characteristics between the Shroud and the images within the Pray Codex. He pointed out that the Shroud is twice the length of the man, that the artist very intentionally copied the difficult herringbone weave pattern, that the man had a beard and long hair, that the body was naked, that the right hand rested over the left, that the nail wounds were on the wrist, that the fingers were long, that no thumbs were showing, that a mark

'Hungarian Pray Codex' date. 1192-1195
Public Domain. Taken from Wikimedia Commons.

above the right eye corresponded to the reverse '3'-shaped blood-stain on the Shroud, and most importantly that there was an 'L'-shaped pattern of holes on the cloth. For many scholars this is *definitive proof* the Shroud of Turin existed before the earliest date given by the 1988 radiocarbon test—1260. *More on that later.*

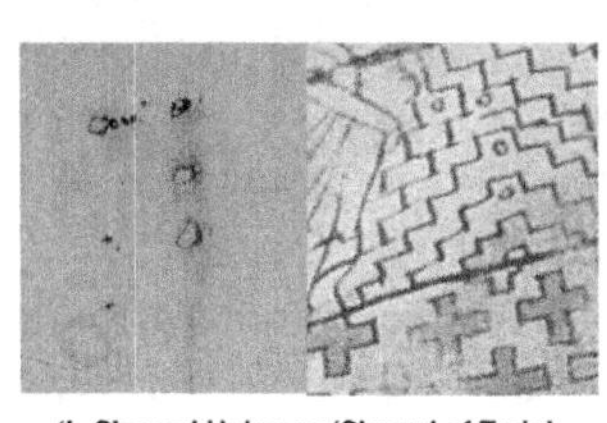

'L-Shaped Holes on 'Shroud of Turin' and 'Hungarian Pray Codex'

About ten years after the Hungarian Pray Codex was completed, the Knight's Templar sacked the city of Constantinople in 1204. The last time we hear about the Mandylion in Constantinople is in 1204 from a pilgrim named Robert de Clari—possibly also a member of the Knight's Templar. He wrote about the church "where was kept the sydoines in which our Lord had been wrapped, which stood up straight every Friday so that the features of Our Lord could be plainly seen there. And no one, either Greek or French, ever knew what became of the sydoines after the city was taken."[82] One of the leading theories of the Shroud's whereabouts from 1204-1355 is that it was in possession of the Knight's Templar who had sacked Constantinople and taken relics with them amongst their other booty. In 2009 a file was discovered in the Vatican archives that held the testimony of a young French Templar named Arnaut Sabbatier. During a 1287 initiation ceremony he was taken into a secret room where "he was shown a long linen cloth on which was impressed the figure of a man, and was told to kiss the feet of the image three times."[83] In 1307 the king of France arrested the Templar leaders in his realm charging them of worshipping a mysterious idol "in the form of the head of a man with a long, reddish beard."[84] The Templar Master of Normandy was a man by the name of Geoffrey de Charny. He was burned at the stake in 1314. Interestingly, the owner of the Shroud of Turin when it first appears in modern historical records in Lirey, France in 1355 is a man by the name of Geoffrey I de Charney. Were these men related? While there is not definitive proof, Ian Wilson writes, "enough has been learned about both individuals during the last three decades to make the family connection near definite."[85] Thus, a probable and reasonable provenance for the Shroud of Turin has been established running back to Edessa in AD 544, and even before that to Antioch and ultimately Jerusalem during the time of Jesus. But, what does the *science* say? Does the Shroud contain scientific clues beyond the 1988 radiocarbon test?

Enter the year 1898. The image that can be seen on the Shroud with the naked eye caused Christians for six centuries (if forged), or nineteen centuries (if not forged), to be in *awe* and *wonder*. Yet, though it had such a grand history of drawing multitudes for showings, there were still skeptics who viewed it as nothing more than a 14th-century *painting*. Such a simplistic dismissal would soon be laughable. For what happened at the turn of the 20th-century was nothing short of an atomic bomb to the modern mind! The story picks up with a forty-two year old lawyer, mayor, and amateur photographer in 1898. The Shroud was being prepared to be shown for the first time in 34 years in celebration of the 50th anniversary of the Italian Constitution. The photographer's name was Secondo Pia, and this was the first time the Shroud was photographed—photography having only been invented about half a century earlier. After the long and arduous process of taking a photograph in that day, as Secondo waited in the dark room for his image to develop, he expected to see a blurry negative image that would ultimately become a positive displaying the ivory covered cloth with the yellowish image of the crucified man on the surface, complete with the reddish bloodstains and scorched fire markings.

Instead, as Secondo watched his photographic plate under the developer begin to reveal itself, he couldn't believe his eyes! Trembling, and almost dropping the plate in astonishment, Secondo was looking at a perfect positive image of a crucified man! Secondo began to think he was the first person since AD 33 to behold the face of Christ as He had lain in the tomb! How was this possible? How could the image people had been looking at for centuries, if not millennia, be a perfect photographic negative? An image of this sort was, and continues to remain, a complete *anomaly* in human history. The 1978 documentary, *The Silent Witness*, has a fantastic reenactment of the emotions that flooded Secondo in this moment. When Pia presented this photograph of the man on the Shroud, the results for many were too spectacular to believe! Rather than allow the Shroud to be photographed again to validate Pia's finding, the Shroud was stored away for another 33 years. Yet, Secondo's photograph stirred the faith of many, some claiming the photograph to be nothing short of a miracle. Others doubted, especially those in the Academy, and even many amongst the hierarchy of the Catholic Church. In light of the disbelief,

Shroud of Turin - Negative Image

Secondo's reputation was attacked and character maligned. He was accused of doctoring and retouching the negative plates.

Enter the year 1931. The Shroud was finally publicly displayed again, and allowed to be photographed for a second time. This time with a professional photographer, more advanced technology, and five other professional photographers who would verify the negative plates were not in anyway retouched. Secondo was also there, and after the two and a half minutes passed for the photo to develop, he exclaimed in joyous vindication, "It's the same!" Now there could be no doubt that the image on the Shroud was a perfect photographic negative on top of a non-photographic sensitive ancient linen cloth! An image that was physiologically and anatomically perfect down to the minutest detail! How could this be? Is it even possible for an artist to reverse engineer an image like this? Could the visibly negative image on the Shroud even have been produced by some sort of dye or paint?

This second round of photos interested a renowned physician by the name of Dr. Pierre Barbet—a man who eventual became president of Paris's Society of Surgeons. Dr. Barbet wrote a book on the Shroud titled *Doctor at Calvary*, and his position enabled him to conduct some unique experiments regarding crucifixion. One thing Dr. Barbet noticed about the

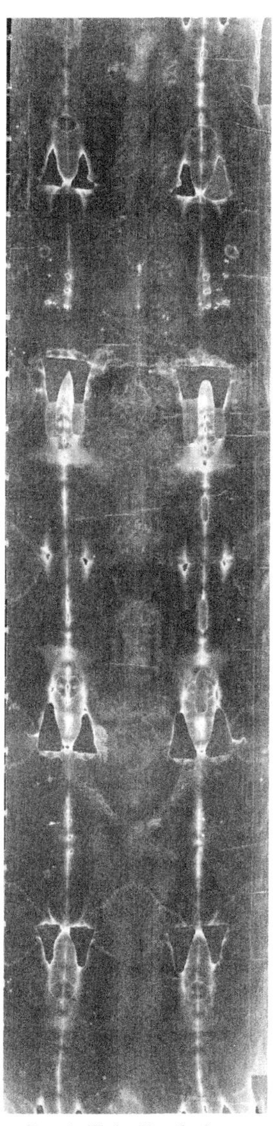

Shroud of Turin - Negative Image

image on the Shroud was that the man was crucified in his wrists rather than through his palms like was seen on *all* religious art until the 17th century, and *most* religious art up until his own day. Having access to unclaimed bodies, Dr. Barbet was able to experiment on some cadavers. He crucified these dead bodies with nails through both the palms and wrists. The body crucified through the palm eventually dislodged by tearing through the hand. However, when Dr. Barbet struck a nail through the 'Destot Space' in the wrist, to his amazement the carpals separated, the nail passed through, and the thumbs immediately snapped behind the palm after hitting a nerve. What's more, the body held in place on the cross. The Shroud not only is by far the earliest image of a crucified man with nails through his wrists, but also shows the thumbs snapped behind the palms! A phenomena unknown to modern physicians until Dr. Barbet's experiments.

During the decades following 1931 many aspects of the anatomy of the crucified man were investigated in detail. For instance, a close evaluation of the scourge marks revealed that there were 372 scourge wounds—159 on the front and 213 on the back. These wounds matched *the exact dumbbell-shape of a Roman flagrum* that was unearthed in the buried city of Herculaneum which was excavated in 1709. Before that time, there was no known Roman scourge in existence. The Roman flagrum was a whip with three strands, with a dumbbell with tiny spikes on the end of each strand. The man on the Shroud was whipped with 124 lashes. Over three times the number allowed by the Old Testament—a *thorough* and *brutal* beating by the Romans who couldn't care less about Jewish law. The man on the Shroud was also scourged naked as there are scourge markings throughout the pelvic region. While the Shroud shows the crucified man naked, no other medieval artist dared to portray Christ in that manner. Concerning the scourge wounds Dr. Antonacci writes, "Photographic enlargement, microscopic examination and ultraviolet lighting show that the skin was torn open and that clot formation and retraction occurred at these sites. These wounds are signs of a savage scourging, probably by two separate individuals."[86] Fr. Andrew Dalton adds, "Each one of these marks is the damage of a third degree burn."[87] The Shroud testifies to a brutal beating—portraying perfect anatomical scourge markings that match an excavated first-century Roman flagrum!

Concerning the elliptical wound in the chest, the Shroud contains an immense amount of real blood and pericardial fluid. The wound itself is the exact size of an unearthed Roman lancea. It is also in the anatomically perfect angle and place it would need to be to strike the heart between the fifth and sixth ribs. The Shroud also shows excoriation across the shoulder blades and possibly the dislocation of the right shoulder—wounds expected to be seen where a crucified man would have carried his heavy crossbeam to the place of execution. The face on the Shroud appears to be beaten as the cheeks and eyes are swollen and the nose is bruised— testifying to the brutal beating at the hands of the Sanhedrin. The head has over thirty wounds on the top, middle, and back, where it was pierced by sharp objects inducing extensive blood flow. The crown of thorns would have been akin to an eastern crown which covered the whole head rather than that of a western crown depicted in most religious art. The man on the Shroud has a cap-like 'bush of thorns' pounded into his head—similar to the ram that was caught in the thicket by the horns (Gen. 22:13). Abrasions, lesions, and scratches on the knee suggest that the man fell while carrying the crossbeam. This would likely have been when he also bruised his nose and dislocated his shoulder—as he could not break his fall. Many other anatomical details, including the blood, will be detailed in a moment.

In 1973 the Shroud was permitted by its owners to undergo a one day examination by a small group of scientists. One of the scientists allowed to see the Shroud was a Swiss police pathologist and Evangelical Protestant by the name of Max Frei. Max collected twelve sticky tape samples from the surface of the Shroud for the purpose of collecting pollen grains. Max was the founder of the Zurich, Switzerland Central Police Scientific Department and was responsible for early pioneering work in Forensic Palynology. By

1976, Frei had identified at least fifty-eight different species of plant pollen from his sticky tapes. These could be used to track the known movement of the Shroud throughout its history. While a small amount of pollens were found from species of plants that grew around Lirey, France and Turin, Italy as *expected*, what was most remarkable was that the majority of the pollen was from Turkey and Israel. In fact, three of the pollen grains were *unique* and *specific* to the region of Edessa, Turkey and thirteen pollen grains were *unique* and *specific* to Jerusalem and northern Judea! This demonstrated *without question* in Frei's mind that the Shroud had spent much of its history in those two locations. A later study at the University of Padua in 2022 corroborated many of Frei's finds.

Another Pia-esque, mind-blowing moment occurred in 1976. That year Dr. John Jackson, a professor of physics at the U.S. Air Force Academy and scientist at the Air Force Weapons Laboratory, took interest in the Shroud. While conducting experiments with a fellow colleague, Dr. Eric Jumper, Jackson made an extraordinary find. When a photograph of the Shroud was placed under a VP-8 image analyzer, the image that was outputted on the analyzer's monitor was an incredibly clear 3D-image. This was astonishing because no other photograph had ever produced a 3D-image! This never happens because the VP-8 analyzer enables shades of white and black to be translated into levels of vertical relief, and a photograph only records variations in light, so it never produces a 3D-effect. The engineer who delivered the VP-8 analyzer to Dr. Jackson, stated, "the results are unlike anything I have processed through the VP-8 Image Analyzer, before or since. Only the Shroud of Turin has produced these results from a VP-8 Image Analyzer."[88] Utilizing the 3D-information sculptors have been able to create life size sculptures of the man on the Shroud. We don't just have a picture of the man, but an entire hologram! Stevenson writes, "Employing sophisticated mathematical analysis, he [Dr. Jackson] showed that no reasonable physical mechanism could produce an image which was both three-dimensional and highly detailed. To achieve clarity, three-dimensionality had to be sacrificed."[89] Dr.

Jackson was able to silence all 'natural' image formation theories with this find. Some type of 'supernatural' interior radioactive and luminescent event was necessary to produce such features, as we will later see.

After the brief examination in 1973, and three-dimensional investigation of Dr. Jackson in 1976, it was becoming increasingly clear that a more thorough scientific examination of the Shroud was necessary. So, in 1978 a team of thirty-three expert scientists was organized under the name STuRP (Shroud of Turin Research Project). This team was comprised of agnostics, atheists, Jews, and Christians. The only qualification necessary for being on the team was excellence in their own field of knowledge. Many of the people assembled for the team knew little to nothing about the Shroud, and some expected the 'supposed relic' would be debunked within five minutes of their investigations. So, loading up eighty crates of scientific equipment weighing eight tons in all, the scientists made their way to Turin, Italy. Upon arriving the team was given unprecedented access to the Shroud. The *Critical Summary* states, "For 120 continuous hours, the Shroud was examined in depth. Such direct research access to the Shroud had not been given prior to this, nor has it been given since."[90] The results would truly be mind-bending and life-transforming for many of these STuRP members. What they examined was nothing short of scientifically inexplicable.

After the investigations the scientists would publish the results of their research in twenty different peer-reviewed scientific journals over the course of the next four years. The STuRP team's official conclusive statement was published in 1981. The statement begins, "No pigments, paints, dyes or stains have been found on the fibrils." It ends with, "there are no chemical or physical methods known which can account for the totality of the image, nor can any combination of physical, chemical, biological or medical circumstances explain the image adequately. Thus, the answer to the question of how the image was produced or what produced the image remains, now, as it has in the past, a mystery. We can conclude for now that the Shroud image is that of a real human form of a scourged, crucified man. It is not the product of an artist. The bloodstains are composed of hemoglobin and also give a positive test for serum albumin."[91]

What is the *image* on the Shroud that is "not the product of an artist"? While the blood soaks into the Shroud, the image itself is *extremely superficial*. A single linen thread on the Shroud is composed of 200 flaxen fibers. The yellowish-brown color that produces the image resides only on the topmost 2 or 3 fibers of each thread, and only on the outer shell of those fibers. The yellowish-brown color is "due to chemical reactions involving the polysaccharides composing the linen fibers: oxidation, dehydration and conjugation."[92] Because the image is so thin it needs to be measured in nanometers (one billionth of a meter). The thickness of a paper is 100,000 nanometers. The image on the Shroud is 200-500 nanometers. Imagine holding a stack of three hundred pieces of paper, and that stack equaled the thickness of a normal piece of paper. The thickness of one of those invisibly thin slices equals the depth of the image on the Shroud! An image easily scraped off with the thinnest of razor blades. On top of that there is *no directionality* to the image. This is another reason why scientists are adamant the image cannot be the work of an artist. Concerning the directionless nature of the image, a chemist on the STuRP team, Dr. John Heller, stated, "It is as if every pore and every hair of the body contained a microminiature laser."[93] As we will see, one of the theories for the image formation has to do with a light burst or radioactive event coming from every pore of the body creating a directionless image. Professional photographer, Leo Vala, said of the image, "I've been involved in the invention of many complicated visual processes and I can tell you that no one could have faked that image. No one could do it today with the technology we have. It's a perfect negative. It has a photographic quality that is extremely precise."[94]

The blood on the Shroud is also remarkable. The blood flows and clots from the wounds are *perfectly flawless*. Around every single scourge wound on the Shroud are blood serum halos that are invisible to the human eye and only were revealed when irradiated by ultraviolet light in 1978. STuRP team members Adler and Heller demonstrated that the blood on the Shroud is *human* blood. Later investigations have gone so far as to say it is type AB blood—the rarest blood type, but also a blood type seen more frequently among Semitic peoples. Niyr writes, "The rivulets of blood on the Shroud also carry distinct characteristics, such as being either *venous* or *arterial* blood in the correct locations for each type of blood. (Knowledge of the difference between *venous* vs. *arterial* blood was not discovered until 1593 by Andrea Cesalpino—centuries after the 1350s.)"[95] A high content of the compound bilirubin has also been found in the blood, indicating the blood was from a man who was severely tortured. Meaning, a forger couldn't have used any old blood, he needed the blood of a tortured man.

The bloodstains on the Shroud also uniquely match another cloth known as the 'Sudarium of Oviedo'—the purported head cloth of Christ that resides in Oviedo, Spain and has a reliable history in that city that dates back to at least the seventh-century. A head cloth would have covered the dead head of Jesus as His followers waited for His body to be granted to Joseph of Arimathea. All of the blood and other bodily fluids that would have flowed from the head, cheeks, nose, and mouth would have stained the head covering in the same way they would have stained the burial shroud once the body was wrapped in it. The head covering would have been part of the "cloths" that John saw lying on the tomb alongside the Shroud and other linen bands that held the body in place (John 20:6). In 1988 the Spanish sindology center began to perform tests on the 'Sudarium of Oviedo' and what they have found since then is remarkable when compared with the Shroud of Turin. The blood type is the same rare AB. The nose on each cloth measures at 8cm (this is measured by the fluid stain on the Sudarium as there is no 'image' like the Shroud). The inverse '3' on the Shroud near the forehead shows up in the same spot on the Sudarium, in serum form. When Alan Whanger's digital overly is applied to both cloths there are 120 points of congruence. What's more, in 2012 after X-ray fluorescence testing was performed on the cloth it came back that the same limestone found on the Shroud on the nose was found on the Sudarium on the nose! (More on that limestone in a bit.) Many scientists believe it is *impossible* for these cloths to have independently received the same bloodstains, bodily fluids, and limestone. The only reasonable conclusion being that they covered the same face of a crucified man who wore a crown of thorns. (And, we only know of one such man in history.) For many, the Sudarium is *clear evidence* that the Shroud of Turin dates to *at least* the seventh-century.

I mentioned the presence of *limestone* on the Shroud. This was something that was discovered by the STuRP team members Roger and Marty Gilbert while performing ultraviolet spectroscopy scanning of the Shroud. With the help of optical physicist Sam Pellicori, and in his words, they were able to determine that there was "dirt" near the soles of the feet. They then found this same microscopic dirt, or limestone, on the knees and nose. The next step was to see what limestone shelf in the world this "dirt" came from. Researchers first compared it to nine different limestone samples throughout the land of Israel. None matched. Finally, the team was able to get a specimen from the Ecole Biblique tomb in Jerusalem. This tomb belongs to the same limestone shelf as the Church of the Holy Sepulcher and the Garden Tomb. To their amazement, it was an exact match! A rare travertine argonite limestone found almost nowhere else in the world! The man of the Shroud was covered in Jerusalem dirt! Even more remarkable, the dirt laid *under* the serum-haloed bloodstains. Meaning, it was there *before the blood*, while the blood was there *before the image*. The blood and dirt could not have been added to the Shroud at any later date but must have been there from the very beginning!

While the STuRP team was busy drawing conclusions on the data they had collected, there was a further confirmation of an earlier theory on the Shroud regarding coins over the man's eyes. In 1954, Francis Filas, a professor at Loyola University had discovered the letters 'UCAI' over the right eyelid while closely examining the

1931 negative photographs. In 1977, Dr. Jackson presented some of his findings from the VP-8 analyzer 3D image, one of which he said was that there were small, round, raised objects over the man's eyes that resembled buttons. He proposed they were coins. In 1979 Filas showed the more defined 3D-image to Michael Marx, a Greek classical coin expert. Marx, agreeing with the suggestion of Ian Wilson before him, suggested that the size, shape, and lettering of the coin might match one of the coins minted by Pontius Pilate between AD 29-32. Niyr writes, "Some of these Pontius Pilate coins still exist today. However, numismatists had never noticed before (until observed on the Shroud) that the abbreviation was misspelled! The correct spelling should have been 'UKAI' (instead of 'UCAI' found on the Shroud). At first, some people insisted that the misspelling was evidence that the Shroud was a fraud. However, subsequent research identified several surviving Pontius Pilate coins still in existence bearing that exact misspelling ('UCAI')."[96] Dr. Antonacci writes, "At least four Pilate coins currently exist that exhibit this misspelling."[97] Alan Whanger used his polarized image overlay technique on the image and the Pilate leptons and found 74 points of congruence. He concluded in the journal *Applied Optics*, "Using the forensic criteria for matching fingerprints, we feel that there is *overwhelming evidence* for the identification of the images and the matches with the coins."[98] Rare Pontius Pilate coins over the eyes of the man on the Shroud? Coins that only became visible in the 20th-century with the help of 3D-technology? Does this sound like the work of a medieval forger?

In 1983 a German physics teacher named Oswald Scheuermann identified faint flower images on the surface of the Shroud and wrote to Dr. Alan Whanger about his find. In 1985 Dr. Whanger also noticed a flower image above the top left of the man's head and for the next four years closely examined the Shroud for any other floral images, comparing them to a six-volume work on the botany of Israel. He ended up identifying 28 different species of plants that had their image imprinted on the Shroud—27 which grew in Jerusalem and one which grew at the south end of the

Dead Sea! Whanger did not publish his findings until confirming them with Avinoam Danin in 1995 and 1997. Danin was the Professor of Botany at Hebrew University in Jerusalem—one of the top authorities on flora in Israel. Danin confirmed Whangers findings and was even able to identify other species. What's more, when the images were compared with Max Frei's sticky tape examination of the Shroud's pollen from 1973, twenty-five of the pollen species matched the flower images that Whanger discovered on the Shroud! Was the Shroud of Jesus covered in 28+ flowers species after being laid in the tomb, along with the bunches of dried myrrh? How did the faint images of these flowers become imprinted in the Shroud? It is also necessary to note that one of the flower images, *Capparis aegyptia,* indicates that the flowers were picked around 3-4 PM. The exact time Christ died! On top of this, Danin stated that the amount of wilting that had occurred on the flowers indicated "their images were made probably between twenty-four and thirty-six hours after being picked."[99] If they were picked at 3-4 PM on Friday, this means the image was likely made early Sunday morning. Was there an event that happened early Sunday morning that could possibly have caused the flowers, coins, blood, and body image to be imprinted on the Shroud?

This brings us to *image-formation theories.* The existing theories can basically be split into three camps between those who think the image occurred as a natural process from a dead body, those who believe a forger was able to contrive a method to artistically imprint all the features of the Shroud, and finally those who believe some sort of light, radiation, or electric field emanating from the dead body was responsible. As of today, there are no credible hypotheses that fall into the first two categories that reasonably make sense of what has taken place in the Shroud or that can duplicate the image of the Shroud on another linen cloth. Many have tried, but all have woefully fallen short. That leaves us with the third option. As early as the 1930s, P. W. O'Gorman came up with a 'flash of heat and light' theory. The basic idea was that the resurrection of Christ was some sort of 'light phenomena' that would have preserved an imprint of the body on the Shroud. If this is true, the Shroud would not simply be a testimony to the Passion of Christ, but also a testimony to the Resurrection! In 1966, Geoffrey Ashe picked up on this idea and wrote, "The physical change of the body at the resurrection may have released a brief and violent burst of some radiation other than heat—perhaps scientifically identifiable, perhaps not—which scorched the cloth. In this case, the shroud is a quasi-photograph of Christ returning to life, produced by a kind of radiance or 'incandescence' partially analogous to heat in its effects."[100] In other words, as Christ came back from the realm of the dead with a burst of new creation light, He took a 'selfie.' Did Christ take the first photographic image, of the most important and powerful moment in human history, that would remain only in negative form until the age of scientific skepticism at the turn of the 20th century? What sort of 'radiance' could create such a 'selfie' of Christ? Scientists have proposed, and even replicated on a very small scale, that a brief flash of high intensity ultraviolet radiation can create rapid dehydration of the uppermost part of the fibrils leaving the yellowish image. But, for ultraviolet light to be able to create such a large image as the Shroud is, one would need the equivalent of 500,000 searchlights worth of energy emanating from the body for one forty-billionth of a second! Any longer, and the linen would be incinerated, any less energy and the image would not be formed. Did an explosive burst of new creation light take place in 'the blink of an eye' from every pore of Jesus' body in a similar way that light burst on the scene in Genesis 1:2? Was this light responsible for imprinting an image of the restful state of the body, covered in all the wounds it endured for our salvation, just before springing to life?

Another 'radiance' theory has to do with particle radiation. In 1989, a physicist named Thomas Phillips proposed that particle radiation had irradiated the Shroud. Dr. John Jackson then proposed something which became known as the 'Radiation Fall-Through Hypothesis.' In this theory, the body under the Shroud became volumetrically radiant and simultaneously mechanically transparent. As the body transformed in this way 'in the blink of an eye', the Shroud would have collapsed inward from both the top and bottom due to a 'vacuum effect.' The Shroud would have passed through the transparent body with the portions of the Shroud that were already resting against the body receiving greater radiation than the points of the cloth that did not begin with contact. The theorists claim this sort of event is able to account for the 3D-image, the perfect negative image, the skeletal features, the coin and flower images, the enduring red-colored blood, the unbroken blood clots, the straight-line vertical directionality of the image, the lack of fading, the straw-yellow coloration, the fibers colored at 360-degrees around the circumference, and many other features. In 2015, Dr. Antonacci endorsed this theory but added his own variation to it. Instead of vacuum ultraviolet light being the source of the image-formation, Antonacci suggested protons were primarily responsible. He wrote, "As the cloth fell through the radiant body region, the very penetrating neutrons, electrons and gamma rays would have passed completely through the cloth without encoding body images. However, the easily-absorbed protons would have evenly deposited their energy to produce a uniform straw-yellow coloration, but only on the topmost two or three fibers."[101] Dr. Antonacci has also proposed several tests that could be performed in the future to demonstrate whether his hypothesis is correct. Something our world could very well see take place in the coming years. William West writes, "After more than a century of trying to replicate the Shroud using human technology, the only hypothesis that can account for what we see on the Shroud is 'something science cannot explain'—radiation from a dead body."[102]

All of this information begs the question of how the men who led the 1988 Carbon-14 dating tests could have been so dismissive of the Shroud. In light of all of the Shroud's extremely unique characteristics that are incapable of being duplicated by any man or instrument in the world, how could they be so ardent and sarcastic in their public statements? One of the three men presenting the findings to the press, Professor E. Hall of Oxford, stated when asked for an explanation of how the Shroud came to be, "There was a multi-million-pound business in making forgeries during the fourteenth century. Someone just got a bit of linen, faked it up and flogged it." Does this sound like a reasonable, undetached, scientific explanation of the Shroud to you? Behind the three men stood a black board with "1260-1390!" written on it. Does that exclamation mark exude 'science', or something else?

While I won't discuss the various theories for the motivation of these men for denouncing the Shroud in such an unscientific manner and with such unscientific terms, what I will do is share the new data related to the reliability of the radiocarbon tests. Were the C-14 tests legit? Do they hold up to scrutiny? One would expect there to be *absolute transparency* of the *raw test data* for laboratories claiming to have conclusive evidence that the Shroud is medieval. Strangely, though scholars regularly requested access to the raw data as early as 1989, their requests were always rejected. It wasn't until 2017, under the legal demands of a FOIA request, that the three laboratories chosen to perform the C-14 tests finally released their raw data. This raw data has proved useful on many fronts. For one, it proved that Dr. Michael Tite and others committed scientific fraud through various statistical manipulations (see Stephen E. Jones work on this). The raw data also indicates the age of the cloth sample decreases steadily as it moves towards the center of the cloth. This information could be indicative of a whole host of things: greater contamination near the edge of the Shroud, less radiation near the edge of the Shroud, or more non-original linen material near the edge of the Shroud. Why was this sort of information not presented at the 1988 press conference? Why did it take a FOIA request 29 years later to reveal it?

Let's get back to the actual test itself. In 1984 STuRP proposed 26 new scientific tests they would like to see performed on the Shroud. One of the proposed tests was radiocarbon dating. In their proposal STuRP scientists recommended that three pieces be taken from the Shroud from three very different pre-analyzed locations on the linen and that a piece of the Holland backing cloth be taken as a 'control' sample. In 1986 archaeologist William Meachum gave a warning at an international symposium about how to date the Shroud. He said the most problematic area of the Shroud for radiocarbon dating was the area the 'Raes sample' was taken from in 1973. (Just as Max Frei was able to get sticky tape samples of the Shroud in 1973, so Gilbert Raes was able to get a small corner piece of the Shroud for examination.) Raes had found traces of cotton in his sample—something that was non-characteristic of the rest of the Shroud. It also was part of the Shroud that had ancient water stain, and was a corner of the Shroud that had been held up by hundreds of hands when the Shroud was on public display throughout its history—opening it to greater contamination. Meachum also agreed with the STuRP proposal of *at least three different locations* on the Shroud, and recommended that seven laboratories test the samples completely blind.

Did the British Museum, and overseers of the Shroud, heed the advice of STuRP and warnings of William Meachum? No. In fact, their sample choice was the worst possible choice that could have been made. They only took *one sample*, and they took it from the exact same place the Raes sample was from! A sample completely unrepresentative of the actual cloth that had many question marks already surrounding it! What's more, in 2010, more information about the sample was released by the head of the Arizona radiocarbon laboratory. He revealed that the "typical warp thread was 30 and for the average weft thread 40." This was the reverse of the warp and weft in the rest of the Shroud! He also reported that "the thickness of the Arizona sample was 250 micrometers (microns)."[103] The STuRP team's measurement of the Shroud's thickness was anywhere between 315-391 microns. Thus, the sample for the C-14 dating of the Shroud was quite a bit thinner than any other part of the Shroud and was not representative of the weave! This certainly should have raised a lot of questions. Unfortunately, no STuRP team members were allowed to participate in the the C-14 test, and this vital information was completely overlooked.

So, why did the C-14 test give the date it did? There are three main hypotheses. The first is that the sample was simply too contaminated, was not properly cleaned, and therefore it did not give a reliable date. The second hypothesis is that the part of the Shroud tested was not original, but was a piece of medieval cloth sewn onto the original. The third hypothesis is that a resurrection radiation event would have caused the Shroud to be radiated with neutrons in a way that would have increased C-14 in the cloth and given it a much younger date. All three hypotheses are possible, but let's look more at the second hypothesis, which seems to have the highest probability. In 2020 Joseph Marino wrote an 804-page book titled *The 1988 C-14 Dating of the Shroud of Turin*. He is a proponent of the second hypothesis and one of the key contributors to this hypothesis early on. For a much shorter synopsis of the reweave theory, one can read Marino's well written 13-page article "Compelling Data Indicating An Invisible Reweave in the C-14 Corner of the Turin Shroud" for free online at shroud.com.

Marino presents a very compelling case. He details the expert testimony of many people from 1988 up to the present day who believe this C-14 sample was in fact a sixteenth-century French reweave. This includes two STuRP chemists, Al Adler and Ray Rogers. In 1996 Adler stated, "You have no way of knowing if the area you took the C-14 sample represents the whole cloth. That's an area which has obviously been repaired." Rogers was not as quick to affirm such a theory and defended the C-14 tests until 2000, but in that year he was presented with new evidence that baffled him and caused him to completely change his stance. After reevaluating the 1973 Raes sample he was able to detect the presence of cotton, encrustation from madder root that was used as a dye, spliced fibers, and vanillin, all of which were not representative of the rest of the Shroud! Rogers also said he could see the sixteenth-century seam that other textile experts also testified they could see. After performing more tests on the Raes sample, Rogers published his peer-reviewed findings in *Thermochimica Acta*. He wrote, "Pyrolysis-mass-spectrometry results from the sample area coupled with microscopic and microchemical observations prove that the radiocarbon sample was not part of the original cloth of the Shroud of Turin."[104] A third STuRP team member, image specialist Barrie Schwartz, pointed to the 1978 ultraviolet fluorescence image showing a much darker color for the corner the Raes Sample—the same corner the radiocarbon sample were taken from. Ray Rogers and others had also been intrigued by the ultraviolet images as it again seemed to indicate different material. Schwartz concluded, "This is further convincing, supportive, scientific evidence that this area is inherently different in composition than the rest of the Shroud."[105] Marino concludes his article along the lines of these three STuRP members, and other textile experts that he sources. He writes, "I maintain that the C-14 sample area having been rewoven is possibly, and likely probably, the most plausible explanation of why the C-14 dating resulted in a medieval date."[106]

The radiocarbon test from 1988 has been proven to be highly suspect in its failure to follow prescribed protocol, in its secrecy, in the highly questionable sample that was taken, and in questions surrounding contamination or possible exposure to radiation. Could other tests besides radiocarbon be conducted to arrive at the age of the Shroud? The answer is, "yes." In fact, five other such tests have been performed on the Shroud since 1988. In 2005 Ray Rogers tested the age of the Shroud by its vanillin content. In his published findings in *Thermochimica Acta* he wrote, "A determination of the kinetics of vanillin loss suggests that the shroud is between 1300- and 3000-years old."[107] In 2014 three new dating test results were released. West writes, "experiments carried out over the past decade by Professor Giulio Fanti and colleagues at the University of Padua using three separate dating methods involving chemical and mechanical dating, established an average age between 33 BC +/- 250 years."[108] This included a Fourier transformed infrared spectroscopy test—based on the decay of enzymes in the cloth, a

Raman laser spectroscopy test, and a mechanical tension and compressibility test. Most recently, in 2022, a wide-angle x-ray scattering test performed by Liberato de Caro dated the Shroud between AD 55-74 (+/- 100 years with a 95% confidence level). Which tests are most reliable? The five tests pointing to a first-century date, or the one test using a highly questionable corner dating to the fourteenth-century?

Disregarding all evidence to the contrary, and for the sake of argument, let's assume the Shroud is a fourteenth-century forgery. In light of all the details discussed above what would a forger have needed to do to create the Shroud? First off, the forger would have needed to construct a loom that was large enough to produce an 8X2 cubit linen cloth—for medieval looms that large did not exist. They then would have needed to travel to Egypt to investigate the first-century ruins of a Roman fort and copy the similar herringbone weave—a weave that did not exist in medieval Europe. After that they would have needed tomb raid some of Masada's first-century tombs to find and copy the only side-stitch pattern similar to the Shroud's. After weaving this very Jewish first-century Shroud, preferably with linen threads that date to the first century that can fulfill the vanillin test by Rogers and stretching tests by Fanti, the forger would have needed to find a Semitic man with type AB blood. After beating this man with his fists and ripping out parts of his beard, the forger would have needed to reproduce old Roman weapons that medieval historians did not possess—like the Roman flagrum and lancea. After reproducing those weapons the forger would have needed to scourge the Semitic man, crown him with Jerusalem grown thorns that were also pounded into his head, forced him to carry a patibulum to create the shoulder abrasions, and then crucified him with nails going through his wrists against every artistic convention in Christian history up until his day. Also, only through this extreme torture could the forger produce the human blood with high contents of bilirubin needed for his forgery, as well as the anatomically perfect body image and blood flows necessary for his image.

After crucifying the man, the forger would then need to figure out the tricky part of creating the image. Would he simply wrap the man in his linen cloth? Or just use the blood and somehow transfer it to the cloth? Whatever the case, first he would need to sprinkle Jerusalem limestone from the same limestone shelf as the Church of the Holy Sepulchre and the Garden Tomb in Jerusalem where the nose, knee, and feet would be. Then he would need to position the blood over that limestone—including the anatomically perfect invisible serum halos. He would also need to make sure the blood positioned near the head matched the blood stains on the Sudarium of Oveido and that the arterial and venous blood stains were in the correct spots even though the difference between venous vs. arterial blood was not discovered until 1593. Only after the Jerusalem limestone and blood of a tortured man was positioned with absolute anatomic perfection could the forger then proceed to figure out how to get a perfect negative image, along with three-dimensional qualities, of the crucified man on the Shroud. The forger then would have needed to find Pontius Pilate leptons and uniquely etch them in a three-dimensional way over the eyes along with twenty-eight plus flora that only grow in Jerusalem and can only have been wilted for about thirty hours. Finally, the forger would have needed to sprinkle the shroud with pollen from many plants that are specific to Jerusalem, Edessa, and Constantinople. The forger also would have had to come to grips with the fact that the vast majority of the features he was creating would be completely undetectable to the public for the first five hundred and fifty years after his forgery was completed!

Lastly, in creating the Shroud, the forger would have needed to do what no other person in human history has been able to do. *Yes, no person has ever been able to duplicate the Shroud.* In fact, no one has been able to come close. It is unduplicable! In 2015 Dr. Antonacci wrote, "These full-length body images and blood marks are so unique they have never been duplicated in any era by any artist, scientist, physician or anyone utilizing any type of artistic, naturalistic or other method."[109] In 2022 the producer of *The Silent Witness* and his updated documentary *Who Can He Be?* offered the British Museum $1,000,000 if they could duplicate the Shroud. Of course, they turned him down, as they could not. To further investigate the Shroud in depth, for free, one can find many great articles at www.shroud.com as well as at www.theshroudofturin.blogspot.com. Many scientists have reached the conclusion that the Shroud is authentic beyond any reasonable doubt. Some would even include evidence for a resurrection event in that category. Summing up the thoughts of many, journalist William West writes, "the Shroud offers powerful evidence for the resurrection – evidence that is now so strong that it should convince any well-instructed jury, beyond a reasonable doubt, that the Shroud is authentic and also that the resurrection did, in fact, take place."[110]

Luke informs us that Jesus' resurrection was accompanied by "many infallible proofs" (Acts 1:3). Maybe, just maybe, Jesus has preserved this one last great "proof" for our skeptical age that is under the great plague of scientism, when the philosophical ungirding of society is perversely bent to prohibit belief in the cardinal doctrines of the Faith. Maybe, just maybe, Christ providentially preserved His burial clothes with a remarkably clear photographic and 3D-image woven into them as a way of reaching out to this skeptical generation in a similar way to how He reached out to His skeptical disciple Thomas (John 20:27). It is as if Christ is holding forth His nail-pierced hands, and lance-pierced side, to all the Thomases of the world, saying, "Will you take time to investigate these wounds?" Will the Thomases be open-minded to the rigor of scientific investigation done on this 2,000 year old linen cloth? To those who are open to this journey, it is quite possible they will become believers like many other skeptics who have poured over these wounds, and end up bowing the knee like Thomas declaring, "My Lord and my God!" (John 20:28)

Remarkably, some who saw the resurrected Christ right in front of them "doubted" (Matt. 28:17). Sight, and even physical evidence, *is not enough*. After Jesus told Thomas to physically examine Him, He still gave the exhortation, "Do not be unbelieving, but believe"

(John 20:27). The Passion and Resurrection of Christ are the deepest truths in human history, but unless we *place our faith* in those truths our lives will remain the same. To place your faith in the truth of the Passion and Resurrection means public confession that Jesus is your Lord and Savior. It means, like the twelve apostles, you will *follow* Him. It means you are no longer your own, for you have been *bought* at a price (1 Cor. 6:20). In fact, the Shroud is an itemized receipt of the world's redemption! It is a beautiful illustration of everything Jesus suffered for *your* eternal salvation! Whether one believes the Shroud to be genuine or not ultimately does not matter when it comes to salvation. But what does matter is that one places their faith in the Man the Shroud testifies to. The God-Man, Jesus. If you have opened your heart to this Gospel truth simply pray, "Father, thank you for sending Your Son to suffer and die for my sin. Thank you, Jesus, for rising again on the third day declaring my justification and Your eternal defeat of death. I believe You are Lord of all and ask You to send Your Spirit into my heart right now. Holy Spirit, thank you for shedding Your love abroad in my heart. Thank you for conforming me to the loving and holy character of Jesus. May I never be the same from this day forward. May I praise You and rejoice at Your marvelously loving redemption for all eternity. In Jesus Name, amen."

Appendix B
The Sacrificial Victim: Scripture's Master Theme

The power and glory of Christ's Passion cannot be fully appreciated by the hearts of men unless seen through the prism of God's revelatory Word. It is essential for one to accept what is presented as a given in the four Passion narratives—*the Old Testament is the interpretive key for understanding everything that happened from Gethsemane to Golgotha.* The Passion was not an unexpected intrusion in history. Rather, it was preached by God from the very beginning. Christ truly is "the Lamb slain from the foundation of the world" (Rev. 13:8). The Passion is an immutable truth in the heart of God that was played out in history in Jerusalem two-thousand years ago. The very moment Adam sinned, God, in accordance with His loving nature, purposed to come in flesh in the person of the Son to die on the cross so that His beloved image-bearers might be liberated from that very sin and its consequent death. The Bible helps us decode history as a great *love story*—an unfolding drama of a Divine Lover who directs history to climax in His own death upon a Roman cross in order to gain a bride. A bride that had previously been deformed by sin, but would become *reformed* and *resplendent* by the work of the Divine Lover on the cross!

The primary image of the cross in the Old Testament is *the sacrificial victim*, and the most prominent sacrificial victim is *the lamb*. The purpose of this appendix is to demonstrate how Jesus on the cross is the fulfillment of those Old Testament sacrificial victims. In fact, we will see how the Spirit designed Scripture in such a way that the Lamb would be its *centerpiece*. The focus will be upon the first four books of Scripture (with special emphasis on Leviticus), before moving to the prophets, and ultimately to the capstone, Revelation.

Genesis (The Sacrificial Victim In The Beginning)

"In the beginning God created the heavens and the earth" (Gen. 1:1). After fashioning the landscape of this world over six days, and furnishing it with beautiful trees, lights, and wondrous creatures, God brought about His crowning work at the end of Day Six. This crowning creature would be fashioned according to His very "image" and "likeness" (Gen. 1:26). After molding man from the dust of the ground, and breathing into him the breath of life, God proceeded to plant a special garden for him in a land called Eden (a place that means 'pleasure' or 'delight'). Eden was on a high plateau, as it pictured the intersection of heaven and earth, and out of this land flowed four crystal clear rivers that brought rejuvenation to the four corners of the earth. As God was fashioning this *special garden sanctuary* for Adam, we can imagine Adam observing God's wisdom and technique as a son observes a father—learning what it means to 'image' the Father in His world. After God finished arranging the garden in the eastern part of Eden, He "placed" Adam there (Gen. 2:8). Adam was right where God wanted him—in a sacred, structured, heavenized zone where God's special presence would be regularly encountered and enjoyed. A place from which Adam could set off on adventures to "take dominion" over the rest of the world—like Cush and Havilah—imaging God in garden planting assignments and establishing new society through multiplication. Likely gathering *gold* and *gem stones* to beautify society before returning to Eden for sabbath seasons.

Immediately after being placed in Eden Adam began to exercise his dominion by naming the animals God had made. Observing the animals, Adam would have learned a lot about himself. For God created the animals to serve as analogues to human life (Prov. 6:6; 1 Cor. 9:9; 1 Tim. 5:18). This is one reason why animals eventually would serve as *representatives* for man. One of the first lessons Adam would have learned through observation is that God's creatures came in complimentary pairs—male and female. Just like the animals, Adam was also created to be a compliment. And God desired to show the connectedness of man and his compliment at a far deeper level than that of the animals. For Adam's compliment would come by means of *sacrifice*. Adam would be put in a deep sleep by God, broken apart, and a 'sacrificial piece' of Adam's side would be used to craft the special creature designed just for him! This creature would be called "woman" for she was taken out of man. Indeed, taken from the place *next to his heart*. A most special creature *born from sacrifice*.

While man is the "glory of God", woman is "the glory of man" (1 Cor. 11:7). In essence she is *the glory of the glory*. The crown jewel of the crown of creation. The strong helper Adam needed to fulfill God's commission to multiply. Though Eve's beauty outshined Adam's, she was still under his authority. He had a duty to "guard" and "keep" her (Gen. 2:15). To love and teach her what God had taught him. Ultimately, he failed. While standing next to Eve, listening to her conversation with the serpent, he allowed her to be *deceived* and eat the fruit God commanded them not to eat (Gen. 3:6; 2 Cor. 11:3). He then high-handedly (deliberately and intentionally) sinned by eating the forbidden fruit himself. This disobedient act against the most basic instruction of their loving Father is commonly referred to as 'The Fall.' Humanity 'fell' from a state of innocence, purity, life, and sweet communion with God on His sanctuary mountaintop. By grasping for the fruit of "the tree of the knowledge of good and evil" before it was granted them, they received a sense of what judicial authority was like. They realized they were naked! Not just naked outwardly, but inwardly. In that moment shame creeped over their souls and overwhelmed them. Fear seized and terrorized their hearts. As God's special presence came strolling in the cool of the day, they ran for cover! Their consciences convicted them, and Adam knew what awaited them. He knew they deserved nothing but *death* (Gen. 2:17).

Though Adam and Eve *deserved* nothing but death, God did not come and smite them with a lightning bolt. Rather, He came preaching the Gospel! Preaching a way of restoration. He did this in two ways. First, through the spoken Word of the coming Seed. Second, through an act of sacrifice. God wanted His promise to be heard, seen, smelt, and felt. He wanted His loved fallen ones *fully saturated* in this promise. In fact, we will see later that God would also want the promise to *even be tasted*. The spoken promise has been called the *Proto-Evangelium* by Christians. Meaning, the First-Gospel. In the presence of Adam and Eve God spoke to the serpent, saying, "I will put enmity between you and the woman, and between your seed and her Seed; He shall bruise your head, and you shall bruise His heel" (Gen. 3:15). Imagine the jubilation that welled up in the hearts of the shame-saturated Adam and Eve as they stood there wearing fig leaves. Eve's seed would crush the serpent's head!? Death would be averted!? There would be an eventual *triumph* over their tragedy!? What a tremendous promise from God's own lips!

After hearing this Promise, and learning about the pain and toil that would result from their sin, "the LORD God made tunics of skin, and clothed them" (Gen. 3:21). In this act their nakedness was not simply covered in a way fig leaves could never cover them, but also a sense of *righteous rule* was restored. The 'tunic' was not some sort of crude caveman-like outfit, but rather a 'robe.' In fact, the next time we see the word used for 'tunic' here is for the 'robe' that Joseph receives from Jacob. After that the term doesn't appear again until the priestly garments that are talked about in Exodus and Leviticus. It is a robe of authority and priesthood. Adam and Eve could again take up the task of fulfilling the cultural mandate God had given them to have dominion over the world. The robe signified restored righteousness at the expense of *a sacrificial victim.*

Remember, these were robes of *skin*. How does one obtain skin? By skinning an animal. This always entails the animal's death. Genesis is showing us that *God enacted the first animal sacrifice.* God had told Adam he would die the day he ate the forbidden fruit (Gen. 2:17). While Adam did become dead in trespasses and sin that day, God in His great mercy and love provided a substitute to undergo the final wage of that sin—physical death. An innocent sacrificial victim took his place. *A picture of Jesus on the cross taking our place.* After being robed in the skin of that animal, Adam could come out from behind the shrubs unashamed. He was restored by God's *promise* and *provision*. Lastly, in an act of both justice and grace, God *expelled* Adam and Eve from the garden so that they would not partake of the tree of life: "He drove out the man; and He placed cherubim at the east of the garden of Eden, and a flaming sword which turned every way, to guard the way to the tree of life" (Gen. 3:24).

The very next verse jumps ahead one or two centuries into the future. It begins with a story about Adam and Eve's children presenting *sacrifices* to God. Why were they sacrificing? Well, seeing that God was positively responding to their sacrifices, it seems Adam and Eve had taught their children how to offer appropriate sacrifices growing up. Re-enacting the primal sacrifice that God had made in the garden. Many theologians have seen these sacrificial events as 'worship services' in the presence of God on the Sabbath. The idea is that the presider of the service (Adam, Cain, Abel, etc.) would have preached about the Seed of Eve who would crush the serpent's head—encouraging all of their family with that powerful principal promise. Accompanying the preaching, the officiator of the service would offer a sacrifice to God. By re-enacting the first sacrifice in the garden the worshippers would essentially confess that they deserved to die for their sin, and then place their faith in the sinless substitute that would be provided to take their place and die the death they deserved. God would meet them in this worship event, showing He was well-pleased with their humility and faith in His promise.

When Abel brought the best of the firstborn of his flock, Scripture tells us God "had regard for Abel" and his gift (Gen. 4:4). This "regard" must have been some sort of *visible/tangible* sign, for Abel experienced it whereas Cain did not. Some have suggested that God came and consumed the sacrifice by His divine fire. Possibly fire emanating from the fiery sword of the cherubim guarding the garden's gate, sort of like how divine fire consumed the sacrifices in the inaugural service of the tabernacle (Lev. 9:24), or how fire came down from heaven for Elijah's sacrifice (1 Kgs. 18:38). Describing what the worship service might have looked like, the sixteenth-century theologian, David Chytraeus, wrote, "When Abel saw that

the lamb had been consumed—indeed, by a fire divinely kindled—
he understood that it signified a different lamb, namely, the coming
Seed…When Abel offered the lamb that was consumed by
heavenly flames, he was admonished by this spectacle so that by
faith he applied the promised benefits of the messiah to himself. He
thus nourished and strengthened his faith."[111] The key takeaway
from this section of Scripture is that God was blessing faithful
'sacrificial worship' the early years after 'The Fall.'

One thing to also consider about this story is that Cain, Abel, and
likely most of the rest of humanity, were still living in the land of
Eden. Earlier I mentioned that the specific sacrificial service where
Abel was 'regarded' and Cain was 'rejected' is happening *one or two
centuries* after Adam's fall. How can we know this? Well, right after
Abel dies and Cain moves out of the land of Eden we are told,
"Adam knew his wife again, and she bore a son and named him
Seth, 'For God has appointed another seed for me instead of Abel,
whom Cain killed'" (Gen. 4:25). A few verses later we are told that
Adam was "one hundred and thirty years old" when Seth was born
(Gen. 5:3). The Septuagint, which very well might have the correct
chronology of the early chapters of Genesis preserved, says that
Adam was "two hundred and thirty years old."

I'm sure that after Adam was restored, and rehearsed the Gospel
promise, he joyfully obeyed God's first command—"be fruitful and
multiply" (Gen. 1:28). Jewish tradition says Adam and Eve had 56
kids. I imagine they had *at least* that many. If we assume a
conservative population growth under a non-contracepting society,
like the growth rate occurring in Somalia today, the population
after 130 years would have been over ten-thousand people. If it had
been 230 years, and it is adjusted for birth happening far later in
life (as Eve apparently has Seth when she is either 130 or 230 years
old), then there is even a possibility the population of the world was
up to one million people at this time. Remember, in 400 years
under less lengthy child-bearing timeframes, the children of
Abraham grew to a population of three million people. In his
magnum opus, *The City of God*, Augustine wrote concerning the first

230 years of history, "are we to understand that…during that long term of years over which one lifetime extended in those early days, there might not have been born very many men, by whose united numbers not one but several cities might have been built?"[112]

Cain and Abel, as the two eldest sons, would have presided over worship for their large families (children, grandchildren, great-grandchildren, great-great-grandchildren, etc.). After worshipping the Lord for decades, if not centuries, with the slain lamb just as Adam had taught him, Cain decided to *innovate*. He brought a grain/tribute offering. Now, this grain/tribute offering was not bad in and of itself. In fact, the second offering commanded by God in the book of Leviticus is a grain/tribute offering. But, what is important, is that the grain offering must always be given after a burnt/ascension offering. We see that is the case in Leviticus, Numbers 28, Joshua 22, and Judges 13. The reason the "burnt offering" was first is because it replicated God's primal offering which symbolized *the death of a substitutional representative in one's place* —also signifying dying to self so that you could rise in new life and communion with God. *Only on the basis of that foundational sacrifice could other faithful worship occur.* Thus, to bring the best lamb first was to come in faith. That is how the book of Hebrews tells the story of Cain and Abel (Heb. 11:4). To bring the sacrificial victim meant you were approaching God the way He designed and desired, "by faith." While Abel's offering is not specifically called a burnt/ascension offering, and also has the idea of "tribute" attached to it, it is likely because Abel offered the tribute on top of the best lamb.

Why would Cain innovate? We aren't told. The only thing we know is that *his innovation demonstrated a loss of faith.* Maybe he didn't like the idea of having to go to Abel for blemishless sacrifices. Maybe over time he thought that the work of his own hands should be more highly respected and was good enough. Maybe he thought his congregation would have thought Abel was better because he raised the sacrifices they needed for worship. Whatever contributed to Cain's loss of faith, he came up with a doctrine that God would respect his own work. But, though he jumps through all the intellectual hoops in his mind, and thinks God will respect his new form of worship, God doesn't. This must have been a deeply *humiliating* experience for Cain. Abel's worship centered around the *slain lamb*, and it was blessed. Cain's worship centered around the *fruit of his own labor*, and it was not blessed. It was *unacceptable* in the eyes of God—like the fig leaves Adam and Eve tried to use before God instituted the slain lamb (Gen. 3:7). When Cain saw God accept the worship Abel offered, but not the worship he offered, he began to *boil* on the inside. His ego had suffered a major blow.

Though God did not accept Cain's sacrifice, He did graciously offer restoration and a way forward. He greatly desired to see Cain worship in faith again. He said to Cain, "Why are you angry? And why has your countenance fallen? If you do well, will you not be accepted? And if you do not do well, sin lies at the door. And its desire is for you, but you should rule over it" (Gen. 4:6-7). The way this verse is taught by most people today is that if you do something bad, sin is at 'the door of your heart' ready to overcome you. That sin is crouching like a demon ready to pounce on you and put you in a strangle hold. Is this what God was saying? Was God instructing Cain to master sinful impulses that wanted to overpower him? Does this interpretation make the best sense of the context of what had just happened at the sacrificial service?

I don't think so. In *The City of God* Augustine says of verse 7, "the obscurity of the passage has given rise to many interpretations, as each commentator on Divine Scripture has tried to explain it according to the rule of faith."[113] The reason there are so many interpretations is because a few of the words in this text can be translated in significantly different ways. For instance, the Hebrew word, חַטָּאת, can be translated as either "sin" or "sin-offering." While most of the time the context *clearly* indicates which translation is demanded, Genesis 4:7 is debated. Many prominent scholars throughout church history have felt "sin offering" is the best translation. This includes Adam Clark, Adoniram Judson, Matthew Henry, and the Young's Literal Translation. Michael Morales, who is one of the leading scholars in the world today on the book of Leviticus, translates the verse like this, "If you do well will not [your countenance] be lifted? If you do not do well, at the door a sin offering is lying down."[114]

In the Morales translation the 'sin offering' is "lying down" at the door rather than "crouching" like in many other translations. The Hebrew word, רֹבֵץ, is used thirty times in Scripture. The other twenty-nine uses are translated as "lie down", "rest", or "sitting." A sin offering, like a lamb, obviously "lies down" in pastures just like the Good Shepherd makes us "lie down" (רֹבֵץ). Yet, because many translators want to see the concept of sin personified here, they adopt the awkward translation "crouch." Another thing to note is that the sin offering is lying *at the door*. The translations that say 'sin is crouching' must interpret 'the door' metaphorically. But those who do not take anything God is saying here metaphorically can easily see that God is simply saying a sin offering (like a lamb or goat) is lying down at the only door we know of. The door to the garden of Eden. Remember, man is offering their sacrifices in the land of Eden. It would make sense that the offerings were brought as close to God's sanctuary domain as they could get. Right to the door. In this sense God would be saying something like, "If you do not do well [i.e., you've approached me sinfully and not in faith], there is a sin offering lying down for you at the door. Its desire is for you and you must make use of him."

Throughout the rest of the Old Testament the Israelites were commanded to bring their sin-offerings to "the door" of the tabernacle (Lev. 1:3). The tabernacle was constructed from the divine blueprint that was given to Moses at the top of Mount Sinai. It symbolically represented God's sanctuary replanted among them —the garden of Eden. To enter the tabernacle was to enter the garden. And there was *only one door* the worshiper could enter—the door at the east end—just like the gate of Eden was at the east of the garden.

For God to provide Cain with a 'sin offering' at 'the door' of His garden sanctuary meant He still desired to have fellowship with

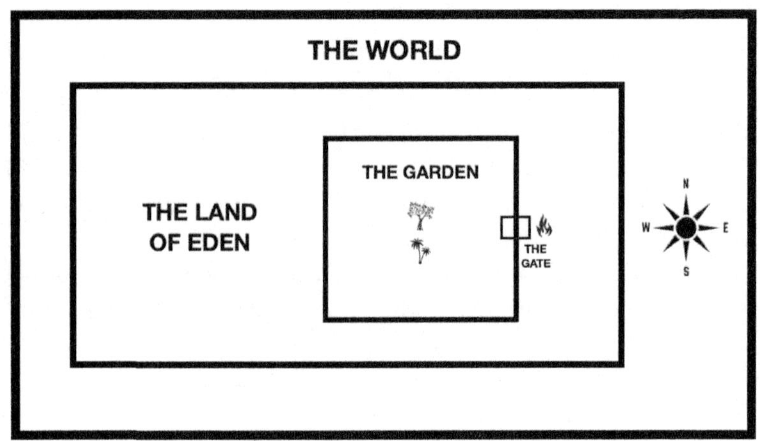

Man's first dwelling place according to Genesis 1-4

him, even after he sinned! At least four of the five offerings God commanded to be offered at the tabernacle in Leviticus were in practice before the time of the tabernacle (ascension, tribute, peace, and sin). Cain skipped the first sacrifice which *undergirded the rest*— the burnt/ascension offering. Because he sinfully jumped straight to the tribute offering, God graciously presented him with the fourth offering in Leviticus—the "sin offering." According to Leviticus 9 this offering, when needed, is presented *before* the ascension offering. God is essentially saying, "Cain! Why has your countenance fallen? Lift your eyes up. Behold, even though you have sinned there is a sin-offering lying down and waiting for you at the door. It desires to be *your* sin-offering. It desires to take the punishment for *your* sin. So lift up your countenance, take hold of the offering, and begin to worship properly again. Then I will regard your worship."

Would Cain "rule over" this sin offering that had "desire" for him? Would he grab hold of this gracious provision, lean his hand upon its head in recognition that he deserved to die, slit its throat, publicly humble himself, and offer it upon the altar? By showing Cain the sin offering that desired him, God was giving Cain a way out of the temptation he had to kill Abel. God always provides us a way of escape (1 Cor. 10:13). He always has an answer for us to nip sin in the bud so it doesn't grow into something bigger. And the way God does this is by showing us His provision of a sin offering. His provision of the cross. He has always wanted us to "behold the Lamb of God who takes away the sin of the world." And when we do sin, like Cain, He wants us to lift up our countenance, grab hold of Jesus, and not push our sin and frustration off on our brothers!

The sin offering's *desire* was for Cain. The Hebrew word desire, תְּשׁוּקָתוֹ, is only used three times in the Bible. It is first used of Eve's desire for Adam, and later of Jesus' desire for His bride in the Song of Songs. In other words, the other two uses of this word have to do with the loving desire of a spouse. God tells Cain that this is the type of desire the sin offering has for him, the sinner. He is painting a picture of Christ's great love and desire for us even in the midst of our sin! Let's look at the passage in the Song of Songs. The bride sings, "I am my beloved's, and his desire is toward me" (Song 7:10). Jesus' desire is toward His bride. While it took the bride a long time in the Song to come to this realization, once she did it changed everything! From that moment on she was prepared to go back into ministry again (Song 7:11). She was ready to be a worker in the vineyard again. To be used by Him. This was the same invitation God gave to Cain. He wanted Cain to continue to be one of His workers in the vineyard. To continue to offer sacrifices and worship Him.

What we've seen is that the first mention of the word 'sin' in the Bible (חַטָּאת) is actually about *the solution to sin*. It is about the *sin offering*. The mention of sin offering comes before the mention of sin. For Jesus is "the Lamb slain from the foundation of the world" (Rev. 13:8). *The provision for humanity's sin has always been accessible from the beginning.* The desire of the Crucified One has never ceased abounding toward man from the moment we fell. God "desires all men to be saved and to come to the knowledge of the truth" (1 Tim. 2:4). The only question is whether men will make use of the provision He has so graciously given. We simply are called to identify with the Gift by faith and trust in the Promised Seed. My own very loose and expanded paraphrase of Genesis 4:6-7 goes like this, "Yahweh said to Cain, 'Why are you upset? And why is your face downcast? You know that if you had offered by faith in the way I had taught you, you would have been accepted. Well, there is still good news for you. Though you have not done well, and have not offered the burnt offering as proper worship, there is a sin offering that is lying down at the garden gate. It desires to be *your* sin offering. It desires to cover *your* sin. So go ahead and make use of it! Lift up your face, see your salvation, move on from your shame, and get back to worshipping properly again!"

The next time in Genesis the sacrificial victim comes into view is in the story of Noah. After fifteen-hundred years the way of faithless Cain had gained ascendency and multiplied on the earth. In view of this decent into wickedness, and the continuous evil intent of man's heart, God decided to purge the earth with His heavenly waters. "But Noah found grace in the eyes of the LORD" (Gen. 6:8). Noah would be shown how to escape the judgment, and he *believed*. The next hundred years Noah was a "preacher of righteousness" as he built the ark for all the world to see (2 Pet. 2:5). He proclaimed that life could only continue for the world if they chose to shelter themselves in the wood of the ark. *The ark is a picture of the cross. The vessel that translates those who come to it in faith from the old creation to the new creation.* What Noah experienced in that ark was nothing short of a new birth. In fact, a careful study of the flood chronology shows that Noah dwelled in the ark for nine months. Noah came out of that ark reborn into newness of life! Ultimately only Noah and his family would *believe, enter the ark,* and *be translated* into the new world. Eight people in all—*the number of new creation.*

What did this new creation people do upon exiting the ark in the new world? They established faithful worship on the basis of *the sacrificial victim.* Moses states, "Then Noah built an altar to the LORD, and took of every clean animal and of every clean bird, and offered burnt offerings on the altar. And the LORD smelled a soothing aroma. Then the LORD said in His heart, 'I will never again curse the ground for man's sake, although the imagination of man's heart is evil from his youth; nor will I again destroy every living thing as I have done'" (Gen. 8:20-21). Note here how God's wrath against sin was not abated by the waters of destruction, but only by the slain sacrificial victim. After smelling the sweet aroma (a picture of Christ as the sinless substitute and fully consecrated man) God gave a sign of peace to the new creation world. He told Noah, "I have set my bow in the cloud, and it shall be a sign of the covenant between me and the earth. When I bring clouds over the earth and the bow is seen in the clouds, I will remember my covenant that is between me and you and every living creature of all flesh. And the waters shall never again become a flood to destroy all flesh. When the bow is in the clouds, I will see it and remember the everlasting covenant between God and every living creature of all flesh that is on the earth" (Gen. 9:13-16, ESV).

God set His "bow" in the clouds. He hung it up on the armory of heaven. In fact, when we see it in the sky it appears like it is *in the firmament* (the barrier between heaven and earth). Every time the rain came God was reminded of His covenant, and man was too. On top of that, man would see that God's bow was not pointed toward them on earth, but rather toward God in heaven. *It is a sign that God would ultimately take the future judgment in order to usher man into new creation life.* Most of the rainbows man sees have the drawstring resting on the earth. Why? Because man would pull that string. We would kill the Man from Heaven, the Author of Life (John 6:38; Acts 3:15). Instead of rain, blood flowed. The One that was slain was a willing victim. A willing burnt offering. He allowed wicked men to kill Him. Instead of liquid judgment falling from the heavens in the form of torrential rain, we had liquid life that would fall in the form of blood. This too is pictured in the rainbow. For the topmost color is red. That rain would first fall as red, then filter through the fiery orange and yellow as the divine alchemy of the love of God reached out to man in the tender touch of indigo and violet. The Sacrificial Victim who sits enthroned in Heaven has this rainbow around His head (Rev. 10:1). He sees man through the covenant He has made with His own blood!

In the story of Abraham we see the sacrificial victim play a prominent role twice. The first time is when God cut a covenant with Abram in Genesis 15. In this chapter the "Word of Yahweh" comes to Abram in a vision (Gen. 15:1). This seems to be a hint that we are to see Yahweh's Word, the Second person of the Trinity, as the primary Actor in this covenant. In this vision the Word takes Abram outside and has him "count", or probably better translated "tell", the stars (Gen. 15:5). Meaning, He wants Abram to gaze at the prophetic significance of the constellations that God had designed as a pictorial prophecy of redemption for the world (Job 38:32; Ps. 19:1).[115] The Word then tells Abram that his seed (singular) would be like that. Meaning, the Seed would be the One who fulfilled the heavenly prophetic redemptive picture—the Seed God promised Eve who would crush the serpent's head. In that moment Abram believed the Word of Yahweh, and Yahweh counted it to him as righteousness (Gen. 15:6). Pure, simple faith. In order to demonstrate to Abram that His promise would come about through His own grace, the Word told Abram to bring five *sacrificial victims*. After Abram put them to death and divided the victims that were mammals, the Word put him into a "deep sleep" (Gen. 15:12). For the covenant would not be fulfilled by Abram, but by the Word of Yahweh on his behalf. Abram would simply *believe* and be at *rest*. As the darkness settled on the land signifying a new day, "behold, a smoking fire pot and a flaming torch passed between these pieces" (Gen. 15:17). Smoke and fire are symbols of the Divine Presence. He is the pillar of cloud by day and fire by night, and on Mount Sinai He comes down in a billow of smoke and fire. *By the act of walking through the slain 'sacrificial victims' God was swearing by Himself that He would fulfill the promise He had just made to Abram.* The promise would not be dependent on man. Man is simply called to believe it, like Abram (Rom. 4). But God Himself would make the bloody walk *alone* to secure an unbreakable covenant!

The second time we see the sacrificial victim in the story of Abraham is in the substitution of Isaac in Genesis 22. God says to Abraham, "Take now your son, your only son Isaac, whom you love, and go to the land of Moriah, and offer him there as a burnt offering on one of the mountains of which I shall tell you" (Gen. 22:2). This, of course, was only a test. For *three days* Isaac was as good as dead in Abraham's eyes (Gen. 22:4). Yet, though Isaac was good as dead, Abraham also had faith that he would be raised from the dead. For he told his servant, "we will come back to you" (Gen. 22:5). He concluded "that God was able to raise him up, even from the dead, from which he also received him in a figurative sense" (Heb. 11:19). A strong young man by this time, Isaac carried the wood for the burnt offering on his own back, just like Christ carried the cross (Gen. 22:6). Ultimately, God stopped Abraham's hand from slaying Isaac (Gen. 22:12). His purpose in having Abraham go through the extreme trial of offering up his "only son" whom "he loved" was solely to give man a picture of what He would one day do as our loving Father (Gen. 22:14). The Father would give the "only begotten Son" as a burnt offering for the world (John 3:16). He would give Him on Mount Moriah. While a ram was the substitute victim for Isaac, two-thousand years later, a lamb was given for the substitution of the world! (Gen. 22:13; John 1:29) The Greater Isaac would truly be *the sacrificial victim*.

The last story I will mention from Genesis is the story of Jacob. Jacob's name was later changed to Israel. In many ways he represents the people of God. God had spoken to Jacob's mother while he was still in her womb that his older twin brother, Esau, would serve him (Gen. 25:23). This theme of divine reversal is prominent throughout the entirety of Genesis. Yet, though God had made it clear Jacob was to receive the blessing, Jacob's father rebelled against God's plan. He wanted to give the blessing to Esau! So, in order to make sure Jacob received the blessing that was promised him, his mother righteously hatched a plan to see Jacob receive the blessing. This plan was based around the blessing coming through the means of Esau's robes and a slain goat. We are told that while Esau was off hunting, "Rebekah took the choice clothes of her elder son Esau, which were with her in the house, and put them on Jacob her younger son. And she put the skins of the kids of the goats on his hands and on the smooth part of his neck" (Gen. 27:15-16). This was *enough* for Jacob to pass as Esau before his aging father and receive the blessing that God said would be his. Isaac felt the goat skin and believed Jacob to be Esau. He smelled the clothes and believed Jacob to be Esau. In a similar manner we are accepted by the Heavenly Father when we are clothed in Christ Jesus! Unlike Isaac though, the Father *wants* us to receive the blessing. He *wants* to see that we have accepted the clothing and sacrificial covering of Christ, and come to Him in faith. Paul says, "For all of you who were baptized into Christ have clothed yourselves with Christ" (Gal. 3:27).

Exodus (The Sacrificial Victim as our Deliverance)

The book of Genesis ends with Joseph lying in an Egyptian tomb. While it began with the fulness of life in the garden, it ends with death in the land of Israel's oppressor, Egypt. If Genesis is a story about "paradise lost", Exodus and Leviticus is a story about "paradise regained", at least, *partially.* The three primary events in Exodus are the deliverance from Egypt, the receiving of the law at Sinai, and the construction of the tabernacle at the base of Sinai. In all three of these events *the sacrificial victim* takes a prominent role. That role being to move Israel from a place of slavery and death into freedom and life with God!

The sacrificial victim first takes center stage in the story of the Passover. In a final act to deliver His people from Egypt, God called on the head of each household to take a male blemishless lamb or goat that would take care of the entire family (Ex. 12:3-5). Next, all of these sacrificial victims were slain at twilight. The family then bunched hyssop plants together to use like a paintbrush, dipped that hyssop in a basin where they had gathered the lamb's/goat's blood, and spread the blood across the sides and top of their doorframe. They then roasted the lamb/goat, and entered the house to eat the lamb/goat alongside unleavened bread and bitter herbs. At midnight, as God went through the land of Egypt bringing His last great judgment, He told His people, "when I see the blood, I will pass over you; and the plague shall not be on you to destroy you when I strike the land of Egypt" (Ex. 12:13). *The blood, which is the life/soul of an animal/person, had taken their place. Because they identified with their substitute, death "passed over" them.* This festival was to be kept every year as a memorial, though with slight modifications. For instance, instead of killing the lamb at their homes they would kill it at God's home. And instead of painting their own doorposts with blood, the blood would be splashed at the base of the altar in God's home (Deut. 16:5-6). God was their Father. So once He had His home constructed among His family, in a sense, they all dwelled in His House. *By the observance of this annual festival God's people were trained to understand that their deliverance from death and the enemy came solely by the means of a blemishless 'sacrificial victim.'*

The end goal of the Passover, and being led through the Red Sea into freedom, was that Israel might "serve" God (Ex. 3:12). Israel was redeemed so that they might become a "kingdom of priests" (Ex. 19:6). They were redeemed to love their neighbor in the same way God had loved them. (See Deuteronomy.) So, after leading His idolatrous people out of Egypt (Josh. 24:14), God sought to see their reformation. One way this would happen was by making a covenant with them in a similar way that a husband and wife make a covenant. One of the problems of course is that God is all-Holy and all-Good, and His people are fallen and wayward. So, when God speaks His ten words from the summit of Mt. Sinai, His people fled in terror! They "stood afar off", and only "Moses drew near the thick darkness where God was" (Ex. 20:21). What could possibly bridge this divide? Only one thing. *The sacrificial victim.* In the very next verse God tells the people how they could draw near. He says, "An altar of earth you shall make for Me, and you shall sacrifice on it your burnt offerings and your peace offerings, your sheep and your oxen. In every place where I record My name I will come to you, and I will bless you" (Ex. 20:24). *The solution for the people to draw near was for the blood of 'the sacrificial victim' to be shed and offered upon the altar.* Immediately after God gave the people the book of the covenant (Ex. 21-23), Israel "offered burnt offerings and sacrificed peace offerings of oxen to the LORD" (Ex. 24:5). Half of the blood was sprinkled on the altar and half was sprinkled on the people. After that, instead of being at a distance, the representatives of Israel drew near! The *blood* had brought about *peace* and seventy elders went halfway up the mountain where "they saw God, and they ate and drank" (Ex. 24:11). What a remarkable contrast with Exodus 19! All because of the blood of *the sacrificial victim.*

The final section of Exodus is largely about God's desire to give the experience He gave to the seventy elders to everyone. He wanted *all* Israel to be able to draw "near" to Him and "eat and drink." So, almost the entirety of the final sixteen chapters concerns the construction of His House. A House which was a large portable tent that mirrored Mount Sinai. In the words of James B. Jordan, "the Tabernacle (and later the Temple), were models of the ladder to heaven, of the holy mountain. Israel did not need to go back to Mount Sinai, or regard it as anything special, after the Tabernacle was built. The Tabernacle was God's portable mountain."[116] At the base of Mount Sinai there was a boundary/fence so that no one could touch the foot of the mountain or approach it (Ex. 19:12). Moses "built an altar at the foot of the mountain" (right at the fence/door to God's abode) and this is where the ascension and peace offerings were offered (Ex. 24:4-5). In a similar manner God told Moses "you shall set the altar of the burnt offering before the door of the tabernacle of the tent of meeting" (Ex. 40:6). The second zone of Mount Sinai was the zone the seventy elders entered along with Moses, Aaron, and Aaron's two eldest sons partway up the mountain. Though they "saw God", their vision was somewhat obscured in that they only saw His "feet" as they looked up through the blue firmament heavens at His throne (Ex. 24:11). A partial vision. This second zone on Sinai corresponds to the Holy Place in the tabernacle which could only be accessed by the priesthood (the representatives of Israel, just as the 70 elders represented Israel). It is in the Holy Place that the priests would eat the bread of the presence every Sabbath (Lev. 24:8-9). The third zone of Mount Sinai was the top portion that was covered in a cloud and consuming fire. Only Moses was allowed to enter that zone of God's Mountain (Ex. 24:12-18). This, of course, corresponds to the Holy of Holies in the tabernacle which could only be accessed once a year by the high priest. Just as the elders only saw God partially, this is also the case with Moses. Though Moses would speak "face to face" with God "as a man speaks to a friend", we are not told He *saw* God's face. God's face was right in front of Moses, but it was veiled. For no one can see the face of God and live (Ex. 33:20). On Mount Sinai Moses was in the midst of the cloud, obscuring a full vision of God. In the tent of meeting God was in a pillar of cloud (Ex. 33:9). Before the high priest would go into the holy of holies on the Day of Atonement he would first burn two handfuls of sweet incense so a cloud would cover the mercy seat on which God was enthroned (Lev. 16:12-13). Though face to face with God as he presented the blood, he also was *shielded from seeing His face.*

Instruction on how to build this 'portable mountain' was given by God in seven speeches (Ex. 25-31). Each speech mirrors the seven days of creation—the final speech being about Sabbath. (See End Note 54.) In essence, the tabernacle was a miniature cosmos, a replanted Eden, where God could come and dwell with His people as the tabernacle and people were continuously purified of sin and uncleanliness by sacrificial victims. When David asks, "LORD, who may abide in Your tabernacle? Who may dwell in Your holy hill?" (Ps. 15:1), we see a parallelism between God's tabernacle and His holy hill. Meaning, they are one and the same. Well, after this new and unique portable holy mountain was set up by God's people according to His divine blueprint, an unprecedented event took place: "Then the cloud covered the tabernacle of meeting, and the glory of the LORD filled the tabernacle. And Moses was not able to enter the tabernacle of meeting, because the cloud rested above it, and the glory of the LORD filled the tabernacle" (Ex. 40:34-35). God moved into His House! For the first time in millennia, God came to dwell with man in the unique and special way He had dwelled with them in the beginning! But there was one big problem. Moses "was not able to enter." Talk about an anticlimax to the book of Exodus. God finally comes down in His Edenic Home, and nobody, not even Moses, could enter! Would there be a solution? Could 'paradise lost' actually become 'paradise regained'? How? In what way could Moses and God's people *enter* His house? In what way could they behold the beauty of the LORD and experience the fullness of joy and pleasures forevermore? Only one way. *The sacrificial victim.* This brings us to, Leviticus.

Leviticus (The Sacrificial Victim as Re-entrance to Eden)

Leviticus sits in the central position of the five books of Moses. As the entirety of Leviticus takes place at Mount Sinai, it is also the center of Israel's wilderness wanderings "with six stations between Egypt and Sinai, and six stations following Sinai to the plains of Moab."[117] Being the Sabbath station in Israel's journey, it makes sense why God essentially has a honeymoon season with Israel here for a year (Deut. 24:5). No wars, no journeys, just God dropping honey wafers in their mouths each morning, shading them with His cloud in the day, warming them with His fire by night, and inviting them to come feast and spend time with Him in the courtyard of His tabernacle.

While many Christians tend to get stuck in the book of Leviticus because of all the sacrificial instruction and at times difficult to understand holiness code, Leviticus in many ways is *the height of the Gospel* in the Old Testament. God is the primary actor. In fact, Leviticus is composed almost entirely of speeches from God—thirty-seven speeches to be exact. The central speech, the nineteenth, is a speech God gives concerning the Day of Atonement (Lev. 16). A Day which has to do with God purging His people and His household from sin. Leviticus can also be divided according to its law/narrative sections. Which breaks down like this: law-narrative-law-narrative-law-narrative-law. The Day of Atonement is not simply the central speech of the book, it is also the central narrative. Ancient writers also organized their works using a literary device called a chiasm (a sequence of ideas/themes

218

presented and then repeated in reverse order). Most scholars of Leviticus see it chiastically structured around the Day of Atonement. *Thus, the center of the central book of Moses is about the Sacrificial Victim who takes away the sin of the world! Leviticus is really God preaching in thirty-seven speeches, with the central speech being the height of Gospel proclamation!* This becomes even more clear if we opt to use the title the Hebrews use. Though most Christian Bibles call this book Leviticus because it has to do with the priests from the tribe of Levi, the Hebrews call it by the first word that appears in the book —וַיִּקְרָא. (Vayikra). This word simply means, "And He called." It is a book about Divine Speech at Mount Sinai. *Divine speech about the most important subject of all—how God's people could be delivered from sin and uncleanliness and brought into loving fellowship with Him.*

God's desire for fellowship is stated beautifully at the end of Leviticus. He says, "I will set My tabernacle among you, and My soul shall not abhor you. I will walk among you and be your God, and you shall be My people" (Lev. 26:11-12). This brings us back to Genesis 2 where God walked with Adam in the cool of the day. The tabernacle is God's ancient mountain repositioned among His people. God would live with His people, love His people, and walk among His people. This happens at an even deeper level in the church. *For after declaring that the church is the temple of God, Paul then quotes this verse from Leviticus as a core reality for Christians (2 Cor. 6:16).* Thinking of the glories of God's palace that has garden imagery, heavenly creatures, sweet-smelling incense, golden architecture, royal purple curtains, and most importantly the palpable presence of God, David sings, "One thing I have desired of the LORD, that will I seek: That I may dwell in the house of the LORD all the days of my life, to behold the beauty of the LORD, and to inquire in His temple. For in the time of trouble He shall hide me in His pavilion; in the secret place of His tabernacle He shall hide me" (Ps. 27:4-5). *There was no better place for the Israelite to be than God's Home.* At the beginning of Leviticus Moses is outside the gates of God's beautiful palace. No one, not even Moses, could presumptuously approach the King. So, the first nine chapters of Leviticus give guidelines on *how* one could come into God's Home. Only after digesting the meaning of the five different offerings, and the role of the priesthood, could Moses and Aaron dare to approach this new Edenic garden in their midst. And all five of these sacrifices pointed toward Jesus, of course! This is why Jesus said, "I am the Way, the Truth, and the Life. No one comes to the Father except through Me" (John 14:6). *There is no other way into the Father's House. One can't innovate like Cain, or the builders at Babel, or Nadab and Abihu. There is only way into God's House—through the sacrificial victims that picture Jesus!*

The first offering God describes in detail to Moses is usually called *the burnt offering* (Lev. 1:1-17). This offering in its entirety is burnt on the bronze altar and turned into smoke. Many scholars believe a better translation of this sacrifice is *ascension offering*, for the Hebrew word literally means "that which ascends."[118] "Ascension" makes even more sense when we visualize the scene at the tabernacle. The last verse of Exodus states, "the cloud of the LORD was above the tabernacle by day, and fire was over it by night, in the sight of all the house of Israel, throughout all their journeys" (Ex. 40:38). The offering was not *obliterated*. Rather, it ascended into the glory cloud of God. In the words of Hicks, it was "transformed, sublimated, etherealized, so that it can ascend in smoke to the heaven above."[119] This pictured a full return to God's Presence by means of a *sacrificial victim representative.*

The Hebrews that had flocks or herds would bring one of their best specimens for this offering. Either an unblemished bull (especially if they were leaders) or an unblemished ram or male goat. For something to be "unblemished" simply means that it lacked defects such as being injured, castrated, blind, or having any open sores or abnormal growths (Lev. 22:17-25). For it to be male meant it was costly as most herds only had one bull for all the cows and most flocks were led by a ram or male goat. As the head of the herd or the flock, the male stood as the *representative head* for them. The fact that these were all domesticated animals, cared for by the owner from their birth, also stressed one's connection to the animal and the fact it had many analogies to their own life. Also, domesticated animals are raised *to give their life as a benefit to others*. Kellog observes, "The carnivora are all excluded; for these, which live by the death of others, could never typify Him who should come to give life."[120] If one was poor, and they did not possess herds or flocks, they were permitted to offer a turtledove or young pigeon (Lev. 1:14). These were two kinds of domesticated doves that were abundant during the time of the Old Testament (Is. 60:8).

The sacrificial victim was to be offered "at the door of the tabernacle of meeting" where the offerer would "put his hand on the head" of the victim and it would be "accepted on his behalf to make atonement for him" (Lev. 1:3-4). The idea is that the Israelite would have to publicly walk through the various tribes, and then through the priestly camps, to the east gate with his offering. Like with the purification offering, he was making a *public pronouncement* before men of his need for atonement. Something Christians are called to do when they place their faith in Christ and His work on the cross (Matt. 10:32; Rom. 10:9). At the entrance they *put their hand on the head* of the animal. The Hebrew word conveys the idea of a 'pressing' or 'heavy leaning' of one's weight on the animal. The concept presented is that of *transfer* and *identification*. We see *transfer of authority or Spirit* with 'hand laying' in the stories of Moses and Joshua (Num. 27:18) and Peter and the Samaritans (Acts 8:17). We see *transfer of identity* when the Israelites lay their hands on the Levites as stand-ins for all the firstborn males of Israel (Num. 8:10, 16). The hand leaning ritual pictures *vicarious substitution.*

After the public confession and substitution ritual, the offerer proceeded to kill the sacrificial victim before the LORD (Lev. 1:6). In the case of the ram or the male goat, which was what was offered by most Israelites, this would happen on the north side of the altar (Lev. 1:11). (The north is the direction from which the enemy comes in Scripture. The victim dies to shield the offerer from the enemy. This is another reason why the table of showbread was on the north side of the Holy Place. It was the table set *in the presence of their enemy.* [Ps. 23:5]) By killing the victim the offerer was demonstrating that they deserved to die but that a blemishless vicarious substitute was taking their place. By actually slitting the throat of the animal they were showing how their own sins contributed to the death of their Savior. They were responsible! After draining the blood and giving it to the priests who would sprinkle it around the altar, the offerer would then skin and cut the animal into pieces. The first pieces they would hand to the priest to put on the altar were the head and the fat. The head was turned into smoke first because it represented the whole of the animal and was specifically what the offerer had leaned his weight upon. The fat was offered next because that was considered the best part of the animal, and it was always given as a portion to God even in the offerings where the offerer or priests were able to eat some of the sacrifice. God deserves the very best, like Abel gave. After that, the rest of the entrails that had been washed of all dirt and excreta, so there would be no curse prosecution against the animal, were laid on the altar and turned into smoke. Thus, *the entirety of the animal ascended into the glory cloud*, with the exception of the skin, which was given to the priests.

This offering was so important to God that it was performed every morning and evening (Ex. 29:38-39). Those who brought personal ascension offerings would offer them after the communal daily ascension offering. 'On top of it,' so to speak. These daily morning and evening ascension offerings especially *typified Christ*. The *propitiation power* of this offering is seen in the story of wrath being averted when David offers ascension offerings on Mount Moriah (1 Chr. 21:26), and when Ahaz neglected the ascension offerings and wrath fell (2 Chr. 29:7-8). The offering typifies Christ's *perfect obedience and consecration* to God on our behalf. For *everything* is given in a blemishless manner on the altar. The personal sacrifices picture one's identification with Christ and their ascent with Christ into heavenly places where they are accepted as a pleasing aroma to God. This sacrifice reminds us that God desires our *total devotion* as living sacrifices to Him. A total devotion that is only fully realized in Christ's life, but one that we must participate in each morning and evening as we recognize Him as our Savior and Lord.

The second offering God describes in detail to Moses is usually called the *grain offering* or *cereal offering* (Lev. 2:1-16). Gordon Wenham writes, "*minhah* often means 'tribute,' the money paid by a vassal king to his overlord as a mark of his continuing good will and faithfulness…The cereal offering is a kind of tribute from the faithful worshipper to his divine overlord."[121] This offering was always offered after the ascension offering—one could not give "tribute" until they confessed in the presence of the King that they deserved nothing but death. We could say that right after one confessed Christ as 'Savior' in the ascension offering, they proceeded to confess Him as 'Lord' in the tribute offering. The cakes were not just given upon the altar for God but also to the priests (Lev. 2:10-11). These cakes were *always salted*—portraying the unchanging quality of their covenantal relationship with God. This was the only offering with no sacrificial victim.

The third offering God describes in detail to Moses is *the peace offering* (Lev. 3:1-16, 7:11-21). The *shalom offering*—the offering symbolizing health, prosperity, and an overall state of well-being with God. Much of the initial offering mirrors the ascension offering—bringing a blemishless sacrificial victim to the gate of the tabernacle, the hand leaning ritual, the slaughter of the victim by the offerer, and the sprinkling of the blood on the altar (Lev. 3:2). Unlike the ascension offering the sacrificial victim could be either male or female—meaning they could offer a cow instead of a bull, a sheep instead of a ram, a female goat instead of a billy goat. Thus it was not necessarily as costly as the ascension offering for the main purpose of this offering was not tied to propitiation or total consecration, but rather *joyful fellowship*.

Only the internal organs with the fat attached to them were offered on the bronze altar—the liver, kidneys, and intestines. In the Bible these organs symbolize the seat of one's emotions, and they were regarded in many ways as the essence of the animal. By offering these inner organs to God one was declaring that God deserved their very 'heart' and that worship was not simply a mechanical exercise. On top of the inner organs, if a lamb was the sacrificial victim the entire 'fat tail' was also offered (Lev. 3:9). Kellog refers to a breed of sheep in the Middle East which have a tail that "grows to an immense size, sometimes weighing fifteen pounds or more, and consists entirely of a rich substance…in the regions where this variety of sheep is found it is still esteemed as the most valuable part of the animal for food."[122] Just as one would normally set aside the choicest pieces of meat for an honored guest, so the choicest parts of the sacrificial victim were set apart for God. Yet, in this feast, God was *host* as much as He was *guest*. For the sacrificial victim that belonged to Him was given back to the offerer as they were invited to sit down and wine and dine with Him in His courtyard. The breast and thigh would be given to the priests officiating the sacrifice, while the rest of the meat of the victim would belong to the family presenting the sacrificial victim(s) (Lev. 7:15, 31-32).

There would be meat, leavened bread, and at some of the other festivals wine and beer would accompany the sacrifice (Lev. 7:13; Deut. 14:26). More than any of the five offerings the peace offering is the closest analogy to the Lord's Supper. A time of feasting and thanksgiving for God's gift of peace through the finished work of Christ. In order, it was the last of the five offerings that were offered on the altar. *Fellowship and feasting in God's House was the end-goal of the offerings.* While only God received the fat and choicest parts in this offering, Isaiah prophesied that a day would come when "The LORD of hosts will make for all people a feast of choice pieces, a feast of wines on the lees, of fat things full of marrow" (Is. 25:6). This banquet of choice meat and aged wine for people from "all nations" would celebrate the day God "will swallow up death forever" (Is. 25:7-8). Was Isaiah prophesying about when the Church would partake the Lord's Supper? For there we eat the body of Christ which is truly the best, *most choice meal* that has ever been! And there we drink wine which powerfully presents us with the joy and rest of the Lord as we celebrate Christ's conquest over death and gift of eternal life! (John 6:51-55) The voluntary 'thanksgiving peace offering' needed to be eaten on the first and second day, and "the remainder of the flesh of the sacrifice on the third day must be burned with fire" (Lev. 7:17). The reason for this is because after the third day it would begin to corrupt. By not eating the sacrifice on the third day or later one was reminded that the sacrificial victim represented the Risen and Reigning Savior whose flesh saw no corruption and who would give them eternal life (Ps. 16:10; Acts 13:37). Jesus is the Incorruptible Sacrifice!

One, of course, must not abuse their feasting time with the LORD and get drunk (like some in Corinth were doing with the Lord's Supper). Properly celebrated, the feast would be a time of communal festive rejoicing with an equal sharing of the good gifts. In Deuteronomy God told His people to come to His Home and bring "sacrifices" and "rejoice before the LORD your God, you and your sons and your daughters, your male and female servants, and the Levite who is within your gates" (Deut. 12:12). This rejoicing would come to a climax in the *peace offering*. For other feasts in Jerusalem they would include one's family, one's servants, Levites, strangers, widows, and orphans (Deut. 16:14, 26:12). The peace offering points to the other festivals which included celebrating with food in God's House and pictures for us *divine hospitality* and *grace overflowing to everyone*. Something to be replicated in His people, as Jesus taught in His parable of the Great Banquet (Luke 14:15-24). The *cross of Christ* culminates with the *table of Christ*. The Sacrificial Victim on the altar becomes the Sacrificial Victim in the chalice and loaf. This was prophetically pictured in the order of the sacrifices in Leviticus.

The fourth offering God describes in detail to Moses is usually called *the sin offering* (Lev. 4:1-5:13). This is a fine translation as the word for the Hebrew literally means 'sin.' Yet, the primary idea in this offering is that of purification, so many have opted to call this offering *the purification offering*, seeing that some of the other offerings also deal with sin. The beginning of the offering follows the same procedure as the ascension and peace offerings—bringing a blemishless sacrificial victim to the gate of the tabernacle, the hand leaning ritual, the slaughter of the victim by the offerer, and the sprinkling of the blood on the altar. Uniquely, we are told that when the offering was for the high priest, or the whole nation, the blood was sprinkled "seven times before the LORD, in front of the veil" (Lev. 4:6, 17). Seeing these sin offerings dealt with either the representative of the nation, or the entire nation, the blood needed to be brought nearer to the LORD. The high priest had access to God's Room, and so his sin pollution needed purification all the way to the veil. The sprinkling of the blood seven times symbolized *complete cleansing*. This foreshadowed the Day of Atonement when the blood would be sprinkled seven times on the ark of the covenant (Lev. 16:14, 19). The purification offering was a *perfect* and *complete* work. A refrain that runs through the purification offering section is that the offerer "shall be forgiven" upon the completion of the offering (4:20, 26, 31, 35). The offerer could rest in this certain word of *forgiveness* after the purification was performed on their behalf.

One unique aspect of the sin offering is that there were three different types of sacrificial victims depending on what class of people needed purification. The high priest and nation both required a bull (Lev. 4:3, 14). Kleinig writes, "Since the bull was the head of the domesticated animals, it was used for the high priest, the ritual head of the congregation."[123] Bulls were used for representative *heads of nations* and *nations* themselves. For instance, during the Feast of Tabernacles, also known as the Feast of Ingathering, seventy bulls were offered over the course of seven days (Numb. 29:12-34). This feast occurred at the end of the harvest season and pictured fields white for harvest being gathered to the LORD. In the Bible seventy always stands for the nations of the world. It is how many nations there are in Genesis 10. The seventy bulls sacrificed for the seventy nations show that Jesus Christ is not only the atoning sacrifice for the sins of Israel, but also the sins of the whole world (1 John 2:2).

For the civil ruler a male goat without blemish was demanded for the sin offering (Lev. 4:23), and for the common Israelite a female goat without blemish was demanded (Lev. 4:28). Kleinig writes,

"Even though rams were the most aggressive and powerful animals in any flock, the dominant male goats led the flock to water and to pasture. Since the male goat represented the leaders of Israel, God's flock (Pss 74:1; 79:13; 95:7; 100:3), it was used for the sin offering of the congregation and its leaders (Lev 4:23; 16:5; Num 7:16; 28:15, 22, 30; 29:5, 11, 16). Female goats and sheep made up the bulk of any Israelite flock. They therefore symbolized the members of the congregation and so were used for the sin offerings of the ordinary people (Lev 4:28, 32; 5:6; 14:19; Num 6:14)."[124]

Another unique aspect of this offering is that the more heavily sin concentrated offerings—the ones that took away the high priest's sin and the sin of the nation—had to be removed outside the camp where its ashes were poured out and it was burned with fire (Lev. 4:12). This is because it signified Christ "becoming sin" for us. This sin needed to be *utterly obliterated*. Thus, this 'sacrificial victim' pictured the sin bearing aspect of Christ's atonement more than the ascension, tribute, or peace offerings. Though the sin offering is concerned with *unintentional sins*, if one "confessed" certain *intentional sins* they could at times be reduced to an *unintentional sin* and forgiven and removed. But, with the emergence of Jesus into the world, *all manner of sin* is capable of being forgiven and removed! Jesus offered forgiveness even to deliberate sinners, like the tax collector (Luke 18:9-14). He forgave high handed sins like the adulterer and murderer (John 8:11; Luke 23:43). John writes, "If we confess our sins, He is faithful and just to forgive us our sins and to cleanse us from all unrighteousness" (1 John 1:9). This is *all inclusive,* not just for unintentional sin and some intentional sin. Jesus, as the ultimate sin offering, is the bull, the male goat, and the female goat who takes away the sin of the world! The sin of every tribe, tongue, nation, and individual! All one must do is *grab hold of this Sacrificial Victim by faith* and *receive His forgiveness* (Acts 26:18).

The fifth offering God describes in detail to Moses is usually called *the trespass offering* (Lev. 5:14-6:7). Other names for it are the *guilt offering* or *reparation offering*. This offering was required of an Israelite on two occasions. The first occasion being if one trespassed against

God and His holy things. This would include things like eating the food reserved for priests, forgetting to fulfill a vow made to God, eating the firstborn animal from your flock that belonged to God, or in some way incurring a debt to God through misuse or abuse. The second occasion this offering would be offered is if an Israelite trespassed against their neighbor's property and either stole it or misappropriated it. If anyone sinned by "deceiving his neighbor in a matter of deposit or security, or through robbery, or if he has oppressed his neighbor or has found something lost and lied about it, swearing falsely" (Lev. 6:2-3, ESV).

In both instances the *sacrificial victim* required for the offering was always the same—a ram. Everyone has the same debt and must pay the same price. The head of the flock, the ram, must die to make things right. While the ram was already a very valuable sacrifice, the offending party also was required to add 20% interest in silver to the offering (Lev. 5:16, 6:5). By requiring a full restitution plus interest, "the guilty person was not allowed to have gained even any temporary advantage from the use for a while of that which he now restored; for 'the fifth part more' would presumably quite overbalance all conceivable advantage or enjoyment which he might have had from his fraud."[125] Furthermore, "In that the sacrifice was prescribed over and above the restitution, the worshipper was reminded that, in view of the infinite majesty and holiness of God, it lies not in the power of any creature to nullify the wrong God-ward, even by fullest restitution."[126] The aspect of the atonement that shines brightest in this offering is *satisfaction*. God's people were reminded by this offering that sin incurs a debt that *must* be paid. In fact, there needs to be an *overpayment*, as well as an innocent *sacrificial victim* on top of the repayment!

Ultimately, humanity has trespassed against an Infinite God, His holy things, and His people in ways we are never able to repay. The awesome and perfect justice of God demands satisfaction and reparation. This perfect justice could only be established one way—through the shed blood of Jesus on the cross. In fact, Isaiah describes the sacrifice of Jesus on the cross as a "guilt offering" (Is.

53:10, NASB). It is at the cross where Jesus *paid for all our sin.* Bowing before the Lamb of God, the choirs of heaven sing, "with your blood you purchased for God persons from every tribe and language and people and nation" (Rev. 5:9, NIV). Neither gold or silver eternally purchased God's people, instead, "the payment that freed you was the precious blood of Christ, the lamb with no defects or imperfections" (1 Pet. 1:19, GNT). Jesus reminds us in His parable of the unforgiven servant that man owed a debt to God that he could never repay (Matt. 18:23-35), yet God, in His infinite mercy, devised the means by which *that debt could be paid in full* and man could be eternally forgiven!

What we see when we put all five offerings together is a comprehensive picture of what atonement through Christ, our Sacrificial Victim, has accomplished for humanity. These offerings (with the exception of the trespass offering—likely because God's Home could not yet be trespassed against) were offered at the inaugural service in Leviticus 9. In that service the sin offering was offered first, followed by the ascension and tribute offerings, with the peace offering coming last (Lev. 9:1-21). This service occurred "on the eighth day" of the first month of the liturgical year. Eight throughout the Bible symbolized new creation, and thus by means of this sacrificial service God's new creation Edenic Home was being reopened to His people. After placing all the offerings on the altar, "Moses and Aaron went into the tabernacle of meeting, and came out and blessed the people. Then the glory of the LORD appeared to all the people, and fire came out from before the LORD and consumed the burnt offering and the fat on the altar. When all the people saw it, they shouted and fell on their faces" (Lev. 9:23-24). This is the first time Moses and Aaron are said to have been able to enter into God's House. Why? Because the appropriate offerings had all been made. This, and this alone, allowed them to enter God's precincts. This, and this alone, allowed them access God's New Creation Home. *Christ, and His cross, is the sole means by which one can come into the presence of God.* Commenting on how the offerings bear witness to Christ's work on the cross,

Wenham observes, "If the burnt offering brings reconciliation between God and man, the purification or sin offerings brings purification, while the reparation offering brings satisfaction through paying for the sin."[127] We might add that the peace offering brings peace with God and enjoyment of fellowship in His House. These five offerings that reestablished right relations with God would be brought to His garden sanctuary in a similar manner to how they were brought in Genesis 4. (See illustration below.)

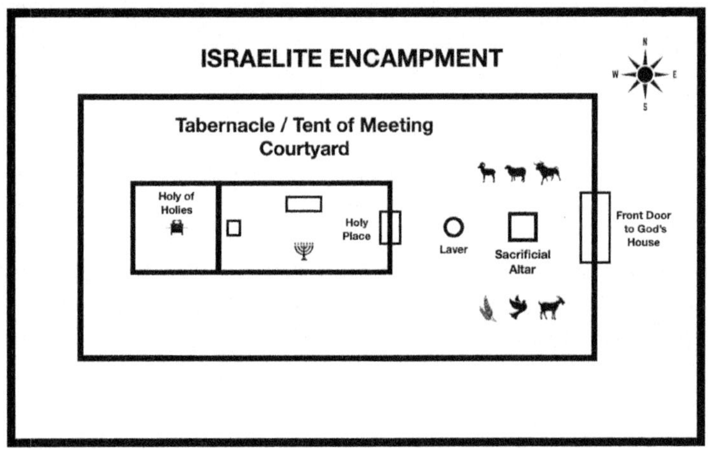

The last portion of Leviticus that deserves discussion regarding 'the sacrificial victim' is the Day of Atonement (Lev. 16:1-34). As we've seen earlier, the book of Leviticus is structured around this chapter from a literary standpoint in three different ways. Additionally, it is the central section of the five books of Moses. This chapter is the height of Gospel revelation in the Torah! It is the mountaintop to which the narrative ascends and descends. For on the Day of Atonement God deals with *all* of the sins that were not dealt with by the five offerings throughout the year. It is a day of *complete purgation* and *cleansing* for God's people, "For on that day the priest shall make atonement for you, to cleanse you, that you may be clean from all your sins before the LORD" (Lev. 16:30). A day that along with Passover beautifully typified Good Friday when Christ brought perfected redemption to His people by His Passion.

The Day of Atonement took place on the tenth day of the seventh month (Lev. 16:29). The Sabbatical month. This was the only day of the year where Israel was commanded to *fast and refrain from all work*. It is termed "a sabbath of solemn rest for you" (Lev. 16:31). In the LXX it is called the "sabbath of sabbaths." Israel could do nothing, not even eat, as they simply stood still and watched the salvation of the LORD. The people simply watched as their representative, the high priest, symbolically climbed to the top of God's mountain in the holy of holies and made atonement for *all* their sins. This complete cleansing is demonstrated through the use of the number seven, symbolizing completeness. The high priest sprinkled the blood "seven times" on the mercy seat and incense altar (Lev. 16:14, 19). Upon deciphering all of the blood manipulations that took place during the four sacrifices on this day and adding them up, Milgrom observes, "The total number of manipulations adds up to forty-nine, or seven times seven. Seven, the number that stands for completion and perfection, is multiplied by itself."[128] Further illustrating complete cleansing, the phrases "the Holy Place" and "the mercy seat" are each mentioned seven times in this chapter. God's abode, throne, and people are perfectly and completely cleansed!

The ceremony itself consisted of *two purification offerings* and *two ascension offerings*. Coming on a cloud of incense into God's throne room, Aaron would offer the blood of the bull on the east side of the mercy seat—a purification for himself as representative head coming from the east to the throne of God (just like the directions in Eden). Aaron would next deal with the purification offering that was for the people. This offering was unique compared to all other purification offerings throughout the year because instead of consisting of one goat, it consisted of two. Yet, the two goats were really one offering. For this reason, the Jews set a precedent of choosing two goats that were *identical*. The Mishnah in m. Yom. 6.1 says, "The two goats of Yom Kippur, it is a mitzvah that they be equal in appearance, height, value and be bought at the same time." Mitzvah means command. The two goats, though performing two different functions, were essentially picturing *one great act of atonement* through a purification offering for the people.

The first goat was slain by the high priest for the people and its blood was sprinkled on the mercy seat, just like the bull's blood (Lev. 16:15). Next, the high priest would handle the living goat. God said, "Aaron shall lay his hands on the head of the live goat, confess over it all the iniquities of the children of Israel, and all their transgressions, concerning all their sins, putting them on the head of the goat, and shall send it away into the wilderness by the hand of a suitable man. The goat shall bear on itself all their iniquities to an uninhabited land; and he shall release the goat in the wilderness" (Lev. 16:21-22). The first thing we notice is that the high priest vicariously confessed all the sins of the people. Not just unintentional sins, but *all* sins. Every sin the people did not confess or purge themselves from that year the high priest confessed on their behalf. One might imagine a mountain of sins piled up on top of the head of the goat. The next thing that happened is the goat was led away outside the tabernacle gate, and taken from the whole camp of Israel to the wilderness. This goat is described as being "for Azazel" (Lev. 16:8, 10, 26, ESV). Azazel was seen as the great demonic power that resided in the wilderness—a picture of Satan. Kellog writes, "As sent to Azazel, he therefore symbolically announces to the Evil One that with the expiation of sin by sacrificial blood the foundation of his power over forgiven Israel is gone. His accusations are now no longer in place; for the whole question of Israel's sin has been met and settled in the atoning blood."[129] God's people overcome Satan (the Accuser) by the blood of the Lamb and the word of their testimony (Rev. 12:11). Their sins are carried to the netherworld and their victory announced!

The psalmist declares, "As far as the east is from the west, so far has He removed our transgressions from us" (Ps. 103:12). This verse does not say "as far as the west is from the east", but rather "as far as the east is from the west." This would have made sense to Israel.

God was always *west* of Israel. In fact, *just barely west* as the high priest could come once a year to the ark of the covenant on the east side. But, *the distance that was infinitely away from them was the eastern direction.* This is why the gate of Eden was on the east, why Cain moved east, why the tabernacle gate was on the east, and why the scapegoat travelled east. *Because that was the direction away from God and His people.* God would send the sins eastward on the second goat back to the originator of sin—Satan. Back to where they belonged. These sins would truly be buried in the netherworld. In the words of Micah, "You will cast all our sins into the depths of the sea" (Mic. 7:19). Carried away by Christ never to be seen again!

Numbers (The Sacrificial Victim as our Strength)

After spending a year at Mount Sinai, and getting their sacrificial system and priesthood up and running, God decided it was time for His people to go inherit the Promised Land. Following the signal of the silver trumpets, the twelve tribal camps would pack up and move out like an army wherever God would lead them. Speaking of their departure from Mount Sinai, Moses writes, "So they departed from the mountain of the LORD on a journey of three days; and the ark of the covenant of the LORD went before them for the three days' journey, to search out a resting place for them" (Num. 10:33). Once the resting place was found we are told exactly where each tribe would set up camp, and how many men of war were in each tribe. *God wanted us to have a visual map of what His camp looked like.* On the east there were 186,400 fighting men, on the west there were 109,100 fighting men, on the north there were 157,600 fighting men, and on the south there were 151,450 fighting men (Num. 2). On the next page is a visual illustration of the camp.

From a mountaintop, as Balaam "saw Israel encamped according to their tribes" the "Spirit of God came upon him" and he prophesied, "How lovely are your tents, O Jacob! Your dwellings, O Israel! Like valleys that stretch out, like gardens by the riverside, like aloes planted by the LORD, like cedars beside the waters" (Num. 24:2-6). The camp of Israel, formed in the shape of a cross, was beautiful—with 'Eden's garden' (the tabernacle) replanted at its center. Every time Israel would be at rest, they would be at rest *in the cross*. This is where true rest for God's people has always come from—the cross. For after we have come to the cross we are freed from our sins and are positioned to *sit* with Christ in

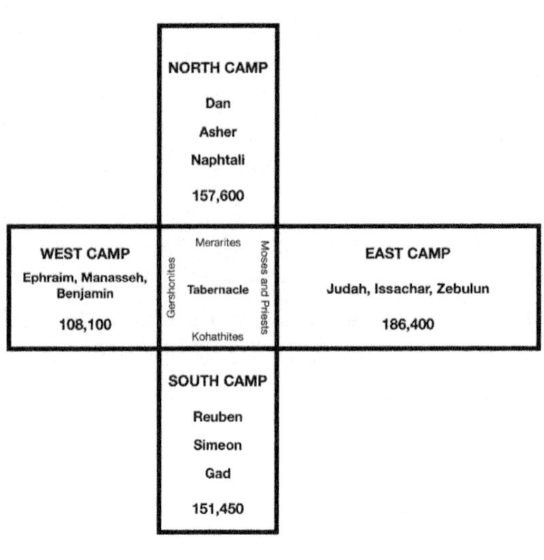

heavenly places (Eph. 2:4-10). As we abide in Him, as Balaam saw, we become *fruitful* and *lovely* (John 15:1-8). From this rested, abiding position, Israel would regularly rise in strength to fight their enemies as they journeyed to the Promised Land. With God as their General leading the way!

The cross would not simply be their rest, but it would also be their *spiritual and physical health.* Later in the book of Numbers when the Israelites forgot how good God had been to them, and began to complain, fiery serpents were sent into the camp and many Israelites began to die. In response, Israel confessed their sin and asked Moses to intercede for them. While interceding God told Moses, "Make a fiery serpent, and set it on a pole; and it shall be that everyone who is bitten, when he looks at it, shall live" (Num. 21:8). In response, "Moses made a bronze serpent, and put it on a pole; and so it was, if a serpent had bitten anyone, when he looked at the bronze serpent, he lived" (Num 21:9). Bronze is a symbol of judgment in Scripture. As Israel looked at the serpent under judgment on the cross, they were healed! We might call this a *cursed sacrificial victim.* A picture of Jesus taking the judgment/curse His people deserved, and giving life in return to those who look to Him in faith (Gal. 3:13; 2 Cor. 5:21).

Isaiah (The Sacrificial Victim as Suffering Servant)

While the sacrificial victim plays important roles in between the time of Moses and Isaiah, it is in Isaiah that the victim's connection to the Passion of Christ becomes strikingly clear. As we've seen, the sacrificial victim was always meant to be *an analogue of human life*. To the extent that it typified that perfect human life—Christ—it was a 'pleasing aroma' to God and restored fellowship. But, the animal sacrifices, in and of themselves, could *not* take away sin (Heb. 10:4). By the time we reach David and the pre-exilic prophets it is made clear that God did not delight in sacrifices and offerings if they were offered simply to fulfill a ritualistic performance (Ps. 40:6; Hos 6:6). For the people to act out the ritual, but not be invested in the ritual at the level of the heart, or see how the ritual pointed toward Christ, meant *they were essentially white-washed sepulchres*. Hypocritical worship was especially the norm for Israel by the time Isaiah arrived on the scene. In fact, at the end of Isaiah's life the worst king in Israel's history was set on the throne—Manasseh. Summarizing his reign, the chronicler writes, "So Manasseh seduced Judah and the inhabitants of Jerusalem to do more evil than the nations whom the LORD had destroyed before the children of Israel" (2 Chr. 33:9). Manasseh would offer sacrifices to Baal, institute child sacrifice, set up worship at the high places, and even had Isaiah "sawn in two" (Heb. 11:37). It was during this season, when Israel and the whole world lay under thick judgment, that God revealed something *new*, even *startling*, about the sacrificial victim.

Before Isaiah reveals God's answer to man's wickedness, he first describes this wickedness, and the judgment it deserves, in detail. In fact, the first thirty-nine chapters of Isaiah are primarily focused on *judgment*. In the first chapter God compares His people to a nation that had degenerated to the level of Sodom and Gomorrah (Is. 1:9). He described them as a "sinful nation, a people laden with iniquity, a brood of evildoers" (Is. 1:4). He says they are sin-sick from the top of their head to the soles of their feet with bruises, sores, and raw wounds (Is. 1:6). In view of their wicked hearts and behavior, God says about their rituals, "What to me is the multitude of your sacrifices? says the LORD; I have had enough of burnt offerings of rams and the fat of well-fed beasts; I do not delight in the blood of bulls, or of lambs, or of goats" (Is. 1:11, ESV). God essentially says, "You guys are just playing church! You come to me with the outward form of worship, but it is meaningless! You are an adulterous, wicked, rebellious bride! You don't truly identify with the sacrificial victim and so there is no transformation or true fellowship. I've had enough of your games!"

This oracle of judgment against Judah billows outward until the whole world stands condemned—the first six chapters speak of Judah's evil, the next six condemn Judah's norther neighbor Israel, the following cluster of chapters have to do with judgment on kingdoms that surrounded Isaiah in his own day, and lastly the whole world is brought under God's judgment with a special condemnation brought against Jerusalem as the priestly people bear the greatest responsibility before God. The judgment section of Isaiah ends with Yahweh declaring, "'Behold, the days are coming when all that is in your house, and what your fathers have accumulated until this day, shall be carried to Babylon; nothing shall be left,' says the LORD. 'And they shall take away some of your sons who will descend from you, whom you will beget; and they shall be eunuchs in the palace of the king of Babylon'" (Is. 39:6-7). Isaiah spoke these words over one-hundred years before they came to pass, and his prophecy happened exactly as it was spoken (Dan. 1). Judgment *prophesied* became judgment *fulfilled.*

Yet, judgment was not the last word. Beginning with chapter 40 of Isaiah there is a change in tone. It begins, "Comfort, comfort my people, says your God. Speak tenderly to Jerusalem, and cry to her that her warfare is ended, that her iniquity is pardoned" (Is. 40:1-2, ESV). Isaiah's name means 'Yahweh is salvation', and the final twenty-seven chapters are focused on this truth. Though the people of Yahweh, indeed the whole world, were leprous and sin-sick, incapable of saving themselves, Yahweh would intervene on their behalf! How? In an unlikely and startling way. He would intervene in the person of the Servant/Slave of Yahweh (Is. 42, 49-50, 53). The climax of this Servant's salvific work would be described in chapter 53. What is so remarkable is that the Servant of Yahweh, who is fully man, is at the same time *Yahweh Himself* stooping to the fallen estate of mankind in order to redeem them. *Yahweh Himself becoming the Sacrificial Victim!* While the sacrificial victims were instituted by God, they simply pointed toward a Sacrificial Victim of a far higher order. One that would not be an animal, but rather a man, a seed of Eve. A perfect, sinless, holy man. Ultimately, a God-Man. Wegner notes that because the sacrificial victim "was only symbolic, it could not fully substitute for a human life. What was required to remove sin was a righteous (i.e. sinless) human (i.e. the servant) to die in the place of the sinful."[130] Yet, this was no ordinary human. *It was the Eternal Word of God made flesh.* In fact, the Servant of Yahweh was the same Being Isaiah saw seated on the heavenly throne in Isaiah 6 when He was 'undone' and given his commission. (Jesus makes that plain in John 12:35-41.) In view of the Almighty King of Isaiah 6 becoming the Suffering Slave of Isaiah 53, J. Sidlow Baxter writes, "The marvel which staggered Isaiah was that the despised, rejected, humiliated, bruised, wounded, pierced, broken, unresisting, meek and lowly, suffering Sin-bearer whom he saw 'led as a lamb to the slaughter' was the very One whom he had earlier seen surrounded by overwhelming heavenly splendor, sitting on the glory-flashing throne, reigning in super-sovereignty over all nations and centuries!…The Sovereign of all becomes the Sin-bearer of all! The regal lion becomes the bleeding Lamb! The most baffling spectacle which angel hosts ever saw was that almighty divine sovereignty fastened by iron spikes to a criminal's cross on this earth."[131]

Isaiah 40-66 is broken up into three equal sections of nine chapters each. Isaiah 53 is the central chapter. After declaring an aspect of Yahweh's salvation, each section ends with a warning, "there is no peace for the wicked" (Is. 48:22, 57:21). Salvation is *offered*, but it must be *received*. Salvation is *accomplished*, but it must be *applied*. Those who continue to obstinately stand against the work of the Servant will not receive His benefits. The central section of the three, Isaiah 49-57, is primarily about *salvation from sin* and this is where three of the four great Servant Songs are found. Salvation from sin climaxes in the central chapter, Isaiah 53, with the central statement of that chapter being, "He is led as a Lamb to the slaughter" (Is. 53:7). *The central statement, of the central chapter, of the second half of Isaiah is about the Sacrificial Victim!* Concerning the phrase 'like a lamb that is led to the slaughter', Gordon Wenham states, "The word used here (seh) is less precise than that used for lamb in Leviticus, and may in fact refer to sheep or goats. An allusion to any type of animal sacrifice is therefore possible and may be intended."[132] By using this less specific term God is wanting us to envision the Suffering Servant who carried the cross to Golgotha as more than simply the *Lamb*. He is also the *Ram*, the *Female Goat*, the *Male Goat*, the *Calf*, and the *Bull*. We might say, "He is led as a Sacrificial Victim to the slaughter." As the Reality and Substance of all of the different animal sacrifices, the Suffering Servant is the fulfillment of every sacrificial victim that God demanded His people to offer. As the Perfect Sacrifice that brought an end to sin, Christ brought an end to the sacrificial victims as their purpose as pointers to His perfected offering now ceased! (Heb. 8-10) While the Christian is still called to sacrificial living, this sacrificial living is not accompanied by sheep, goats, and bulls. Instead, every time we participate in the Lord's Supper we are reminded of the Final Sacrifice of Christ and how we identify with that Sacrifice. Our 'sacrifices of praise', and 'the offering of our body as a living sacrifice', is accomplished *in and through the once and for all Sacrifice of Christ* (Heb. 13:15; Rom. 12:1). Instead of entering the Father's House with a sacrificial victim, we come to the Father solely with Jesus our High Priest and Sacrifice (Heb. 4:15-16), our Representative and Mediator (1 Tim. 2:5).

Many have referred to Isaiah 53 as 'the fifth gospel.' Augustine said of Isaiah, "Some say he should be called an evangelist rather than a prophet."[133] Alongside of Psalm 22 this chapter in Scripture gives us the greatest visual representation of what happened at the cross. One cannot read this chapter and not immediately think of the Passion Narrative. In fact, many Jews who hear this passage think it is from the New Testament! The reason for this is because this chapter has been excised from public readings in many synagogues. The readings simply jump from Isaiah 52 to Isaiah 54, so many modern Jews are completely unaware this prophecy concerning the Messiah even exists. Yet, Isaiah 53 does something even more than Psalm 22 or any other passage that describes the crucifixion of Christ, it gives us *a theological interpretation of the cross*—an in depth analysis of 'why' Christ needed to die this way.

As if looking upon the Crucified Christ alongside Mary and the beloved disciple, Isaiah proclaims, "He was like someone people turned away from; he was despised, and we didn't value him. Yet he himself bore our sicknesses, and he carried our pains; but we in turn regarded him stricken, struck down by God, and afflicted. But he was pierced because of our rebellion, crushed because of our iniquities; punishment for our peace was on him, and we are healed by his wounds. We all went astray like sheep; we all have turned to our own way; and the LORD has punished him for the iniquity of us all" (Is. 53:3-6, CSB). The word 'bore' is the same word that is used in the book of Leviticus to describe the action of the scapegoat who bore away the sin of the people (Lev. 16:22). Christ on the cross is the scapegoat who bears away the sin and sickness of the world! Though the crowds thought Christ was being punished by God for His own sins, Isaiah shows us that He was being punished as a substitutional representative. Pierced *because of our rebellion*. Crushed *because of our iniquities*. Cut off from the land of the living *because of the people's rebellion* (Is. 53:9).

Though some Christians are afraid of the concept of 'penal substitution', as they think it impugns the character of God, the truth is the concept runs throughout the narrative of Scripture and reaches a height in Isaiah 53. The Isainic scholar, J. Alec Motyer, writes, "Verse 4 demands the noun 'substitution', and verse 5 adds the adjective 'penal'."[134] The coherence of 'penal substitution', and its biblical and philosophical underpinnings, have been ably defended in William Craig's recent work *Atonement and the Death of Christ*. While there are some perverse presentations of penal substitution that pit the Father against the Son, a true explication will do no such thing. Rather, when explained within proper biblical/theological parameters, both the Father and Son shine brilliantly as the Loving and Just eternal God they are. A perverse form of penal substitution might insinuate that an 'unloving Father' needed to be appeased by a 'loving Son' so that He would could love mankind again. This, of course, is heretical. For the mutual love of the Father and Son is what sent the mission of the Son in motion (John 3:16, 1 John 4:10). J. I. Packer states, "Since all this was planned by the holy Three in their eternal solidarity of mutual love, and since the Father's central purpose in it all was and is to glorify and exalt the Son as Savior and Head of a new humanity, smartypants notions like 'divine child abuse' as a comment on the cross are supremely silly and as irreverent and wrong as they could possibly be."[135] J. Sidlow Baxter adds, "The Sinbearer is the 'Word made flesh,' God the Son, which means that in its deepest meaning the Cross was not so much God's laying our penalty on *another*, it was God himself shouldering our burden and bearing the damning load as our Substitute!"[136] In Paul's words, "God was in Christ reconciling the world to Himself" (2 Cor. 5:19).

In the last three verses of Isaiah 53 we learn, "the LORD was pleased to crush him severely. When you make him a guilt offering, he will see his seed…my righteous servant will justify man, and he will carry their iniquities…because he willingly submitted to death, and was counted among the rebels; yet he bore the sin of many and interceded for the rebels" (Is. 53:10-12, CSB). Notice how the Servant is made "a guilt offering" (Is. 53:10, CSB)—the fifth offering in Leviticus that has to do with payment, satisfaction, and compensation. The Servant on the cross, as the Guilt Offering

Ram, pays for the sins of the world! In the words of Kellog, "His soul He made a guilt-offering for our trespasses! Isaiah's words imply that He should make full restitution for all that of which we, as sinners, defraud God."[137] God is completely satisfied by His own Guilt Offering. The church was "purchased with His own blood" (Acts 20:28). Paid in full! There is no outstanding debt after the finished work of Christ!

We have learned from Leviticus that the death of the sacrificial victim is not its end. Rather, it rises in smoke to join God in the glory cloud. This is the case with the Servant. Isaiah 53 shows us His death is not the end of the story. For the Servant "shall see the labor of His soul, and be satisfied", and He "will divide Him a portion with the great, and He shall divide the spoil with the strong, because He poured out His soul unto death" (Is. 53:11-12). The One who was crushed and pierced to death not only *sees* the fruit of His death, but actually is seen as the Commander *dividing* the spoils after a great victory. Isaiah 53 ends with triumph, rather than tragedy. A triumph over sin and death (Col. 2:15). This is in total contrast to the other kings of the world who live glorious lives that end in painful demise in Sheol. Motyer observes, "In 14:9-17 Isaiah depicted earth's royalty in Sheol, clutching their now meaningless dignities, actually weak, as are the rest, and with their pretensions in life exposed as pitiable foibles. Death has dethroned them. In the case of the Servant, however, death ushers him into sovereign dignity and power, with his own hand administering the saving purposes of the Lord, and as victor taking the spoil."[138] *The Sacrificial Victim rises on the clouds to the Ancient of Days to Reign Supreme!* A theme that becomes utterly clear in the last book of the Bible…

Revelation (The Sacrificial Victim as Supreme Ruler)

Revelation begins with a vision of the Risen and Glorified Christ. He is described as "the ruler over the kings of the earth" and One "who loved us and washed us from our sins in His own blood" (Rev. 1:5). The first words from Jesus are, "I am the Alpha and the Omega, the First and the Last" (Rev. 1:11). He is Lord, Savior, and

God Almighty! The description of what Christ looks like in many ways parallels the tabernacle and temple, as He is the Living Temple (John 2:21). Part of this physical description is that He holds the churches/lampstands in His right hand, just as the lampstand in the tabernacle/temple resided on the right side of the Holy Place (Rev. 1:12-20; Ex. 26:35). The fact there are *seven* churches in His Right Hand shows us that the *fullness* of the church is held by the *strength* of Christ. He is the Chief Shepherd over the church who dictates letters to the Church for their edification and health (1 Pet. 5:4; Rev. 2-3). There is no question about Jesus Christ's omnipotence and the fact that He "overcame and sat down" with the Father "on His throne" (Rev. 3:21).

This, of course, is something that has *already taken place*. It is not as if 'one day' Christ will reign. No! Christ reigns, *right now*. He is seated on the throne with the Father, *right now*. He reigns over the kings of the earth and His church, *right now*. Revelation in many ways is a spiritual vision of Christ's reign over all things seen and unseen, *right now*. Revelation 4-5 speaks of Christ's inauguration on that highest of thrones. John is invited to "come up" into the highest of heavens and get a glimpse of what happened after Jesus ascended on the clouds (Rev. 4:1). He sees a scroll with seven seals on it clasped in the hand of the Ancient of Days. The scroll that had been sealed during the time of Daniel and needed to be unsealed as the old age and old covenant were coming to an end (Dan. 12:4). Yet, no one was found in heaven or earth who was *worthy* to open the scroll. This caused John to weep profusely (Rev. 5:4). While distraught that history could not move forward, one of the twenty-four elders approached John saying, "Do not weep. Behold, the Lion of the tribe of Judah, the Root of David, has prevailed to open the scroll and to loose its seven seals" (Rev. 5:5). John would likely have caught on that this was a reference to Jesus. He probably expected to see Jesus shining in strength again as a Roaring Lion. Yet, he sees nothing like that. Instead, John writes, "And I looked, and behold, in the midst of the throne and of the four living creatures, and in the midst of the elders, stood a Lamb as though it had been slain, having seven horns and seven eyes, which are the seven Spirits of God sent out into all the earth" (Rev. 5:6). Instead of seeing a Lion, John sees a little Lamb as though it had been slain. He sees the Sacrificial Victim! He sees Jesus covered in all His covenantal markings. It is this Man who emerges from the "midst of the throne" as "worthy" to unlock the next steps of covenantal history. It is this Man who emerges as the *All Powerful Administrator* in the highest heavens. The Lamb of God!

This Lamb is described as having seven horns, seven eyes, and seven spirits. Horns in the Bible speak of power. The Lamb is all-powerful, omnipotent. Eyes speak clear vision and point to knowledge, wisdom, and the ability to pass judgment. The Lamb is omniscient. Seven spirits in all the earth speak of the fullness of presence. The all-powerful, all-knowing Lamb, is also omnipresent. Though Jesus was beaten to a bloody pulp, crucified in nakedness, ridiculed by Jerusalem and Rome, and buried in weakness, *this same Jesus now sits enthroned with the Father as the Supreme Ruler for all eternity.* The wounds that He bore for the world's salvation forever remain. They are the covenantal sign of the price of our redemption. As this 'worthy Lamb' receives the scroll, all of the highest creatures in the heavenly places explode in thunderous worship! Falling down on their faces with harps and golden bowls full of the prayers of the saints, the twenty-four elders sing, "You are worthy to take the scroll, and to open its seals; for You were slain, and have redeemed us to God by Your blood out of every tribe and tongue and people and nation, and have made us kings and priests to our God; and we shall reign on the earth" (Rev. 5:9-10). The voices of one hundred million angels join the song of the elders singing, "Worthy is the Lamb who was slain to receive power and riches and wisdom, and strength and honor and glory and blessing!" (Rev. 5:13) As if this wasn't enough praise, John tells us "every creature which is in heaven and on the earth and under the earth and such as are in the sea" began to sing, "Blessing and honor and glory and power be to Him who sits on the throne, and to the Lamb, forever and ever!" (Rev. 5:13) The entire cosmos is singing praises to the Lamb! The

One who was despised, rejected, mocked, spit upon, scourged, and crucified has been exalted above all created things, seated on the throne of God! Baxter writes, "God has put the Lamb in the place of absolute supremacy and centrality. Let us keep him where God has put him! He is central in prophecy and history, central in the worship of heaven, central in the adoration of saints and angels, central in the government and ultimate homage of the whole universe, central in his atonement as the one true Savior of men; central in his exaltation as the one true King of all creation."[139] The Sacrificial Victim spoken about in *the very center* of Leviticus and the books of Moses, and in *the very center* of the redemptive prophecies of Isaiah, is the One who now reigns on the Throne of God at *the very center* of all existence! All hail the Lamb! He has come on the clouds to the Ancient of Days and reigns supreme forever and ever! (Matt. 26:64, ESV; Dan. 7:13)

The Lamb is so central to Revelation that He is mentioned twenty-nine times. He opens seals, receives adoration and praise, pours out wrath, and washes robes white in His own blood (Rev. 6:1, 6:16, 7:9, 7:14). The saints overcome the Enemy by the blood of the Lamb and the word of their testimony (Rev. 12:11). The undefiled "follow the Lamb wherever He goes" (Rev. 14:4), whereas the wicked are tormented in fire and brimstone "in the presence of the Lamb" (Rev. 14:10). Though kings rise up to make war against this Lamb, "the Lamb will overcome them, for He is Lord of lords and King of kings" (Rev. 17:14). Amazingly, this Lamb that reigns supreme does not want to be alone. He was put to sleep on the cross, and His side was opened, so that He too could receive a bride. This is how the Good Book ends—*with the bride of the Lamb.*

The last two chapters of Revelation describe this bride. When John is shown the bride he sees a massive, bedazzled, garden-city with pearly gates and streets of gold. John says, "the wall of the city had twelve foundations, and on them were the names of the twelve apostles of the Lamb" (Rev. 21:14). This, of course, is a symbolic picture of the church. For the church is "built on the foundation of the apostles and prophets, Jesus Christ Himself being the chief cornerstone" (Eph. 2:20). After the harlot, old-covenant Jerusalem, that had become like become like Sodom and Babylon was destroyed, the New Jerusalem took its place (Rev. 11:8, 18:2-21). John saw "the holy city, New Jerusalem, coming down out of heaven from God, prepared as a bride adorned for her husband" (Rev. 21:2). The Lamb isn't married to a literal city, of course. The Lamb is married to the redeemed who are the 'living stones' and 'pillars' of this city. *The church is the bride of the Lamb (Eph. 5:32).* Within the New Jerusalem is no temple for "the Lord God Almighty and the Lamb are its temple" (Rev. 21:22).

This reality is not solely future. While the fulness of the New Jerusalem will not be experienced until the last enemy (death) is destroyed and Christ makes all things new, we do have an *already/ not-yet experience* of the New Jerusalem even today. For the book of Hebrews states that the church "has come" to "the city of the living God, the heavenly Jerusalem" (Heb. 12:22). In light of *already having come* to the Heavenly Jerusalem, and in one sense *already being betrothed* to the Lamb, we can experience the glories of the Glorified Lamb even today. Speaking of the life source of this city, John writes, "he showed me a pure river of water of life, clear as crystal, proceeding from the throne of God and of the Lamb. In the middle of its street, and on either side of the river, was the tree of life, which bore twelve fruits, each tree yielding its fruit every month. The leaves of the tree were for the healing of the nations. And there shall be no more curse, but the throne of God and of the Lamb shall be in it, and His servants shall serve Him" (Rev. 22:1-3). From the throne of God, on which sit the Father and the Lamb, that same throne John had seen in Revelation 5 where millions of creatures were bowing in worship, now flows a beautiful crystal river cascading *into* the New Jerusalem—the Lamb's bride! It is the River of Living Water Jesus said would flow to the believer after He was glorified (John 7:37-39). His very life! The Holy Spirit Himself! This River of Life that flows from the Lamb to His bride makes the bride fruitful, vibrant, healthy, and capable ministers to the world! (Rev. 22:2-3)

Just as the Sacrificial Victim's desire was for the sinner, Cain, at the beginning of Scripture, so the Sacrificial Victim's desire is for the all the sinners of the world at the end of Scripture. For God is "not willing that any should perish but that all should come to repentance" (2 Pet. 3:9). For this reason, the Spirit that proceeds from the Lamb's throne joins with the Bride of the Lamb in crying out to everyone outside of the city gates to come into the New Jerusalem. Speaking to the "dogs and sorcerers and sexually immoral and murderers and idolaters, and whoever loves and practices a lie", John writes, "the Spirit and the bride say, 'Come!' And let him who hears say, 'Come!' And let him who thirsts come. Whoever desires, let him take the water of life freely" (Rev. 22:15, 17). Have you *received* this invitation from the Lamb and the Spirit? Have you *accepted* it? Have you *entered* the Heavenly Jerusalem? Have you *bent the knee* to the Lamb who is the Supreme Ruler over all things seen and unseen? He died for *you*. He desires *you*. He wants to spend eternity with *you*. Open your heart and say, "Lord Jesus, thank you for dying for me. Thank you for Your Passion. I believe that You reign as Lord over all. Come and fill my life right now with that Crystal River that flows from Your innermost being. Father, Jesus promised that You would not withhold the Spirit from anyone who asks You for it (Luke 11:13). I ask that You fill me with the Holy Spirit right now. Thank you. In Jesus Name, amen."

Bibliography

Ambrose, Isaac. *Looking Unto Jesus*. 1658. Repr. Harrisonburg, VA, Sprinkle Publications, 1986.

Antonacci, Mark. *Test the Shroud*. Forefront Publishing, 2015.

Augustine of Hippo. *The City of God (Books 11-22)*. translated by William Babcock from Latin. Hyde Park, NY: New City Press, 2013.

Augustine. *On The Gospel of St. John*. In vol. 7 of *The Nicene and Post-Nicene Fathers*, Series 1. Edited by Philip Schaff. 1886-1889. 14 vols. Repr. Peabody, Mass.: Hendrickson, 1994.

Bainton, Roland. *Here I Stand*. Nashville, TN: Abingdon Press, 1950.

Barbet, Pierre. *A Doctor at Calvary*. translated by the Earl of Wicklow from French. Issoudun, France: Dillen & Cie, 1950.

Baxter, J. Sidlow. *The Master Theme of the Bible*. Wheaton, IL: Tyndale House, 1973.

Bellarmine, Robert. *The Seven Last Words From The Cross*. 1618. Repr. Providence, RI: Cluny, 2016.

Bock, Darrell L. *Luke 9:51-24:54*. Grand Rapids, MI: Baker Academic, 1996.

Brown, Raymond. *The Death of the Messiah Volume 1*. New York, NY: Doubleday, 1994.

Brown, Raymond. *The Death of the Messiah Volume 2*. New York, NY: Doubleday, 1994.

Brown, Raymond. *The Gospel According to John XIII-XXI*. Garden City, NY: Doubleday, 1970.

Carsidoni, Ignatius. *Meditations on the Passion and Death of Christ*. 1895. Repr. Charlotte, NC: TAN, 2018.

Cicero, Marcus Tullius, *The Orations of Marcus Tullius Cicero*, trans. C. D. Yonge from Latin. London: George Bell and Sons, 1903.

Constantinou, Eugenia Scarvelis. *The Crucifixion of the King of Glory*. Chesterton, IN: Ancient Faith, 2021.

Coverdale, Myles. *Fruitful Lessons upon the Passion, Resurrection, Ascension, and of the Sending of the Holy Ghost*. 1540.

Craig, William L. *Atonement and the Death of Christ*. Waco, TX: Baylor University Press, 2020.

Edersheim, Alfred. *The Life and Times of Jesus The Messiah.* 1883. Repr, Peabody, Mass.: Hendrickson, 1993.

Edersheim, Alfred. *The Temple Its Ministry and Services.* 1874. Repr., Peabody, Mass.: Hendrickson, 1994.

Farrar, Frederic W. *The Life of Christ.* 1874. Repr., Salt Lake City, UT: Bookcraft, 1995.

France, R. T. *The Gospel of Mark.* Grand Rapids, MI: Eerdmans, 2002.

France, R. T. *The Gospel of Matthew.* Grand Rapids, MI: Eerdmans, 2007.

Gerhard, Johann. *Meditations on Divine Mercy,* translated by Matthew C. Harrison. Saint Louis, MO: Concordia, 2003

Gorman, Ralph. *The Last Hours of Jesus.* 1960. Repr., Manchester, NH: Sophia, 2 2017.

Groenings, James. *The Passion of Jesus and its Hidden Meaning.* 1900. Repr. Charlotte, NC: TAN, 2012.

Hall, Joseph. *The Works of Joseph Hall Vol. II.* Oxford: D. A. Talboys, 1837.

Harris, Murray J. *The Seven Sayings of Jesus on the Cross.* Eugene: Cascade, 2016.

Hengel, Martin. *The Cross of the Son of God,* translated by John Bowden from the German. 1977. Repr. London: SCM, 1986.

Henry, Matthew. *A Commentary on the Whole Bible Vol. 5.—Matthew To John.* 1706. Repr., Iowa Falls, Iowa: World Bible Publishers, 1993.

Irenaeus. *Against Heresies.* In vol. 1 of *The Ante-Nicene Fathers,* Series 1. Edited by Philip Schaff. 1886-1889. 14 vols. Repr. Peabody, Mass.: Hendrickson, 1994.

Jackson, John. *The Shroud of Turin a Critical Summary of Observations, Data, and Hypotheses.* The Shroud of Turin Center of Colorado, 2017.

Jeffrey, David Lyle. *Luke.* Grand Rapids, MI: Brazos Press, 2012.

Jordan, James B. *Through New Eyes.* Eugene, OR: Wipf and Stock, 1988.

Josephus. *Antiquities of the Jews.* Translated by A. M. William Whiston. 2 vols. London: Bohn, 1862.

Josephus. *The Wars of the Jews.* Translated by A. M. William Whiston. 2 vols. London: Bohn, 1862.

Justin Martyr. *Dialogue with Trypho.* In *The Apostolic Fathers with Justin Martyr and Irenaeus.* The Ante-Nicene Fathers 1, edited by Alexander Roberts and James Donaldson. Grand Rapids, MI: Eerdmans, 1989.

Kellog, S. H. *The Book of Leviticus.* Minneapolis, MN: Klock & Klock, 1978 reprint.

Kempis, Thomas à. *Meditations on the Life of Christ*. translated by Archdeacon Wright and S. Kettlewell. Repr. Createspace, 2014.

Kleinig, John W. *Leviticus*. Saint Louis, MO: Concordia Publishing House, 2003.

Köstenberger, Andreas J. and Justin Taylor. *The Final Days of Jesus*. Wheaton, IL: Crossway, 2014.

Leithart, Peter. *The Gospel of Matthew Through New Eyes Volume Two: Jesus as Israel*. West Monroe, LA: Athanasius Press, 2018.

Liguori, Alphonsus. *The Passion of Jesus Christ*, translated from the Italian by Eugene Grimm. Edited and language modernized by Darrell Wright, 2016.

Luther, Martin. *Sermons on the Passion of Christ*, translated by J. T. Isensee and E. Smid. Louisville, KY: GLH Publishing, 2021.

Ludolph of Saxony. *The Life of Jesus Christ Part Two Volume 2, Chapters 58-89*, translated by Milton T. Walsh. Collegeville, MN: Liturgical, 2022.

McGovern, Thomas W. *What Christ Suffered*. IN: Huntington, 2021.

Milgrom, Jacob. *Leviticus 1-16*. New York, NY: Doubleday, 1991.

Miller, Stephen M. *Eyewitness to Crucifixion*. Grand Rapids, MI: Our Daily Bread, 2020.

Missler, Chuck and Mark Eastman. *The Agony of Love*. Coeur d'Alene: Koinonia House, 2018.

Morales, Michel. *Who Shall Ascend the Mountain of the Lord?* Downers Grove, IL: InterVarsity Press, 2015.

Motyer, Alec J. *The Prophecy of Isaiah*. Downers Grove, IL: InterVarsity Press, 1993.

Niyr, Mark. *The Turin Shroud*. Morgan Hill, CA: Bookstand Publishing, 2020.

Packer, J. I. *In My Place Condemned He Stood*. Wheaton, IL: Crossway, 2007.

Pink, Arthur W. *The Seven Sayings of the Saviour on the Cross*. 1947. Repr. Grand Rapids, MI: Baker, 2005.

Schilder, Klass. *Christ Crucified*, translated from the Dutch by Henry Zylstra. Repr. Minneapolis, MN, Klock and Klock, 1978.

Schilder, Klass. *Christ in His Sufferings*, translated from the Dutch by Henry Zylstra. Repr. Minneapolis, MN, Klock and Klock, 1978.

Schilder, Klass. *Christ on Trial*, translated from the Dutch by Henry Zylstra. Repr. Minneapolis, MN, Klock and Klock, 1978.

Senoir, Donald. *The Passion of Jesus in the Gospel of John*. Collegeville, MN: Liturgical Press, 1991.

Sheen, Fulton J. *Life of Christ*. 1958. Repr. Garden City, NY: Image Books, 1977.

Spurgeon, Charles. *12 Sermons on the Passion and Death of Christ*. Repr., Grand Rapids, MI: Baker, 1994.

St. Philaret of Chernigov, *On The Passion of Our Lord Jesus Christ*, translated from the Russian and edited by the St. Herman of Alaska Brotherhood. Platina, CA: St. Herman of Alaska Brotherhood, 2015.

Tauler, John. *Meditations on the Life and Passion of Christ*. Repr., Ithaca, NY: Just and Sinner, 2020.

The Apostolic Fathers: Greek Texts and English. Edited by Michael W. Holmes. Grand Rapids, MI: Baker, 2007.

Tholuck, August. *Light From the Cross*, translated from the German. Philadelphia, PA: William S. & Alfred Martien, 1858.

Thompson, John L, ed. *Reformation Commentary on Scripture Genesis 1-11*. Downers Grove, IL, InterVarsity Press, 2012.

Wegner, Paul D. *Isaiah*. Downers Grove, IL: InterVarsity Press, 2021.

Wenham, Gordon J. *The Book of Leviticus*. Grand Rapids, MI: Eerdmans, 1979.

West, William. *Riddles of the Shroud*. 2022.

Wilcox, Robert. *The Truth About the Shroud of Turin*. Washington, DC: Regency, 2010.

Wilson, Ian. *The Shroud*. London: Bantam Books, 2010.

Wright, N. T. *Jesus and the Victory of God*. Minneapolis, MN: Fortress, 1996.

More Resources from Joshua Hershey...

* The initial sermons many of these devotions were based on can be found on the 'Gethsemane to Golgotha' playlist on the 'Mission City Church' YouTube channel (@missioncitychurch4771). To stay connected with the teaching ministry of Joshua Hershey subscribe to the YouTube channel as well as the 'Mission City Church w/ Pastor Josh Hershey' Podcast, follow the 'Mission City Church' Facebook page, and visit the church website at missioncitychurch.us
* To buy *Gethsemane to Golgotha* visit amazon.com or contact Joshua Hershey for special bulk order rates by calling (818) 365-5502
* Other books by Joshua include: *Beloved, Relationships,* & *A New Day Dawns.*

End Notes

1. Bellarmine, *The Seven Last Words From The Cross*, 70.

2. Two days before the Passover arrived Mark informs us that the chief priests did not want to arrest Jesus during the Passover and the Feast of Unleavened Bread (Mark 14:1-2). Thus, they needed to *act quickly*. They followed their plan and arrested Jesus the next evening, which was the beginning of Nisan 14 the day of the Passover. But the Passover festival technically didn't start until noon when the lambs were slaughtered and the next night when the meal was eaten. So, Jesus was still technically arrested *before* the festival as the Gospels indicate. Jesus, thus, ate the Passover Meal with His disciples on Nisan 14. This was the beginning of Nisan 14, as Jewish days began at sunset. Also, Jesus tells His disciples to make preparations for their meal *on the day* when they sacrifice the Passover lambs—i.e., Nisan 14 (Mark 14:12). He must have made this statement around sundown. The Gospel writers make clear they were observing the meal a day *prior* to the day everyone else would. The New Testament scholar, R. T. France, states, "If, then, we accept that the last supper took place on the Thursday evening which began Nisan 14, it was a day in advance of the official Passover. Yet the case for its being nonetheless a Passover meal in intention, based on the Synoptic accounts, seems overwhelming. It therefore seems most likely that Jesus deliberately anticipated the official date in his anxiety to hold a Passover with his disciples while it was still possible (cf. Lk. 22:15), aware that by the official date he would not be there to do so. The failure to mention a Passover lamb as part of the last supper might then suggest that Jesus and his group, in common with Jews who had to celebrate the feast away from Jerusalem (and with those who continued to celebrate it after the destruction of the temple), held the meal without a lamb, since the lamb must be slaughtered in the temple and the official date for the sacrifice there had not yet come." (France, *The Gospel of Mark*, 560-561) Jesus, of course, would be the Passover Lamb, as this devotional will make clear throughout. He would be slain as the Passover Lamb the exact time all the other passover lambs were slain. Yet, Christ's 'last supper' would still be filled with all the symbolic power of a typical Passover meal as it pictured the New Exodus of God's people that would happen *in Christ Himself* as Christ provided an *eternal redemption* by His broken body and shed blood.

3. Jesus was called "out of Egypt" and saved as an infant just like Moses (Ex. 2; Matt. 2). Jesus' ministry began with being "led" by the Spirit into the wilderness to be tested for forty days (Matt. 4:1). Similarly, Moses and the nation of Israel were "led" by the Lord to be tested for forty years (Deut. 8:2-3). At the beginning of Jesus' ministry, "He went up on a mountain" (Matt. 5:1) and delivered a message from God. Moses also "went up on the mountain" (Ex. 19:3) and delivered a message from God at the beginning of his leadership. Moses walked through the midst of the waters and Jesus walked on top of the waters (Ex. 15:21; Matt. 14:26).

This happened "around the time of the Passover" and right after this event Jesus fed the 5,000 and referred to Himself as "bread which came down from heaven" (John 6:4, 58). Similarly, Israel was fed with manna after crossing the Red Sea. After Moses spoke with Jesus on the mount of transfiguration, a voice from heaven from heaven commanded Peter, James, and John to "Hear Him!" (Matt. 17:5). Moses himself had prophesied of this moment when he said, "The LORD your God will raise up for you a Prophet like me from your midst, from your brethren. Him you shall hear" (Deut. 18:15). This "hearing" of Jesus in Matthew's Gospel comes in five neatly arranged teaching sections—Sermon on the Mount (5-7), Mission Sermon (10), Kingdom Parables (13), Sermon on the Church (18), and Sermon and Parables on the End of the Age (24-25). Moses wrote five books, and in Matthew Jesus gives fives major teachings. Ultimately, Moses instituted the Passover Meal and Jesus is the Last Passover who institutes the Lord's Supper (Ex. 12; Matt. 26:26-29). The entire life of Jesus, climaxing in His Passion, is the New Exodus that Isaiah and the rest of the prophets longed for. The much greater Exodus. The Exodus that would be for the whole world and would have an everlasting impact. Allusions and connections between Jesus and Moses could be multiplied, but this is sufficient to demonstrate that Jesus is a New Moses bringing His people (Jews and Gentiles who believe in Him) into all of His promises.

4. Sheen, *Life of Christ*, 321.

5. Irenaeus, *Against Heresies*, 454. In defending the true humanity of Jesus, Ireneaus states if He did not have the true humanity from Mary He would not "have sweated great drops of blood." Clearly taking Luke's statement *literally*, as many early interpreters did.

6. Dr. Barbet, *A Doctor at Calvary*, 70.

7. Loredo, J. (2022, June 17). *The holy shroud: A twenty-First Century gospel*. The American TFP. https://www.tfp.org/the-holy-shroud-a-twenty-first-century-gospel/

8. Fr. Ignatius, *Meditations on the Passion and Death of Christ*, 2.

9. Spurgeon, *12 Sermons on the Passion and Death of Christ*, 17.

10. Brown, *The Death of the Messiah Volume 1*, 248.

11. Sheen, *Life of Christ*, 325.

12. Edersheim. *The Life and Times of Jesus The Messiah*, 843.

13. Josephus, *Antiquities*, 20.9.1-2.

14. McGovern, *What Christ Suffered*, 68.

15. France, *The Gospel of Matthew*, 1032-1034.

16. Tauler, *Meditations on the Life and Passion of Christ*, 87-88.

17. Philaret, *On The Passion of Our Lord Jesus Christ*, 262.

18. Groenings, *The Passion of Jesus and its Hidden Meaning*, 116-117.

19. Luther, *Sermons on the Passion of Christ*, 68-69.

20. Schilder, *Christ on Trial*, 254.

21. Ludolph of Saxony, *The Life of Jesus Christ*, 114.

22. The Apostolic Fathers, *The Epistle to Diognetus*, 709-710.

23. Thomas à Kempis, *Meditations on the Life of Christ*, 116.

24. See Appendix A.

25. Miller, *Eyewitness to Crucifixion*, 5.

26. Groenings, *The Passion of Jesus and its Hidden Meaning.*, 218.

27. Groenings, *The Passion of Jesus and its Hidden Meaning.*, 219-220.

28. Edersheim, *The Temple Its Ministry and Services*, 173.

29. Luther, *Sermons on the Passion of Christ*, 113.

30. Henry, *A Commentary on the Whole Bible Vol. 5.—Matthew To John*, 824.

31. Josephus, *War*, 6.3.4.

32. Brown. *The Death of the Messiah Volume 2*, 927.

33. Hengel, *The Cross of the Son of God*, 113.

34. Tauler, *Meditations on the Life and Passion of Christ*, 189.

35. Thomas à Kempis, *Meditations on the Life of Christ*, 128.

36. Brown, *The Death of the Messiah Volume 2*, 965.

37. Harris, *The Seven Sayings of Jesus on the Cross*, 13.

38. Cicero, *The Orations of Marcus Tullius Cicero*, 2.5.165.

39. Miller, *Eyewitness to Crucifixion*,17.

40. Josephus, *Wars*, 5.11.1.

41. Miller, *Eyewitness to Crucifixion*, 27.

42. Cicero, *The Orations of Marcus Tullius Cicero*, 2.5.165.

43. Bellarmine, *The Seven Last Words From The Cross*, 1.

44. Fr. Ignatius, *Meditations on the Passion and Death of Christ*, 152.

45. Ludolph of Saxony, *The Life of Jesus Christ*, 243.

46. Pink, *The Seven Sayings of the Saviour on the Cross*, 75.

47. Tauler, *Meditations on the Life and Passion of Christ*, 269.

48. Farrar, *The Life of Christ*, 650.

49. Brown, *The Death of the Messiah Volume 2*, 1075.

50. Harris, *The Seven Sayings of Jesus on the Cross*, 77

51. Missler, *The Agony of Love*, 84-85.

52. Harris, *The Seven Sayings of Jesus on the Cross*, 77.

53. Edersheim, *The Life and Times of Jesus The Messiah*, 893.

54 Throughout Scripture the seven-fold (heptamerous) sequence of creation frequently repeats itself so it should not be strange for us to expect this sort of Spirit-inspired sequence to be woven into the seven statements of Jesus from the cross. For example, God tells Moses how to construct the tabernacle in *seven* speeches in the book of Exodus. The tabernacle is a picture of heaven on earth. It is a "new heaven and new earth" among God's people. So, it shouldn't surprise us that it follows the pattern of the seven days of creation. In the first speech (Ex. 25:1-30:10) God separates the priesthood from the rest of Israel and instructs that the priests maintain the burning light of the menorah from evening to morning. Just as the Spirit hovering over the water shined brightly on Day 1, so the bearers of the Spirit (the priesthood) maintained the entrance of light into their new creation abode. In the second speech (Ex. 30:11-16) the males are separated from those *above* twenty-years old and those *below* twenty years old for the giving of a temple tax to support the maintenance of the heavenly zone. So, on Day 2, a firmament separated things above from things below. In the third speech (Ex. 30:17-21) God commands Moses to construct the bronze laver that would hold the water at the tabernacle. On Day 3 God created the seas. In the fourth speech (Ex. 30:22-33) all the furnishings of the tabernacle were anointed and set apart for sacred use. It could now properly function for 'signs' and 'seasons' for Israel just as the heavenly bodies did on Day 4. In fact, Psalm 89 speaks of God's throne in the tabernacle as "the sun" what will be established forever like "the moon" (Psalm 89:36-37). In the fifth speech (Ex. 30:34-38) God commands Moses to make a mixture of incense that included "onycha" that would be burned before the ark. Onycha was made by grinding mollusks (sea creatures) into powder, thus linking to the sea creatures of Day 5. In the sixth speech (Ex. 31:1-11) God told Moses He would "put wisdom in the hearts of all the gifted artisans" to construct the tabernacle and specifically fill Bezalel with the Spirit. On Day 6 God creates man as His image-bearers and breathes the breath of life into them. In the seventh speech (Ex. 31:12-17) God solemnly commands that the Sabbath be observed by all Israel. This, of course, maps on to Day 7 where God rests and sanctifies the seventh day. Another example would be the seven signs of Jesus in the Gospel of John. The first sign, water into wine, is described as Christ *manifesting His glory* (John

2:11). There is an unveiling of who He is. Light shining in darkness as in Day 1. In the second sign, the healing of the noble man's son, Christ heals *at a great distance*—just as heaven and earth are separated at a great distance by the firmament on Day 2. In the third sign, the healing of the lame man, a crowd surrounds a large pool of water—fitting nicely with the seas created on Day 3. During the fourth sign, the feeding the 5,000, the people want to make Jesus king by force (John 6:15). This maps on with the sun, moon, and stars as rulers. The fifth sign, walking on the Sea of Galilee, is associated with God creating all the sea creatures on Day 5. In the sixth sign, the man born blind having his sight restored, Jesus uses *clay* to restore the man's sight. In a similar manner, God formed Adam out of clay on Day 6. The New Creation Man, Jesus, recreates fallen man into someone new. The seventh sign, the raising of Lazarus, points forward to the last/eighth sign—His own resurrection. Jesus' resurrection is the entrance of new creation. As he stands before that tomb where Lazarus is *resting in sleep* (John 11:11), He calls Him out into His *new creation life* (John 11:25). (I am thankful for the insights of Peter Leithart and Alastair Roberts in helping me think through some of these 'signs' in John.) Many other heptamerous examples could be given such as the seven feasts in Scripture, Psalm 104, and the many seven-fold structures throughout the book of Revelation.

55. Edersheim, *The Life and Times of Jesus The Messiah*, 894.

56. Ludolph of Saxony, *The Life of Jesus Christ*, 288.

57. Constantinou, *The Crucifixion of the King of Glory*, 306-307.

58. Edersheim, *The Temple Its Ministry and Services*, 174-177.

59. Justin Martyr, *Dialogue with Trypho* 40, ANF 1:215.

60. Augustine, *On The Gospel of St. John*, 434.

61. Ludolph of Saxony, *The Life of Jesus Christ*, 303.

62. Thomas à Kempis, *Meditations on the Life of Christ*, 210-213.

63. Tauler, *Meditations on the Life and Passion of Christ*, 302-303.

64. Ludolph of Saxony, *The Life of Jesus Christ*, 299.

65. Myles Coverdale, *Fruitful Lessons upon the Passion, Resurrection, Ascension, and of the Sending of the Holy Ghost.*

66. Joseph Hall, *The Works of Joseph Hall Vol. II.*, 498.

67. Isaac Ambrose, *Looking Unto Jesus*, 374.

68. Fr. Ignatius, *Meditations on the Passion and Death of Christ*, 187-189.

69. Groenings, *The Passion of Jesus and its Hidden Meaning*, 397-398.

70. Josephus, *Antiquities*, 4.8.6.

71. Sauter, M. (2023, April 5). *How was Jesus' tomb sealed?* Biblical Archaeology Society. https://www.biblicalarchaeology.org/daily/archaeology-today/biblical-archaeology-topics/how-was-jesus-tomb-sealed/

72. Ludolph of Saxony, *The Life of Jesus Christ*, 373.

73. Bainton, *Here I Stand*, 303.

74. Wilson, *The Shroud*, 113.

75. Jackson, *The Shroud of Turin a Critical Summary*, 26.

76. Wilson, *The Shroud*, 177.

77. Jackson, *The Shroud of Turin a Critical Summary*, 11.

78. Stephen E. Jones: 2020. "Antioch #10." http://theshroudofturin.blogspot.com/2020/01/antioch-turin-shroud-encyclopedia.html. Accessed October 20, 2023.

79. Jackson, *The Shroud of Turin a Critical Summary*, 19.

80. Jackson, *The Shroud of Turin a Critical Summary*, 22.

81. Wilcox, *The Truth About the Shroud of Turin*, 105.

82. Jackson, *The Shroud of Turin a Critical Summary*, 30.

83. Wilcox, *The Truth About the Shroud of Turin*, 225.

84. Wilcox, *The Truth About the Shroud of Turin*, 225.

85. Wilson, *The Shroud*, 274.

86. Antonacci, *Test the Shroud*, 279.

87. Fradd, Matt, host. "New Evidence for the Shroud of Turin 2/ Fr. Andrew Dalton." *Pints With Aquinas*, 6 Jan. 2023. www.youtube.com/watch?v=HAbuG-oVq1Q

88. Wilson, *The Shroud*, 46.

89. Jackson, "Problem of Resolution Posed by the Existence of a Three-Dimensional Image on the Shroud," in Sevenson, K.E., ed., "Proceedings of the 1977 United States Conference on the Shroud of Turin," Holy Shroud Guild: Bronx NY, 1977, 223-33.

90. Jackson, *The Shroud of Turin a Critical Summary*, 3.

91. Jackson, *The Shroud of Turin a Critical Summary*, 43-44.

92. Jackson, *The Shroud of Turin a Critical Summary*, 71.

93. Antonacci, *Test the Shroud*, 9

94. Wilson, *The Shroud*, 44.

95. Niyr, *The Turin Shroud*, 47.

96. Niyr, *The Turin Shroud*, 49-50.

97. Antonacci, *Test the Shroud*, 72.

98. Alan D. and Mary Whanger, "Polarized Image Overlay Technique: A New Image Comparison Method and its Applications", *APPLIED OPTICS*, Vol. 24, No. 6, 15 March 1985, 766-772.

99. Danin, et al., 1999, p. 16; Danin, A., 1999, "Botanical Evidence Indicates 'Shroud of Turin' Originated in Jerusalem Area Before 8th Century,' XVI International Botanical Congress, St. Louis, MO, *Science Daily*, August 3; Wilson & Schwortz, 2000, p. 86.

100. Wilcox, *The Truth About the Shroud of Turin*, 138.

101. Antonacci, *Test the Shroud*, 234-236.

102. West, *Riddles of the Shroud*, 203.

103. Jackson, *The Shroud of Turin a Critical Summary*, 95.

104. Rogers, Raymond N.: 2005. "Studies on the radiocarbon sample from the Shroud of Turin." Thermochimica Acta, 425: 189-194. http://bit.lv/2ZXcuFi. Accessed October 20, 2023.

105. Schwortz, Barrie: 2003-2011. "Some Details About The STURP Quad Mosaic Images." http://bit.ly/2ZW7clf. Accessed October 20, 2023.

106. Marino, Joseph: 2019. "Compelling Data Indicating An Invisible Reweave In The C-14 Corner Of The Turin Shroud." https://shroud.com/pdfs/ n90part1.pdf. Accessed October 20, 2023.

107. Rogers, Raymond N.: 2005. "Studies on the radiocarbon sample from the Shroud of Turin." Thermochimica Acta, 425: 189-194. http://bit.lv/2ZXcuFi. Accessed October 20, 2023.

108. West, *Riddles of the Shroud*, 182.

109. Antonacci, *Test the Shroud*, 4.

110. West, W. (2023, April 6). *New evidence supporting Shroud of Turin is too strong to ignore, says journalist.* The Catholic Weekly. https://www.catholicweekly.com.au/ new-evidence-supporting-the-shroud-is-too-strong-to-ignore-says-journalist/

111. David Chytracus, "4:1-7 Cain and Abel Bring Offerings To The Lord," in *Reformation Commentary on Scripture* (ed. John L. Thompson), 190-191.

112. Augustine, *The City of God*, 149.

113. Augustine, *The City of God*, 145.

114. Morales, *Who Shall Ascend the Mountain of the Lord?*, 57.

115. See Appendix A of my book *A New Day Dawns* for more thoughts on the Mazzaroth and how it relates to Scripture and the Gospel of Jesus Christ.

116. Jordan, *Through New Eyes*, 213.

117. Morales, *Who Shall Ascend the Mountain of the Lord?*, 86.

118. Milgrom, *Leviticus 1-16*, 172.

119. Milgrom, *Leviticus 1-16*, 161.

120. Kellog, *The Book of Leviticus*, 37.

121. Wenham, *The Book of Leviticus*, 69.

122. Kellog, *The Book of Leviticus*, 86

123. Kleinig, *Leviticus*, 113.

124. Kleinig, *Leviticus*, 114.

125. Kellog, *The Book of Leviticus*, 160.

126. Kellog, *The Book of Leviticus*, 161.

127. Wenham, *The Book of Leviticus*, 110.

128. Milgrom, *Leviticus 1-16*, 1039.

129. Kellog, *The Book of Leviticus*, 270.

130. Wegner, *Isaiah*, 401.

131. Baxter, *The Master Theme of the Bible*, 80-81.

132. Wenham, *The Book of Leviticus*, 110.

133. Augustine, *The City of God*, 308.

134. Motyer, *The Prophecy of Isaiah*, 430.

135. Packer, *In My Place Condemned He Stood*, 22.

136. Baxter, *The Master Theme of the Bible*, 295.

137. Kellog, *The Book of Leviticus*, 172.

138. Motyer, *The Prophecy of Isaiah*, 440-441.

139. Baxter, *The Master Theme of the Bible*, 60-61.

Printed in Great Britain
by Amazon

60220467R00147